FIFTY YEARS IN CONSTANTINOPLE

AND

RECOLLECTIONS OF ROBERT COLLEGE

BY

GEORGE WASHBURN, D. D., LL. D.

Commander of the Princely Order of St. Alexander (Bulgaria)
Grand Officer of the National Order of Civil Merit (Bulgaria)

FORUM
TAURI

CHRISTOPHER R. ROBERT

George Washburn
Fifty Years in Constantinople
And Recollections of Robert College
First Edition: 1909

ISBN 978-605-74621-6-9

FORUM TAURI Press
9211 Orbitan Rd, Parkville, MD, 21234, US
contact@forumtauri.com
www.forumtauripress.com

Editor: Erdal K.
Graphic Design: Ergun Kocabıyık
Cover Design: Aynur Küçükyalçın

December 2023

PREFACE

This book has been written at the request of many friends of Robert College. It embodies a history of the College from its foundation to the close of its fortieth year, 1903. I have chosen to make it a record of personal recollections, because this seemed to be the only way in which I could write freely of events and personalities as they appeared to me at the time, without compromising the present administration of the College or making it responsible in any way for my opinions or actions.

It has been my purpose to make it as far as possible a history of the College, but the picture of a college in Constantinople during these years could not be drawn without a background of incidents, personalities and events, such as would have no place in the story of a college in America. On the other hand, it did not seem wise to make the background more attractive than the picture, or even to set the latter in the frame of a detailed history of the Turkish Empire. The Introduction is a review of the events of the last fifty years which have led to the recent revolution in Constantinople.

CONTENTS

ILLUSTRATIONS

INTRODUCTION

CONSTANTINOPLE has long been the queen city of Europe. It has been an imperial city for sixteen hundred years; once the chief city of Christendom, the centre of Christian missions, but since 1453 the capital of the Turkish Empire and of the Mohammedan world; for centuries the one defense of Europe against the advance of the Moslem hordes of Arabia; for three centuries the terror of the Christian world; during the last century the chief battle-ground of European diplomacy over the Eastern Question.

When I first knew it, in 1856, it was no longer the city of Suleiman the Magnificent, or of Mahmoud II, the great reformer, who first undertook to check the progress of decay and save the empire by introducing something of European civilization. His son, Abd-ul-Medjid, owed his throne to the intervention of the European powers, and they used their influence, under the inspiration and direction of Lord Stratford, the English ambassador, to europeanize the government still further. This period of reform under outside influence ended with the Crimean War, and the treaty of Paris in 1856, when Turkey was formally recognized as one of the family of European States and her integrity guaranteed by treaty. Great changes had taken place in the empire. It had been consolidated and the government centralized. Much that was picturesque in Constantinople in the costumes of the people had disappeared; the Janissaries had been massacred; the turban had given place to the red fez; but, after all, it was an Asiatic and not a European city. The Turk himself was unchanged. The Sultan was an irresponsible autocrat, as his ancestors had always been. The Turks generally were as ignorant and uncivilized as when they came from Central Asia in the thirteenth century. There were schools of theology, but otherwise education was unknown. The highest officials were often unable to read or write their own language. Still, there were great men among them, and one could not meet the humblest Turk without realizing that he belonged to the ruling race.

For a few years after the Crimean War, Constantinople probably enjoyed more freedom than ever before, and more than most of the capitals of Europe at that time. The government was weak, but feared nothing from the people, and left them very much to themselves. As the people of Constantinople were theoretically the guests of the Sultan, there was no conscription for the army and very few taxes of any kind. There was but little crime among the natives, and the police did not interfere with their private life. There was great freedom of speech, anything might be discussed in the bazaars or the coffee-shops, and as the Turks had not begun to read newspapers, there were no laws to limit the freedom of the press. There are no class distinctions among the Turks. Every Turk belongs to the ruling class and may aspire to the highest offices in the government. There was nothing to interfere with their individual liberty so long as they observed the conventionalities of their Faith.

There was a restfulness in life in Constantinople in those days which was refreshing to an American. No Turk was ever in a hurry. Time was of no account. If a Turk moved, it was with deliberation and dignity. If he smoked, it was a *tchibouk* or a *nargileh*, and it was the business of the hour. No modern improvements had come to disturb the peace of the city and complicate the simple life of the people. A few small steamers had begun to ply on the Bosphorus, but it was still picturesque with thousands of graceful caïques and hundreds of sailing craft. I remember one day when more than a thousand ships passed up the Bosphorus. I counted more than three hundred in sight at once, all under full sail.

All this has passed away. The Constantinople of fifty years ago will never be seen again. It is still an Asiatic city, still wonderfully beautiful, still the place of all others where I would choose to live, so long as I could enjoy the exceptional privileges of ex-territoriality secured to foreigners by the capitulations. For the subjects of the Sultan, the easy-going, happy-go-lucky government of fifty years ago was an era of relative liberty and comfort, which they have since learned to regret.

But it was in those days that a few young Turks first woke up to a sense of their ignorance and the need of education. They founded a society and started a periodical to promote the progress of knowledge among their people. They used to come to the American missionaries for aid and counsel. It was a new thing for the Turks, and the feeble beginning of the movement which has revolutionized the government. In later years one of these young men was Minister of Public Instruction for the empire.

In 1861 the reign of the weak but well-intentioned Abd-ul-Medjid came to an end, and his brother Abd-ul-Aziz ascended the throne, — a genuine Turk of the old school, as determined an autocrat as his father, but of unbalanced mind; wildly extravagant, to such an extent that he reduced the empire to bankruptcy; fond of cock-fighting and similar amusements. He once decorated a successful fighting-cock with the first class of the Order of the Medjidie. On another occasion he smashed the furniture and mirrors in his palace, in a fit of rage.

During the first ten years of his reign, French influence was supreme in Constantinople, and two of the Turkish Ministers, Fuad and Aali Pashas, were recognized in Europe as statesmen of unusual ability. They induced the Sultan to ignore the traditions of his ancestors and make a tour through Europe to visit the Emperor Napoleon. He was careful to take with him the next heirs to the throne, his two nephews, Murad and Hamid, to guard against a revolution during his absence.

On the occasion of his return and of the visit of the Empress Eugénie after the opening of the Suez Canal, we had the most magnificent fêtes on the Bosphorus that Constantinople had ever seen. During these ten years of French influence there was comparative peace in Constantinople, except for the conflict between the Greeks and Bulgarians over their church relations. The Sultan was building palaces, buying ironclads for his navy, and making foreign loans to pay for them. The people were generally prosperous and contented, and there was always talk of reforms in the empire.

But the influence of the great changes going on in Europe stirred the subject races of European Turkey to revolt against the Turkish rule. Servia, Wallachia and Moldavia were successful. The Cretans defeated the Turkish armies again and again, and maintained an heroic struggle for liberty for three years, aided by the Greeks; but the powers of Europe allowed them to be subdued at last.

The fall of the French Empire put an end to French influence in Constantinople; and as Bismarck had no interest in the Eastern Question, there was a battle royal between England and Russia to win the confidence of the Sultan and control his policy. It was the object of Sir Henry Elliott, the British ambassador, to maintain and strengthen the Turkish Empire as a barrier against the advance of Russia, while General Ignatieff, the Russian ambassador, hoped to free the Slavic provinces of European Turkey from Turkish rule, and make of them a bridge by which Russia could come to Constantinople. While the secret agents of Russia were everywhere encouraging the Slavs to rise in rebellion against the Turks, Sir Henry Elliott was conspiring with the Turks to dethrone the Sultan, and at the same time to put down the revolutionary movements in the European Provinces with fire and sword.

The English ambassador cast in his lot with what was then first known as the Young Turkey party, the leader of which was Midhat Pasha. This party at that time was a sort of "Cave of Adullam"; the only thing in which they agreed was the desire to throw off the tutelage of Europe and restore the strength and independence of the Turkish Empire. For some of them this meant a great panislamic revival and the restoration of the ancient power of the Caliph. Others dreamed of a new Turkey, in which Moslems and Christians should unite together to throw off the yoke of Europe, and build up a great and prosperous Ottoman Empire by themselves. A few were republicans, a few anarchists. Midhat Pasha himself had been a very successful provincial governor, an able administrator, devoted to road-making and other public improvements, self-educated, and a most interesting talker on political affairs. His personal following was never very large, but his intimate relations with Sir Henry Elliott made him an important conspirator.

The conflict went on until, in May, 1876, General Ignatieff appeared to have been defeated along the whole line. Sultan Abd-ul-Aziz was deposed, and a week later either murdered or allowed to commit suicide. First Murad and then Hamid was put upon the throne by Sir Henry and his Turkish allies. Midhat Pasha was Grand Vizier, and General Ignatieff's protégés in the European provinces were slaughtered without mercy. It was dramatic, — a revolution and three sultans within three months, — but it was a barren victory for both Sir Henry Elliott and Midhat Pasha. Within a year Sir Henry was retired and Midhat Pasha sent into exile, to be finally assassinated in Arabia, while Turkey was plunged into a war with Russia which resulted in the loss of most of her European possessions. There was one force which Sir Henry resolutely ignored, and that was the public opinion, the sympathies of the Christian world. The outside world did not care whether the Sultan was Aziz or Murad or Hamid, but the wholesale massacre of unarmed Christian people by the Turks in Bulgaria made a European intervention inevitable, and when, at the end of the year 1876, the Conference of Constantinople opened a way for a peaceful settlement in a partial autonomy for the Christian provinces, Sir Henry and Midhat Pasha made the mistake of believing that Europe could be satisfied by the pretense that Turkey had suddenly become a constitutional government under which Moslem and Christian were to have equal rights. After this, war was inevitable, and no Christian state dared to ally itself with Turkey. This unhappy constitution of Midhat Pasha, which the Sultan had accepted to humbug Europe, had to wait thirty-two years before the autocratic rule of Abd-ul-Hamid had driven the Turks themselves to revolt and to seek refuge in its establishment.

Life in Constantinople during these years of massacre, revolution and war, from 1875 to 1878, was anything but peaceful. They were years of wild excitement, sometimes of joy, sometimes of despair, on the part of the Turks. When they had beaten the Servians, terrorized Bulgaria, defied Europe by rejecting the demands of the Conference, and declared war with Russia, they were full of enthusiasm and hope. During the first months of the war, when the Turks had checked the advance of the Russians, the Christian population of the city was alarmed for its own safety. When the tide turned and the city was filled with disbanded soldiers and starving Turkish refugees, the Christians prayed for the speedy coming of the Russians. The horrors of that winter can never be forgotten. Thousands of these poor Turks, men, women and children, died in the streets and mosques of starvation and of pestilence. They were too far gone, when they reached the city, to plunder it. Then came the Russian armies, which camped outside the city, and at whose headquarters the Sultan agreed to the treaty of San Stefano, which provided for the dismemberment of his empire. It was with great difficulty that the Sultan was dissuaded from abandoning Constantinople and retiring to Broosa. But for the arrival of the English fleet, he would probably have gone and the Russians would have occupied the city.

The intervention of England led to the Congress of Berlin, in which Prince Bismarck professed to act the part of "an honest broker" between the Powers. The treaty of Berlin, which took the place of the treaty of San Stefano, humiliated Russia without helping Turkey, while it ignored the rights and interests of the people of the provinces of which it disposed. It was a triumph for Lord Beaconsfield, but it was a misfortune for England, and has been a source of trouble in Europe ever since.

When the war was over, peace concluded and the treaty of Berlin signed, Sultan Abd-ul-Hamid set himself to his task of rebuilding the shattered fabric of his empire. To those who knew Turkey best it seemed a hopeless task — the treasury bankrupt, credit gone, the richest provinces lost, the army defeated and demoralized, the people disheartened or disloyal, and neighbors awaiting the chance to strike another blow. All honor to Sultan Hamid that he undertook this task with unshaken faith in the destiny of his country. He bore the burden alone, a solitary autocrat, trusting no one but himself, least of all his appointed ministers. He reigned supreme for thirty years after the war, and proved himself more than a match for all the diplomats of Europe. The story of these thirty years, up to the time when his autocratic rule was brought to an end by the revolution of July, 1908, ought to have been heroic. In fact it is pitiful, and the pity of it comes from two fatal mistakes. He was a self-constituted prisoner in his palace, and undertook to hold the whole administration of the empire in his own hands. As no man could do this work alone, he surrounded himself with irresponsible attendants, secretaries, valets, astrologers, spies and other vagabonds of various Moslem races, some of them the worst characters in the empire. He was possessed by the idea that he was in danger of assassination, and his attendants made him believe that it was only by their care that his life could be preserved. They were but little better than a band of brigands, and there was no conceivable crime which they did not commit under the protection of the Sultan. Their chief object was plunder, and as they were the real rulers of the empire, no one was safe from their extortions. There was no escape from this palace camarilla except in revolution. Europe would no doubt have intervened years ago, but for the fact that the German Emperor took this camarilla under his special protection.

The Sultan himself had some ideas which were worthy of a great sovereign, and which he attempted to carry out. He saw the need of education and ordered the establishment of a great number of schools for Turks, even for girls. He saw the need of training for the officers of the army and induced the German Emperor to loan him a number of distinguished officers for this purpose. He encouraged the building of roads and railways. He interested himself in the sanitary condition of the empire, built a number of admirable hospitals and reorganized the medical schools. He favored the development of the mineral resources of the country and was no doubt interested in its general prosperity. The palace camarilla had no interest in any of these things except so far as they afforded them opportunities for plunder. Death or exile was the fate of those who opposed them. They made the Sultan believe that his schools were fostering sedition, and that the officers trained by the Germans were not to be trusted. They organized a system of espionage which employed thousands of spies and created a reign of terror for all intelligent Turks and Christians. Hundreds were secretly put to death, and many thousands sent into exile. Many others secretly escaped from the country. These were condemned in their absence, and their property was confiscated. The suffering of the people all through the empire under this régime was terrible. Even the army was half starved and clad in rags.

The Sultan took his religious rank as Caliph of the Mohammedan world more seriously than his immediate ancestors did, and in this he seems to have been encouraged by the palace camarilla. How far his motives were religious and how far political, it is impossible to say. One of his intimates assured a friend of mine that the Sultan was an agnostic, with no faith in any religion; but he certainly did his best to rouse the militant spirit of Mohammedanism, not only in Turkey but all over the Moslem world, and also to break down the influence of his own Christian subjects. He would have taken away all their established rights, if Russia and other Christian powers had not intervened in their behalf.

The treaty of Berlin had a special article in the interest of the Armenians, but the Turks soon discovered that England was the only power interested in enforcing it, and nothing was done. The more loudly the Armenians appealed to Europe, the heavier was the hand of the Sultan; until finally, in 1894, the work of extermination was commenced in ancient Armenia. In 1895 there was a massacre of about a thousand in Constantinople, and as the powers tolerated this, the massacres went on for a year all over Asiatic Turkey, culminating in the great massacre in Constantinople in 1896, when some ten thousand were slaughtered in the streets of the city, which literally ran with blood. Even worse than the killing of so many was the tireless plunder and persecution that went on from 1880 to 1908. It was only the palace camarilla and its agents that profited by this. It was through its influence that the Sultan approved it, while the better, more enlightened class of Turks felt that this plunder and massacre of the Christians was a political blunder and a great moral wrong, whatever provocation had been given by the Armenian revolutionists in their attempts to attract the attention and secure the support of Europe.

The palace camarilla made a similar mistake in encouraging the revolutionists in Egypt, under the impression that in so doing it was working in the interest of panislamism, and strengthening the hands of the Caliph. The result was the occupation of Egypt by England. Turkey had the opportunity to join England in the occupation of the country, but failed to improve it. The loss which was most keenly felt at the palace was the cutting off of the golden stream of backsheesh which was always coming in from the Khedive.

Following closely upon the loss of Egypt came the revolt of Eastern Roumelia, in 1885, and its annexation to Bulgaria. In this case Turkey happily followed the lead of England and refused the demand of Russia that she should reconquer the province. The Czar had his revenge in stirring up the Servians to attack Bulgaria, and, when they were beaten, in kidnapping and dethroning Prince Alexander; but Bulgaria lived and flourished in spite of his enmity.

These changes in Egypt and Bulgaria brought about great diplomatic conflicts in Constantinople, which added not a little to the interest of life in that city.

In the summer of 1894 Constantinople was severely shaken by an earthquake, which caused the death of some fifteen hundred persons, most of whom were buried in the ruins of the bazaars, and great numbers of people camped out for a month, while the shocks were repeated almost every day.

The same year the Greeks in Constantinople resented the action of the palace in restricting their rights, by closing all their churches, and Russia intervened in their behalf. In 1889, 1896, and 1897, there were revolts of the Greeks in Crete, which resulted in a war between Greece and Turkey, in which the Turks, aided by German officers, easily defeated the Greeks, and were prevented from occupying Athens only by the intervention of Europe; but, as generally happens in such cases, Turkey was not allowed to reap the fruits of victory. The European powers took possession of Crete, and nothing was left of the Turkish rule over the island but a small Turkish flag on an island in Suda Bay.

In 1903 the storm-centre in Turkey was transferred to Macedonia. The condition of the province had been pitiable ever since the

Congress of Berlin had recommended that it be made an autonomous province by Turkey. The Turks refused to carry out this plan, and the Christian population was given over to be exterminated by Albanian brigands and Turkish officials. As Europe would do nothing to help them, the people finally revolted.

This movement was directed by a committee of Bulgarian revolutionists which had brought the whole Christian population under its control by systematic terrorism; and for a while it was successful. From that time up to July, 1908, the state of the country was such as to force the European powers to intervene. That nothing was accomplished by successive interventions was due to the fact that Russia and Austria were allowed to take the lead, and neither of them desired any permanent settlement of the question. It was only the Western powers which had any real sympathy for the people of the province. The Turks might have put an end to the existing anarchy, but they preferred to encourage the conflict of races and religions which was going on and destroying the Christians. We may find some excuse for the Turks, but the conduct of the European powers, including Greece and Bulgaria, admits of no excuse. For five years Constantinople was constantly agitated by the different phases of this question.

The revolution of July, 1908, was the triumph of a process of enlightenment which has been going on for many years among the Turks. They have ruled over the many conquered races of the empire for six hundred years in the spirit of Asiatic despots, and have shown themselves to be the most remarkable race that has ever come out of Central Asia to trouble the peace of Europe. Fifty years ago they were essentially unchanged from what they were when they first appeared in Asia Minor. This immobility has undoubtedly come from the unchangeable character of Mohammedanism. It is only since the Crimean War that any number of them have come under the influence of Christian civilization. Thirty years ago, in the time of Midhat Pasha, we first heard of a Young Turkey party, which proposed to modernize the form of government; but it was too weak to influence Sultan Abd-ul-Hamid, and the palace camarilla waged an incessant war against the Christian nationalities which naturally sympathized with the Young Turkey party.

The sudden and astonishing success of the revolution was due to many causes, first of all to the universal fear and hatred for the existing government, and next, to the wisdom and tact of the

Committee of Union and Progress which directed it. It was a wonderful inspiration which led them to attempt nothing at Constantinople, and, after having secured the support of the army, to strike their blow from Macedonia and revolutionize Constantinople by telegraph. The palace camarilla and the regiments of the Sultan's body-guard could do nothing. There was nothing in Constantinople for them to strike.

Of course, behind all these things was the rapid progress of enlightenment among the Turks during these thirty years. This was due in some measure to the acts of the Sultan himself. He had seen the necessity of education for the Turks, and founded many schools of all kinds. He had brought German officers for his military schools, and German doctors for his medical schools and hospitals, who inspired the Young Turks with modern ideas. Every enlightened Turk sent into exile in the interior became a centre of light, and every one who managed to escape to Europe was filled with new ideas of society and of government.

Other influences have been potent. Every missionary station, and every school and college, has not only elevated its Christian students and the few Turks who attended these schools, but it has shown to all the value of education and made them more or less familiar with the progress of Christian civilization. The influence of education on the Bulgarians made a profound impression upon the Turks, even upon the Sultan himself.

In addition to all these things, intelligent and patriotic Turks were moved by the rapid decline of their power and the dismemberment of the empire. They had a great history to stir their pride, and felt that by nature they were the equals of any other race while even in the Mohammedan world their influence was waning. They felt that their only hope lay in the transformation of their government, the education and general enlightenment of the Turkish people.

It was a Turkish revolution in the interest of the Turks and designed to strengthen their power, but its leaders took for their watchwords, Liberty, Justice, Equality and Fraternity, for all the races and religions of the empire, with equal rights and equal duties for all. As we in America proclaimed these principles in 1776, and have not yet been able to put them in force in all parts of our country, we may expect to wait some time before they can be fully carried out in Turkey; but there is no reason to doubt the honesty and sincerity of the Young Turkey party in proclaiming them.

Abd-ul-Hamid professed to accept the new order of things which had transformed him from an autocrat into a constitutional sovereign, but at heart he resented the dictation of the Young Turks and secretly plotted for their destruction. April 13, 1909, he startled the world by a counter revolution at Constantinople and the massacre of many thousand Christians in Asia Minor and Syria. In a few days his triumph seemed complete, but eleven days later the Young Turks, with an army from Macedonia, stormed and captured the city. Abd-ul-Hamid was taken prisoner, deposed and transported to Salonica, while his brother was proclaimed Sultan Mahomet V and reigned in his stead.

How far the conquered races in Turkey, Moslem and Christian, will heartily accept this new form of Turkish rule and give it their support remains to be seen. The wild enthusiasm and joy of the first days of emancipation from the tyranny of the palace camarilla have passed, and already some of these nationalities have come to remember that what they have desired was not the reform but the destruction of the Turkish Empire. Russia and Austria are not likely to discourage this feeling, which has been the basis of their policy for more than a century.

However this may be, we have to-day a new Constantinople hastening to be transformed into a European city. The old Asiatic Constantinople of a hundred, or even fifty years ago will soon disappear.

BOSTON, 1909.

CHAPTER I
THE FOUNDING OF ROBERT COLLEGE

ROBERT COLLEGE was founded by Mr. Christopher Rheinlander Robert, a New York merchant descended from a French Huguenot family of Rochelle, France.[1]

There is still an impression in some quarters in America, that the idea of founding a Christian college in Constantinople was a whim of Mr. Robert's, a notion which sprang from his brain as did Athena from the head of Zeus, and it is often spoken of as Mr. Robert's college. The truth is that the College grew out of the natural development of American missions in Turkey, in which Mr. Robert had long been interested. The policy of the missionary boards at that time was opposed to the expenditure of missionary funds for education. A resolution was passed at the annual meeting of the A. B. C. F. M. in 1856, that the only work of the missionary was to preach the Gospel, "the oral utterance of the Gospel in public or in private"; but the time had come when some at least of the missionaries in the field saw the necessity of a new departure, saw what a Christian college might accomplish in the elevation of the people. Mr. Robert was the first man of means in America to see and appreciate this necessity, the man whom God chose to meet this want in Turkey, and to turn the tide of missionary work in other parts of the world in this direction. The fact that he was the treasurer of the American Home Missionary Society, which had already discovered this need in the newer states of the West, was perhaps one reason why he became a leader in this movement. Mr. Robert himself always felt that he had been providentially directed to the sacrifices which he made to found and sustain the College. It

---

1 Mr. Robert was descended, in the fourth generation, from Daniel Robert of Rochelle, who was believed to have been a direct descendant of Count Robert of Normandy, the son of William the Conqueror, King of England. Daniel Robert was a Huguenot, and emigrated to New York in 1701, after the revocation of the Edict of Nantes, when he became a British subject. His grandson, Mr. Robert's father, was a graduate of Columbia and Edinburgh Universities, a physician by profession, who, after living ten years in the British West Indies, returned to New York in 1784 and bought a large estate on Long Island, where Mr. Christopher R. Robert was born March 23, 1802. When fifteen years old he went into a merchant's office in New York, and continued in business all his life.

was the Lord's work, not his.

There were good reasons why the first American college of this kind should have been founded at Constantinople. Not only had the attention of the Christian world been concentrated upon the Turkish Empire by the Crimean War, but the people of Turkey had been aroused to new life and were beginning to seek for education. It was believed that a new era of tolerance and liberty had dawned upon the East, that the government, as well as the people, was desirous of encouraging progress in every form, that at last there was an open door in Turkey. Sultan Abd-ul-Medjid was a reformer, Fuad and Aali Pashas were enlightened statesmen. The Hatt-i-houmayoun was a charter of liberty for all. This was the general belief of the Americans in Turkey.

The French and the Roman Catholics had been quick to see and improve the opportunity for political and religious propaganda. They had established a number of schools of a low grade, and had induced many of the wealthy families to send their sons to Paris. French influence was already dominant here. There were but few native schools of any kind. There were some Mohammedan schools for small children connected with the mosques, as well as naval, military and theological schools. There were a few Protestant and Catholic mission-schools, and here and there the Christian nationalities had established schools, in some of which there were teachers who were doing good work; but there was nothing corresponding to an American college in the empire. More than anywhere else in the world at that time, there seemed to be an open door and a great work to be done. Constantinople was the natural place to begin it. It was not only the capital of the empire, but it had been for fifteen centuries the centre of life and power in this part of the world.

The idea of founding a college at Constantinople was first suggested to Mr. Robert in 1857 by Messrs. James and William Dwight, the sons of Rev. Dr. H. G. O. Dwight, then a missionary here. They were young men of high character, graduates of Yale College and Union Theological Seminary. They called upon Mr. Robert, as a well-known philanthropist and friend of missions, and stated that they had for some time contemplated founding a school at Constantinople, not in any way connected with the Mission and tolerant of the religious prejudices of the natives, which they hoped would soon become self-supporting, and they proposed to associate with themselves an Armenian, also a graduate of Yale.

Mr. Robert was interested in their plan, and in October, 1857, a meeting was held at his house to consider this proposition. Those present were Rev. Drs. Wm. M. Adams, A. D. Smith, G. W. Wood, M. Badger, D. B. Coe, W. G. Schauffler and E. Riggs (the last two from Constantinople), Hon. Geo. P. Marsh, Messrs. Robert, Ely, Moore, Ransom and Schiefflin. No decisive action was taken at this meeting beyond the suggestion of six names for trustees of the proposed school. Five of these gentlemen appear to have met once in March, 1858, and in May the Messrs. Dwight called on Mr. Robert again, and he wrote to Dr. Hamlin to ask his opinion of the plan; but, so far as I can learn from the correspondence in my hands, no money was ever pledged by any one to carry out this project, and it was abandoned. The reasons for the failure of the Messrs. Dwight to secure support appear to have been their youth, lack of confidence in the person associated with them, the financial crisis in America at the time, and a difference of opinion as to the religious status of the school. The Messrs. Dwight proposed to make the school purely secular, while Mr. Robert and others, to whom they appealed, felt that there was no reason why they should give money for a school in Constantinople, unless it was to be distinctively Christian. Dr. Hamlin had written to the Messrs. Dwight in 1856, that it must be "a decided, thorough Christian school from its very commencement," or it would not secure the confidence of the people. A school without a religion would be an inexplicable anomaly in Constantinople, and, as he said in another letter, "would be regarded as a trap to cheat the devil."[2]

Mr. Robert had become too much interested in the idea of founding a college in Constantinople to let it drop when the Messrs. Dwight gave it up, and he naturally turned to Dr. Cyrus Hamlin, whose acquaintance he had made when he visited Constantinople during the Crimean War, at the time when Dr. Hamlin was fur-

---

2 In justice to the memory of the Messrs. Dwight it should be stated that in the original circular which they issued in 1856 they say," It is desirable that the leading object of this institution should be to cooperate with the direct labor of others in the work of Protestant Evangelization, by giving the whole instruction a decided and unmistakable Evangelical influence, though it may be important that it should be distinctly recognized as standing on its own separate and independent basis." It appears to have been in the discussion of practical details that a serious difference of opinion arose.

nishing the British hospitals and soldiers with bread. He had previously consulted him as to the project of the Messrs. Dwight and January 3, 1859, in a postscript to a letter, he wrote: "Since writing a few lines this morning it has occurred to me to ask confidentially whether, in view of the great importance of the institution referred to, it may not be your duty to take charge of it. I think thirty-five to forty thousand dollars can be secured for it with comparative ease, if you do, and I doubt if it can be without. My idea is to have the Messrs. Dwight as your assistants. You may write me fully on the subject."

Apparently Dr. Hamlin either failed to notice the postscript, or did not take it seriously. Mr. Robert wrote him again March 15, repeating the question. To this Dr. Hamlin replied at length. After calling attention to the fact that he had certain disqualifications for the place; that he was not *a persona grata* with the Turks, and had a very meagre knowledge of the Turkish language; that he had not the requisite scholarship for the post, and that his work in Bebec Seminary had aimed only at preparing young Armenians for the ministry by a short course of study, he concluded as follows: "This letter will be quite as unsatisfactory to you as to me. I do not see clearly what course the thing will take, and I wish to know the position of the Dwights before I go farther, also to ascertain the opinions of my associates and some good friends and advisers like Count DeZuylen, the pious and excellent Dutch ambassador, Dr. Millingen, and others."

Without waiting for a reply to his letter, Mr. Robert commissioned Rev. Drs. Coe and Badger to address to Dr. Hamlin a formal invitation to devote himself to this enterprise, which they did March 28, 1859, without mentioning Mr. Robert's name. Dr. Hamlin concluded that Mr. Robert had inspired this proposal, and wrote to him April 26: "I shall write to Messrs. Coe and Badger as soon as any light dawns upon my path. If I should feel it to be my duty to do anything for this great undertaking, it would be only to get it fairly started and leave it in abler hands. . . . It is of the Lord and cannot fail, whether I have anything to do with it or not."

Mr. Robert wrote again June 27, to press the question, and August 22 Dr. Hamlin replied that he had laid the subject before his associates in the Mission, and that the majority had expressed a decided opinion in favor of his undertaking the work. Two weeks later he wrote again: "I have, with feelings of deep solemnity and sorrow, written my request to be released from the service of the Board as soon as my place can be supplied. ... I tremble at the responsibility I have assumed, but I trust that He who has upheld me through many trials and labors will not forsake me here."

It appears from Dr. Hamlin's autobiography that what finally determined his acceptance of Mr. Robert's proposals was that he regarded the educational policy of the American Board as suicidal, and that the action of the Mission in accepting this policy and removing the Mission Seminary from Bebec to Marsovan put an end to the work to which his whole missionary life had been devoted. The proposed college would be a continuation and enlargement of that work.[3]

Mr. Robert and Dr. Hamlin were now both fully committed to the work of founding a Christian college in Constantinople, and it was agreed that Dr. Hamlin should come to America to consult with Mr. Robert as to their plans and also to secure additional funds, but it was thought best that he should first secure a site for the College. This did not prove to be an easy task. At first, the majority of his advisers, rather against his judgment, favored a location in old Stamboul and proposed the purchase of the old palace of Constantine Porphyrogenitus on the city wall. A meeting of the friends of the College at the Dutch Embassy, in January, 1860, finally approved of the site on the Bosphorus near the Castle of Europe, where the College now stands; but the owner of this site, Achmet Vefik Pasha, then Turkish ambassador in Paris, absolutely refused to sell at any price. This was a bitter disappointment, but Dr. Hamlin purchased what he considered to be the next best available site, the land on the hill above the village of Kourou Tcheshmé. We held this property until 1904, when I sold it to the Scheik-ul-Islam for a little less than it cost. We had never been able to find a buyer for it before, at any reasonable price. When Dr. Hamlin returned from America a year later, it was found that Achmet Vefik Pasha had returned from Paris, needed money, and was willing to sell the land at Roumeli Hissar. After some months of negotiations, Dr. Hamlin, with Mr. Robert's approval, bought about half of the lot, about six acres, for sixteen hundred pounds sterling. Some years later, I bought the other half for about eighteen hundred pounds sterling. It was an essential part of Dr. Hamlin's agreement with Achmet

---

3 *My Life and Times*, pp. 413, 414.

Vefik Pasha that no money should be paid for the land until the necessary permission had been given to erect a building upon it for the College. This was December 2, 1861. In March, 1862, the Minister of Foreign Affairs having informed the English ambassador and the American minister that the government had given its consent to the erection of the College on this site, and the Minister of Public Instruction having authorized the establishment of the College, the money was paid over to Achmet Vefik Pasha. Dr. Hamlin and his friends here felt that they had every reason to be jubilant. There is no more beautiful site for a college anywhere in the world, and no place on the Bosphorus to equal it. All the city wondered that such a site had been granted to an American college.

Dr. Hamlin went to America in the summer of 1860, and returned in June, 1861. It was not a favorable time to raise money, as the whole country was absorbed in the conflict between the free and the slave states, the Presidential election and the outbreak of the Civil War, but he had no little success in awakening an interest in the proposed college. Harvard University took it up with considerable enthusiasm, and it was under its auspices that he had a very successful meeting in Boston. His visits to England in going and coming were also of importance in gaining friends for the College there. But the great object of his visit was to come to a full understanding with Mr. Robert as to the character and purpose of the College, and to make such arrangements as were possible for its organization and the erection of a building. A Board of Trustees was legally established, consisting of C. R. Robert, Wm. A. Booth, Milton Badger, David B. Coe, Wm. L. Lambert and David Hoadley, all personal friends of Mr. Robert, and I believe all associated with him in the management of the American Home Missionary Society. Wm. A. Booth was President, and David B. Coe Secretary of the Board, and they held their offices until they died, many years after the death of Mr. Robert. They were his chosen advisers in everything concerning the College, and, for years after his death, the trustees were always guided by their judgment.

In 1864 they were formally incorporated by act of the Legislature of New York, under the name of *"The Trustees of Robert College of Constantinople,"* and the College was included with other state institutions in the University of the State of New York. This established the legal status of the College in America.

The outbreak of the Civil War was a great blow to Dr. Hamlin and Mr. Robert, but neither of them was a man to turn back, when once he had put a hand to the plough, and they determined to go on and put up the building for the College. Dr. Hamlin spent much time in preparation for this. He interested Mr. Corliss of Providence in it, who gave him a steam-engine and other machinery for use in the woodwork of the building. He studied plans and bought considerable material. Most of all, he and Mr. Robert came to understand and trust each other, so that they could work together harmoniously.

As has already been explained, Dr. Hamlin, on his return from America, abandoned the site which he had bought at Kourou Tcheshmé and bought the site at Roumeli Hissar. After some delay he received permission to build on this site, and believed that his troubles were ended. This was in March, 1862. It proved to be not the end but the beginning of serious trouble. He was destined to wait more than six years, until December 20, 1868, before he could begin work on this site. The new era and the open door in Turkey supposed to have been won by the Crimean War seemed to have disappeared. This change was undoubtedly due in some measure to the death of Sultan Abd-ul-Medjid and the accession of Abd-ul-Aziz, in June, 1861, — a man of totally different character, who soon changed the whole spirit of the government. Whatever else might be said of it, it was no longer weak. It soon became a strong government, whether for good or evil. But I think Dr. Hamlin was right in believing that the opposition to the College did not originate with the Turks. If left to themselves they would probably have regarded it as a matter of very little importance in any way. The powers that he had to contend with were France, Russia, and the Roman Catholic Church. Their influence was pushed to the utmost to prevent the establishment of a college which would promote and extend the use of the English language and the influence of Protestant, English and American, ideas in the East. They were formidable enemies because at that time our friends were weak. America, engaged in a great civil war, had little influence here, Prussia and Holland were friendly but without much influence. England, at the close of the Crimean War, had lost her dominant position at Constantinople. This had been won by France, and under Sultan Abd-ul-Aziz Russia regained much of her former influence here. England was still a power to be reckoned with, but, at the time when the college question came up, she was represented here by Sir Henry Bulwer, a brilliant but unprincipled man, who was ready to sacrifice anything to his own personal interest. At first he supported Dr. Hamlin, but in the end abandoned his cause to secure a bribe which finally cost him his place. The permission to build had been granted through the influence of Achmet Vefik Pasha, then a minister; but, only a few days after it was given, he was removed from office and his enemies were glad to do him any injury in their power.

Under these unpropitious circumstances, and with the forces arrayed against the College, it was natural for the Porte to oppose the erection of the College, and in Turkey it is always easy to find excuses for delay. *How not to do it* is the perfection of Turkish diplomacy. The permission to build was never formally revoked, but six years of wearisome and often exasperating negotiations followed. When Lord Lyons came from Washington to the British embassy here in 1865, he took up the question with vigor, but unfortunately he was transferred to Paris in eighteen months. The last thing that he told me before he left was that he had finally settled the college question with Aali Pasha. If he had remained here, that would have been the end of it; but he had no sooner gone than a new reason for delay was found. For Dr. Hamlin and Mr. Robert these years were alternations of hope and despair. Nothing that they could do here or in Washington seemed to be of any avail and the prospect was never darker than in 1868.

The final settlement was brought about most unexpectedly by a providential combination of agencies, unconsciously working together, and was long a mystery to Dr. Hamlin. The ball was set in motion by Mr. George D. Morgan of New York, a gentleman who had never heard of the proposed college until he came to Constantinople as a traveler, in the winter of 1868. He saw Dr. Hamlin, investigated the case, and was so much interested that, when he returned to America a few months later, he went to Washington on purpose to persuade Mr. Seward to take action in behalf of the College. He first interested Senator Morgan and Mr. Evarts in the case, and they three went together to Mr. Seward, who had special reasons at that time to wish to please them. He was persuaded, sent for Blacque Bey, the Turkish minister, and pressed his demands in such a way that the minister wrote to Constantinople that this question must be settled at once or there would be serious trouble. This letter reached Constantinople not long before the arrival of Admiral Farragut at the Dardanelles, who insisted upon coming up to Constantinople in his flag-ship. His appearance in these waters at this time had nothing to do with the revolution in Crete, but to the Turks it seemed suspicious. They allowed him to come to Constantinople after some delay, and received him with great honors. To please his little son, now a professor in Columbia University, Dr. Hamlin took him to call on the admiral, and by chance met a gentleman there who knew him well and introduced the subject of the College and its difficulties. The admiral was so much stirred by the injustice involved that he promised to speak to the Grand Vizier about it unofficially, if he had a chance. He found his opportunity at a grand dinner given in his honor, as Dr. Hamlin afterwards learned. No one at the College knew anything at that time of the action of Mr. Seward or the dispatch of Blacque Bey, but the Turkish government put all these things together, and evidently believed that Admiral Farragut's real mission here was to settle the College question, with the possibility of his taking his ships to Crete in the background. They settled it, granting even more than had been asked, giving the College a *toghrali iradé*, or imperial charter, as an American college under the protection of the United States with ex-territorial rights, and with all the privileges granted to educational institutions in Turkey. Indeed, they were so friendly and cordial that Dr. Hamlin wrote to Mr. Robert that, in case more money were needed, he should apply to the Sultan, who would undoubtedly give it. But he never applied. The *iradé* was issued by the Sultan in September, 1868, but not communicated to the United States Legation until December 20, 1868. In October Aali Pasha informed the American minister that Dr. Hamlin "could go on and build as soon as he pleased and that an *iradé* would appear in due time"; but Dr. Hamlin had been deceived so often that he did not care to act on this intimation.

CHAPTER II
THE OPENING OF THE COLLEGE AT BEBEC

WHEN it became probable in the summer of 1862 that the contest over the site at Hissar would be a long one, Mr. Robert and Dr. Hamlin began at once to consider the possibility of opening the College elsewhere. The building belonging to the mission at Bebec, the suburban village on the Bosphorus just below Hissar, where Dr. Hamlin had for many years conducted the Mission school, was vacant, and no further permission from the government was necessary to open the College there. The American Board at Boston offered it rent free. Dr. Hamlin made extensive repairs, and the College was opened there September 16, 1863, with 4 students, 3 English and 1 American, all residents of Constantinople. Two professors had been appointed in 1862, Rev. H. A. Schauffler and Rev. G. A. Perkins, and Mr. Robert had sent one to Germany and one to Yale to complete their preparation for the work in the College. They were present at the opening, and three or four native assistants had also been employed. Before going to Germany Professor Schauffler raised twenty-one hundred and twenty dollars towards the foundation of a library for the College, and Harvard University contributed some two hundred volumes. Mr. Corliss of Providence, Mr. B. M. E. Durfee of Fall River, Mr. Wheelwright of London, and Mrs. J. C. Whitin of Whitinsville added to this fund, so that when the College went to Roumeli Hissar the library contained some five thousand volumes. It now (1907) contains over twelve thousand volumes, has a card catalogue and is open to students every day.

Before issuing a prospectus Dr. Hamlin felt that it was necessary to give a name to the College, and his advisory committee discussed the question without reaching any satisfactory conclusion, although many names were suggested. Mr. Robert had called it the American College, but this was rejected on the ground that it had a political significance. Finally Dr. Hamlin proposed Robert College as a neutral name, which could be spelled in all the languages of the East.[1] This was adopted with acclamation. Mr. Robert protested against it as unwise and contrary to all his principles,

---

1 This is more important than it may appear. My name, for example, cannot be spelled in any of these languages.

but Dr. Hamlin replied that it was too late to change it. The name had already been adopted in all the languages and was universally accepted as the best.

The discussion of the character, organization and curriculum of the College commenced in 1859. Mr. Robert wrote June 27, 1859: "In my judgment the time has come for you in connection with some of your wisest associates and any others in whom you may think dwells the spirit of true wisdom to draw out the plan of a college, taking as a pattern the best in our country as to the course of study, government, Faculty, etc. The beginning of course must be small but let the plan be such that it can be enlarged to meet the wants of the community in which it is situated. The foundations therefore must be broad and deep, but looking to a gradual execution of the plan in its completeness. A rapid and hasty growth must not be expected or desired."

The religious status of the College was made clear in the constitution adopted by the trustees. It was to be unsectarian and open to all without distinction of race or religion. It did not aim to destroy or weaken the ancient Christian churches of the East, but to develop the moral and spiritual life of its students, their faith in God and their purpose to obey his law. The constitution states that "it is to be founded and administered on the principles of the Bible: it is hereby declared and ordained that, while it is to be a scientific and literary institution, God and His word shall be distinctly acknowledged and honored therein: the Scriptures, as published by the American or British and Foreign Bible Societies being read and prayers offered at least once each day of each collegiate term, and Divine worship held on the Sabbath, at which services the Faculty are expected to be present, and all the students shall attend unless for special and imperative reasons some are excused by the Faculty and teachers."

Dr. Hamlin replied at great length to Mr. Robert's letter of June 27, proposing in substance English as the language of the College, Preparatory and Collegiate Departments, a governing Board of Trustees in New York, a local Board of Managers (or *Advisers* he wrote later) at Constantinople, a Faculty of a president and three professors, a course of study essentially the same as in American colleges, with the omission of Latin and Greek and the addition of French and the native languages, with some legal studies.

There were two special reasons for making English the language of the College. It was necessary to have a neutral common language for students of many races and tongues and this could only be some European language. Among these it was natural for us to choose English. Moreover, there were no text books to be had in any native language and no means of pursuing any science or other subject such as was offered by the literature of England and America. The use of English has attracted many students to the College for its own sake.

Mr. Robert objected to the exclusion of the classics, and since the second year's graduates in 1869 Latin has always been required for the degree of A. B. Otherwise the European universities would have refused to recognize our diplomas. The local Board of Managers was organized and was probably useful for a time, but died a natural death in a few years. Dr. Hamlin proposed to confine the study of the native languages to the Preparatory Department, but it has been found necessary to give them special prominence and continue them through the whole course. This helps the College to give a thorough education to students of different nationalities without denationalizing them or unfitting them to become the leaders of their own people.

Dr. Hamlin was not discouraged by the small number of students the first year, 1863-64. Before the close of the year 20 had been registered, all but 2 Europeans or Americans. Towards the end of the year 2 Greeks came.

The second year, 1864-65, opened with 23 students, and 28 in all were registered during the year, of whom 4 were Greeks, 1 Armenian and 1 Bulgarian. This year was a very trying one for Mr. Robert and Dr. Hamlin, aside from the troubles in regard to the site. The two professors constituted a majority in the Faculty, and even during the first year there were serious differences of opinion between them and Dr. Hamlin as to the management and discipline of the College. These culminated early in the second year, and the trustees were called upon to decide whether to accept the resignation of Dr. Hamlin or of the two professors. They did the latter, and Dr. Hamlin was left alone in the middle of the year to carry on the College as best he could with his native assistants.

In addition to this difficulty Dr. Hamlin had to expel for immorality four students belonging to the best European families in the city, and this stirred up new enmity against the College. One peculiarly Eastern method of injuring an enemy was experienced during the year. Some one secretly introduced into the dormitories a piece of an old garment swarming with lice, which was not discovered until the evil had spread among the boys.

The year closed with one of those terrible calamities which used to be so common in Constantinople. The Asiatic cholera carried off some seventy thousand persons in three months. The College was closed early, before there had been any cases in Bebec, and Dr. Hamlin and his family went to the Princes Islands to regain his health. He was suffering from insomnia and nervous prostration. I remained in Bebec, and one of my sons, about two years old, was the first victim of the epidemic there, after which Mrs. Washburn and I devoted ourselves to the care of the sick in the village for two months. I had to go to town frequently to attend to my work there, where Dr. Long and Mr. Trowbridge had given themselves entirely to the care of the sick in the public khans. It would require the pen of a De Quincey to describe the scenes which I witnessed, pathetic, grotesque, horrible, a dance of death among men who had lost their hold upon the humanities of life.

The epidemic passed away with a great fire in Constantinople which consumed some ten thousand houses and seemed to disinfect the city.

What with the cholera and the fire it was not strange that the third college year, 1865-66, opened with only 8 students. The number gradually increased, and the whole number registered was 51, of whom 20 were Armenians, 9 Bulgarians and 6 Greeks.

In place of the two professors Mr. Robert sent out two tutors, Messrs. Ostrander and Rodger, for a period of three years. This was the beginning of a plan which has continued in force all through the history of the College. In the Appendix of this volume will be found a paper which was drawn up by Mr. Robert and sent by him to the colleges where he was seeking candidates for this position. I think that this is the latest form of it. He had modified it from time to time as his practical experience with the men sent out suggested weaknesses to be avoided. I remember when he inserted the clause *not conscientiously obstinate*. It is well worth reading, not only as illustrating Mr. Robert's character but also his idea of the work which the College ought to do.

Probably his ideal was never realized in any one tutor; in fact, one college president wrote to him that no such men existed in this world, but many of those who have filled this position in the College have been men of rare ability and the highest character. Their personal influence over the students has been a very important factor in the work of the College, as they lived with the students and came into more intimate relations with them than was possible to the professors. It is the almost unanimous testimony of the men who have filled these positions that their years spent in the College were the most fruitful years in their preparation for their life-work. They gained here new and broader conceptions of life, of the world as a whole and of men and individuals, besides enjoying rare opportunities for study and travel.

The names of all the professors and American tutors who were connected with the College during the first forty years will be found in the Appendix.

At the beginning of this year Dr. Hamlin secured the services of an English lady, Mrs. Julia Calluci, as matron of the College.

There can be no doubt that the close of the Civil War in America and the final triumph of the national government added much to the prestige of the College among the people here and was one cause of the increase in the number of students.

It was also a great relief and great joy to Mr. Robert and Dr. Hamlin. They were men of strong convictions and deep feeling, devoted patriots, whose hearts were bound up in this struggle for national life and freedom for the slave. Their letters are full of it, and when peace came a great burden was removed from their minds and hearts.

Mr. Robert at once interested himself in the education of the poor whites in the South, bought the United States Hospital buildings, with the land and furniture, on Lookout Mountain near Chattanooga, Tenn., and established a school there under the direction of Mr. Bancroft, who in later years became the famous principal of Phillips Academy, Andover. Mr. Robert's letters show that his interest in this school was quite as great as his interest in Robert College.

The fourth college year, 1866-67, opened with a large increase of students. The whole number registered during the year was 96, of whom 19 were Armenians, 13 Bulgarians and 18 Greeks. There was nothing to disturb the peace of the year but a terrific storm of which Dr. Hamlin gives a graphic account in his letters and which very nearly swept the college building into the Bosphorus.

Dr. Hamlin's sympathies were deeply stirred during the year

by the long and serious illness of two of the students, one of whom, a very promising Bulgarian, died, and the other, a German, was disabled, so that he was a cripple for life, although he finally recovered so far as to graduate in 1869.

One of the questions much discussed during the year and in regard to which Mr. Robert and Dr. Hamlin never agreed was that of beneficiaries, of receiving a certain number of students at a reduced rate. To satisfy Dr. Hamlin the trustees in 1864 voted that "the President select any number, not exceeding six, talented youth of high moral character, one from each of the large nationalities of the Turkish Empire, who shall enjoy the privileges of the College by paying one-fourth to three-fourths of the ordinary charges." In 1867 it was added that "those so received should sign a pledge that they will diligently pursue the prescribed course of instruction not less than three years." In fact, a much larger number had been received by Dr. Hamlin and he also rejected the last regulation as "needless, useless and injurious." In 1868 one-fourth of the students were beneficiaries and the amount deducted for them from the regular charges was about twenty-five hundred dollars, about five hundred dollars of which was specially contributed for this purpose by friends in England and America. Dr. Hamlin writes: "Both for scholarship and character the students thus aided are the glory of the College. Of four prizes these men won three."

The intensity of Dr. Hamlin's feeling on this subject will be appreciated when we remember that his chief ambition was to make the College self-supporting, and that his own salary at this time was only three hundred and seventy-five dollars a year and the board of his family in the College, a salary fixed by himself against the protest of Mr. Robert.

Serious efforts have since been made to raise a substantial fund for beneficiaries but with limited success, and the College has regularly expended from two thousand to three thousand dollars a year from its common funds for this purpose. It is understood however that we do not receive *free* students, and the aid given depends on scholarship and conduct.

Dr. Hamlin, in his annual report, writes very confidently of the steady improvement in the character and intellectual progress of the students and very hopefully of the religious influence of the College. No difficulties had arisen from the religious services or the teaching of the Bible in classes, and the students seemed interested in both.

At the close of the year the trustees at the suggestion of Mr. Robert voted to invite Dr. Hamlin to visit Paris during the great Exposition and appropriated five hundred dollars to meet his expenses. He went there and also attended the meeting of the Evangelical Alliance in Holland. He enjoyed this trip very much, especially the opportunity he had to make the acquaintance of many distinguished men and to purchase in Paris some new and interesting scientific apparatus for the College.

He returned by way of the Danube to escape quarantine, and Messrs. Paine, Grosvenor and Wilcox, the new American teachers, came with him. As none of them had passports they were arrested when they reached Turkish territory at Rustchuk. Dr. Hamlin got through on the ground that he belonged to the suite of the Dutch ambassador's wife who had come with him from Holland, but the tutors were held until Dr. Hamlin could get orders at Constantinople to allow them to come on.

This fourth year of Robert College was the first year of the Syrian Protestant College founded at Beirut under the presidency of Dr. Daniel Bliss, an old college-mate and dear friend of mine. It was the first fruit of the influence of Robert College in leading to the foundation of similar institutions in all mission fields, and it was incorporated in the state of New York in the same act with Robert College. Dr. Bliss had been in America and in England since 1862 to raise funds for it. The first class of 16 entered in 1866. It has been a triumphant success, although like Robert College it has passed through many trying experiences.

The fifth college year, 1867-68, opened with a full number of students. One hundred and two were registered during the year, of whom 14 were Armenians, 16 Bulgarians, 33 Greeks, but Dr. Hamlin in his report at the close of the year complains that many, especially of the Greek day scholars, "came only to try it. Not liking it, after a few lessons half learned, they left," so that at the end of the year there were but 75 students present. He speaks in the highest terms of the work done by Messrs. Grosvenor and Wilcox, the new tutors.

The College bore fruit this year of a very different kind from the sister college at Beirut. The French ambassador here and M. Boré, the Director General of the Jesuit Missions, had failed to prevent the opening of Robert College; but they took advantage of the visit of Sultan Abd-ul-Aziz to Paris in 1867 to induce the Emperor

Napoleon to extract a promise from the Sultan that on his return to Constantinople he would found a grand Lycée, the teachers in which should be appointed by the Emperor, the language should be French and the whole cost should be paid by the Turkish government. In spite of the opposition of the Turks, the Russians and the English, the French government had influence enough to hold the Sultan to his promise. The Lycée of Galata Serai was opened in 1868 in magnificent buildings, on a site unsurpassed in beauty by any other in Pera. Everything was done to make it attractive in every way and provision was made for six hundred students. The Emperor sent out a distinguished and experienced man as director with a large staff of able professors. Both our friends and our enemies felt that this would be the end of Robert College, especially as provision was made in the Lycée for a large number of free students. Dr. Hamlin was anxious but not disheartened, and there is no reason to believe that the Lycée of Galata Serai or any other of the numerous schools that have since been established in Constantinople has seriously affected the work of Robert College. The fall of the French Empire and the decline of French influence in Turkey led to great changes in the character of the Lycée. The language is still French and there are some eight hundred students, but it has long been a Turkish rather than a French school. It was destroyed by fire last winter (1907) but is to be rebuilt.

There was considerable correspondence during the year between Mr. Robert and Dr. Hamlin in regard to the organization and the discipline of the College, suggested in some measure by troubles which had been experienced at Lookout Mountain. Dr. Hamlin did not think that it was desirable to attempt a systematic classification of the students, but preferred to deal with them individually. At the close of the year he selected two of them, Hagopos Djedjizian, an Armenian, who had been two years in the College, and Petco Gorbanoff, a Bulgarian, who had been there three years, to graduate and received the degree of A. B. He justified this action in a detailed statement of the acquirements of the two young men, each far advanced in certain studies and far behind in others, but both mature in age and character. Both of them became teachers in the College the following year. The former has long been a professor in the College. The latter has held many important posts in Bulgaria.

The first "Commencement Exercises" of the College were held at the close of the public oral examination of the various classes, which in former years had attracted considerable attention. This year the audience was as large as could be accommodated, and all were enthusiastic over the orations of the two graduates and the speaking of other students in Turkish, Armenian, Bulgarian and French. The diplomas given were unique, long sheets of parchment, on which the conferring of the degrees was written, in fancy penmanship, in four languages — English, French, Turkish and Armenian or Bulgarian. I believe that similar diplomas were given in 1869.

The sixth college year opened with 80 students, and 95 in all were registered during the year, of whom 11 were Armenians, 41 Bulgarians, 17 Greeks.

The all absorbing event of the year, which transformed Dr. Hamlin from an educator into an architect, builder and mechanic, was the permission to build at Hissar, which was given informally at the beginning of October and officially December 20, 1868. In the evening of that day a general meeting of thanksgiving was held at the College and Dr. Hamlin writes, "It is a great triumph of right over wrong, and the Providence of God in bringing it about is truly wonderful and demands our warmest gratitude and daily thanksgiving." All Constantinople had come to have an interest in this prolonged contest, and it had long been predicted that the College would fail in its efforts to overcome the *vis inertiæ* of the Porte. They regarded Dr. Hamlin's final triumph with wonder and admiration.

Dr. Hamlin was determined to put up the college building himself without the aid or interference of any architect or builder, and I suppose that no one who reads his autobiography is surprised when he finds him undertaking this work. He would say: "It was just like him. He was that sort of a boy and man." He firmly believed that he could erect a better building at a less cost than any one else, and he undertook this Herculean task with a light heart. After the middle of the year he did not attempt to do any work in the College at Bebec except in the evening. He commenced excavations on the site April 7, 1869. All the teachers and students with many friends were present, and, after speeches in eleven languages, each one in turn took a spade, filled a barrow with earth and wheeled it away. In May, 1869, he received a visit from Mr. W. A. Booth, president of the Board of Trustees, and in consultation with him made some changes in his plans. By Monday, July 5, he was ready to lay the corner stone. The day was unfavorable. Mrs. Hamlin was very ill, and there was a pouring rain all the morning, but quite an assembly gathered on the grounds and there were appropriate addresses in five languages. The ceremony of laying the stone was performed by Hon. E. Joy Morris, the American minister. Sir Philip Francis, Judge of the Supreme Consular Court, and Canon Gribble, Chaplain of the British Embassy, represented England and made sympathetic addresses. It was nearly two years before the building was ready for occupation. During those years, while the work of construction was going on, Dr. Hamlin was always at Hissar, but one never knew where to find him. He might be in the water at the bottom of the well mending the force pump, or at the top of the building standing on an iron girder with forty feet of empty space below him. He might be setting up a steam-engine or doctoring a horse or teaching his masons how to lay stone. He might be entertaining some Turkish gentleman or using his rich vocabulary of invective on some wild Kurdish laborer. He made a sort of hut for himself in a pile of lumber near the building, and you might find him there taking a five minutes' nap in his chair or sharing his meagre lunch with a tailless green lizard which had made friends with him. If you came at the right time, you might be treated to a delicious cup of coffee made by himself. You might see him losing his own fingers as he stumbled on to a buzz saw or tenderly dressing the wounds of some unfortunate workman. Wherever you found him, you saw that his whole mind and heart was concentrated upon the building. He had endless difficulties, but was never discouraged and never daunted by any new and unthought-of problem which presented itself in the building. I think that those were the happiest days of his life.

I shall have much to say of Dr. Hamlin in my personal recollections of the College after I came into it a few weeks before the close of the sixth year, in June, 1869, but it seems desirable to preface this by a brief statement of dates and details drawn from the correspondence of Mr. Robert and Dr. Hamlin, which do not directly relate to the work in the College and which may also supplement the statements in his autobiography.

After a full discussion of the situation with Mr. Robert he went to America in September, 1871, to raise an endowment for the College, leaving his family in Bebec. He returned to Constantinople in June, 1872, and remained here until October, 1873, and while here he erected the Study Hall annex to Hamlin Hall, which was a temporary structure, but which served its purpose until 1906. In

October, 1873, he went to America with his family to continue the work of raising an endowment and never returned. In 1877 he resigned the office of president of the College.

His letters to Mr. Robert bring out still more strongly than his autobiography his utter aversion to the work of raising money, and his ill success strengthened this feeling; while Mr. Robert, who was a man of moderate means, never a millionaire, I believe, as the expenses of the College increased, was more and more impressed with the necessity of an endowment and with the belief that Dr. Hamlin was the only man who could raise it.

As early as August 21, 1867, Dr. Hamlin proposed to Mr. Robert that as soon as Robert College was well under way he should give himself to the founding of a college for girls at Constantinople. He writes: "It is not desirable that Robert College should remain in my hands after age begins to dim the eye and abate the natural force. I should then ruin it and I pray God in His infinite wisdom and mercy to keep me from it. I fear it now, but perhaps after a few more years I shall begin to think myself the only man who can carry it forward. In a female seminary I should not be exposed to anything of that sort. The work itself is necessary to the completeness of Robert College. The two institutions should have no connection with each other, but naturally female education should and must have a certain correspondency to that of the other sex. This has long been in my mind, but the time has not yet come for more than the mentioning of it."

Dr. Hamlin pressed this plan upon Mr. Robert frequently in special letters and in 1874 almost persuaded him to agree to his giving his time to raising money for this object rather than for Robert College. It was due in some measure to his influence that the Woman's Board of Missions in Boston took the matter up and founded a school which finally developed into the American College for Girls at Scutari, a part of Constantinople situated on the Asiatic shore of the Bosphorus.

Dr. Hamlin, however, writes to Mr. Robert in August, 1873, that "a girls' college in Constantinople should have no connection with any missionary society, but be governed by a corporate board like that of Robert College, with no woman in it, unless insisted on by the donor or donors and then I would weep in secret places over the necessity. As a general thing woman has not, and I pray she may never have, the business education that would fit her for such duties."

CYRUS HAMLIN

Mr. Robert finally insisted on Dr. Hamlin's devoting himself exclusively to the work of Robert College, and he reluctantly consented. What Mr. Robert thought of Dr. Hamlin at that time may be gathered from a letter written to me in November, 1874. "If I do not greatly mistake, those who come after us, fifty or one hundred years hence, will see more clearly than we ever shall that those who laid the foundations of the College were guided by the wisdom that cometh down from above. Although Dr. Hamlin is now highly appreciated by those who know him best it is only an index of far greater honor that will be showered on his name in after generations."

The following years up to 1877 were very trying ones to both Dr. Hamlin and Mr. Robert. Dr. Hamlin had labored in vain to raise an endowment, and now he felt that the great crisis of revolution and war in Turkey had made his task hopeless. No one who has had experience in such work can fail to sympathize with his feeling that he could endure it no longer, and, this given up, he felt that he had no place and no work in America. Mr. Robert was broken down in health. The troubles in Constantinople threatened the very existence of the College, and the burden of expense, with yearly increasing deficits, was greater than he was able to meet. No one who has ever found himself weighted with a burden too heavy for him to carry, but which could not be thrown off, can fail to sympathize with him. Rightly or wrongly, he felt that, in the interest of the College, it was not wise for Dr. Hamlin to return to Constantinople at that time. The question was discussed between them several times, and in June, 1877, Dr. Hamlin resigned the place of president and accepted an appointment for one year in Bangor Theological Seminary. He and Mr. Robert kept up a constant correspondence during the year, and October 23, 1877, Mr. Robert wrote to Dr. Long, then acting as director of the College, "I suppose that the faculty at Bangor will wish to make his appointment permanent, but I have not much fear that he will stay if the College needs his services next year, as I hope that it will."

The office of president was not filled until June, 1878, just as Mr. Robert was leaving for Europe, broken down in health, to die a few months later in Paris. Dr. Hamlin remained in Bangor to the sincere regret of his old associates in the College at Constantinople.

CHAPTER III
LAST TWO YEARS AT BEBEC. 1869-1871

I CAME to Constantinople in 1858 as treasurer of the Missions of the American Board, and up to 1869 my connection with the College was only incidental. When Dr. Hamlin went to America in 1860 he left me in charge of a well to be dug on the Kourou Tcheshmé lot. After going down about one hundred feet through solid rock without finding water I gave it up, and there it remains to this day.

When Dr. Hamlin was left alone by the resignation of the two professors, 1865, I taught several classes until the end of the college year. When he was trying to secure permission to build at Hissar I was living in Pera, and for about two years I had charge of all the negotiations with the American Legation and with the British Embassy. We depended chiefly at that time upon Lord Lyons, who had just come from Washington, who was an enthusiastic friend of America and who saw clearly that Robert College would strengthen English influence in Turkey. Dr. Hamlin was so disgusted with what he felt to be a want of sympathy on the part of the American minister that he had broken off personal relations with him, and the situation was farther complicated by the fact that the minister and his first secretary and dragoman were not on speaking terms. Yet all the official communication with the Porte had to be carried on through the American Legation. Happily I was on good terms with all the parties concerned. Dr. Hamlin told me what he wanted and I went first to the minister and got his promise to act; then I went to the dragoman and persuaded him to act on the same line, in both cases listening to the complaints which the one had to make against the other. It was the most curious experience that I ever had in diplomacy. In 1868 Dr. Hamlin resumed direct intercourse with the American minister.

I have already mentioned the aid given by Mr. George D. Morgan of New York. In January, 1868, Mr. Morgan and his family met at their hotel in Constantinople Mr. C. C. Coffin of Boston, the well-known war correspondent, who was a friend of mine. Mr. Morgan was ill, but Mr. Coffin brought the family to a prayer meeting at my house in Pera, and the next morning I went to see what I could do for Mr. Morgan. In the course of our conversation I told him the story of Dr. Hamlin's conflict with the Turkish government. He was so much interested that he gave up a day to go to Hissar with me and see the site. I took him to Bebec to call on Dr. Hamlin, and there he carefully examined all the documents connected with the case. He told me that evening that he should not return to America before May or June, but that he would make it his first business after his arrival to go to Washington and settle this matter with Mr. Seward. He kept his promise, and this was the beginning of the end of the struggle for permission to build the College.

I left Constantinople in the spring of 1868 with no expectation of ever returning to work here. I had other plans in view. In the winter of 1868-69 I was at my father's house on a visit, when one morning I received a telegram from Chicago asking me to take charge of a church there, a letter from two gentlemen in New York offering to furnish all the money needed for the carrying out of the plans which I had in view when I left Constantinople, and a letter from Mr. Robert, who wrote that it was absolutely necessary for me to go to Constantinople to look after the work of the College while Dr. Hamlin was engaged in erecting a building at Hissar. I declined the invitation to Chicago and went to New York to see Mr. Robert and to consult my friends there. I got their consent to postpone my work in New York for two years, and agreed with Mr. Robert to go and assist Dr. Hamlin for that length of time if he wished me to come, knowing as he did that I had no special preparation for such work. He had expressed some doubt about my health and my willingness to come, but approved of Mr. Robert's proposal fully when he found that another man whom he had invited had declined to go. I had no thought of making this my life-work, but I believed in the College. I loved and admired Dr. Hamlin and I was willing to sacrifice two years to help him out. I suppose that the one thing which led Mr. Robert to insist upon my going was the fact that my wife was Dr. Hamlin's eldest daughter.

Dr. Hamlin telegraphed me to come at once, and we arrived in Constantinople in season to be present at the laying of the corner stone of the new building at Hissar, July 5, 1869, and went to live in one of the college buildings at Bebec just opposite the main building. The College was still in session. Dr. Hamlin writes, "We welcome the Washburns with great rejoicing, for all these difficulties so absorb my time that the college year would wind up badly without him." My official position was that of Professor of Philosophy.

Robert College in 1869 was a unique institution. It occupied an old wooden house, built in 1798, on the side of a steep hill in the midst of the village of Bebec. It was entered from a court, with three stories below this level and three above. At the opposite end of the court was the kitchen. Dr. Hamlin's family lived in the story on the level, and the students occupied the rest of the building. They also occupied part of a house on the opposite side of the street which Dr. Hamlin had built some years before for a flour mill and bakery. I lived in the upper story of this house. The main building was very picturesque, but there were very few conveniences in either house, and what there were were chiefly the handiwork of the president. Not a penny which could be saved was ever wasted on the place, and the College was practically self-supporting. It was generally known as Dr. Hamlin's College. There was one professor when I came who had already resigned and who left in July. There were two American tutors, Grosvenor and Wilcox, and four assistant teachers for French and the native languages. Dr. Hamlin was the College. If the tutors were wise and tactful enough to understand and carry out his ideas, they were a help. Sometimes they were a hindrance. There were no regular college classes. Every student was treated as though he were the only one and given such studies as were adapted to his capacity. Every year those who were advanced were selected and formed into a class to graduate at the end of the year. With the small number of students then in the College this system worked very well. We have had no graduates who have distinguished themselves in later life more than those who were under Dr. Hamlin's personal influence. He had a marvelous power of impressing his own personality on his students. He was a great teacher and he lived with the students, ate at the same table, and managed, in spite of the variety of his occupations, to see much of them. He believed in righteous anger and sometimes came down upon a student like a cyclone, but behind this there was a tenderness of heart and a sense of humor which I think invariably won the affection of the students.

I have found among my papers an old document in Dr. Hamlin's handwriting which illustrates his methods of discipline, which were often as unique as this, and almost always successful. It relates to two brothers, Italians, who were always quarreling.

ARTICLES OF PEACE BETWEEN
SILVIO AND PIERRE BISCUCHIA TERMINATING
THE WAR OF 1867 & 1868
MARCH 7, 1868

The two high contracting parties agree:

1. That in order to preserve peace, amity and good will and to confirm a strict brotherhood to all future generations one shall not call the other an ass or a dog or a pig or a thief, robber, rowdy, pezevenk or other opprobrious epithet in Italian, French, Turkish, Greek, English, Bulgarian, Armenian or any other language spoken at the tower of Babel or since that day.

2. Silvio shall in no case strike Pierre nor Pierre Silvio.

3. If either is guilty of any injustice toward the other the injured party shall state it to the Principal in writing and judgment shall be rendered according to the evidence.

Witnesses: (Signed)
    GUSTAVE CAZE.   SILVIO BISCUCHIA.
    HENRI COIDAN.   PIERRE BISCUCHIA.
    YANKO AGELASTO.

These boys left the College soon after, and some years later one killed the other in a quarrel.

He was as supreme in the kitchen as in the schoolroom and generally superintended the making of the morning coffee himself. Although he knew nothing of book-keeping he managed the financial affairs of the College with success, as he had managed his bakery and laundry in the time of the war.

About three-fourths of the students boarded in the college, 35 in all. They studied in the study hall, slept in dormitories, 12 or 15 together, bringing their own bedding, ate in the dining-room, played in the small court, made their ablutions in a small lavatory or in the open court, got exercise by walking and occasional games on the hills above Bebec. They had prayers conducted by Dr. Hamlin at 6.30 in the morning and any student who failed to be present lost his breakfast. Lunch was at 12.30 and dinner at 6. The study hours were 4 in the morning, 2.30 in the afternoon and 1.30 in the evening. Every student was in bed and all lights extinguished at 10. I think that Dr. Hamlin himself seldom slept more than four hours in the night, with some five-minute naps during the day. Each dormitory had a tutor's room next it, and the tutors were expected to keep a surveillance over the students at all times, but especially in the study hall and the dormitories. No student could leave the building without special permission.

Most of the boarders at this time were Bulgarians, and for twenty years the great majority of the graduates were of this nationality. During the previous decade the Bulgarians had awakened from the sleep of centuries. They had thrown off the yoke of the Greek Patriarch of Constantinople and began to dream of escaping from that of the Turk. It was a nation of peasants, held in ignorance by a double bondage. When they began to seek for enlightenment their attention was first directed to Robert College by Dr. Long, then an American missionary in Bulgaria and later a professor in the College. Although Dr. Hamlin had interested himself in the Bulgarians in 1856 and used his influence to have missions established in Bulgaria, it does not appear from their correspondence that either he or Mr. Robert had ever thought of them as possible students in the College, and Mr. Robert died without knowing that he had played an important part in founding a new state in Europe.

When I reached Constantinople Dr. Hamlin had been absorbed for some time in the work of building at Hissar, and, having no head, the College had fallen into confusion; but it was soon reduced to order, the examinations were satisfactory and Dr. Hamlin looked upon the Commencement exercises as a great success. Five Bulgarians and one German were graduated and eighty persons attended the exercises. Dr. Hamlin writes to Mr. Robert August 6, 1869: "Our Commencement was the best we have ever had and left a very excellent impression. The orations of the graduating class were sober, manly, dignified, earnest and full of Christian thought. I would have wished you no greater luxury than listening to them. Mr. Washburn will put things in shape and keep them there. You will enjoy having a business man to correspond with instead of a busy man. I think he will do grandly."

The seventh college year opened September 15, 1869. Dr. Hamlin continued in charge of the boarding department. Otherwise he was absorbed from the very early morning until evening at Hissar, but always ready to give me advice. Two new tutors arrived from America, Wetmore of Michigan University and Anderson of Hamilton College, and together with Mr. Grosvenor they entered into the work with enthusiasm and whole-hearted devotion. There were six assistant teachers.

October 6 there were present 53 boarders and 18 day scholars from the vicinity of the College, making 71 in all, of whom 35 were Bulgarians, 10 Greeks, 8 Armenians, 6 Americans, 4 English, 2 Dutch, 2 Syrians, 2 Christian Osmanlis, 1 Persian prince, 1 German. Dr. Hamlin could pick out only one student who could be called a Senior, an Armenian, but I managed during the year to organize a Junior class of five Bulgarians.

Up to this time the Sabbath services at the College had been in charge of Rev. Dr. Schauffler, who had been for many years the pastor of a church made up of missionaries and foreign residents, which held regular services in the building which Dr. Hamlin had rented for the College. The students attended this service. Dr. Schauffler resigned this work at the end of 1879 on account of feeble health. The College then became responsible for the services. The preaching was done by Dr. Hamlin and myself with what help we could get from the missionaries. The Bible classes had always been a part of the college work, and Dr. Hamlin was nowhere more successful than in this department.

In March the number of students had increased to eighty-three, but an epidemic of measles, brought into the College by a day scholar, created a panic, and thirty boys, mostly day scholars, left, some of them not to return. None of the cases proved fatal, but it was a serious interruption to our work. Mr. Robert was seriously ill in New York at this time and came to Europe to regain his health. This also was a source of great anxiety to us. We were greatly refreshed by a visit from Professor Park of Andover and Professors Smith and Hitchcock of New York. Their enthusiastic interest in the College and in the building at Hissar gave us all new courage. I do not think that a gift of five thousand dollars would have done us as much good. They were great and good men and their hearty indorsement of our work, which many of the missionaries looked upon unfavorably, confirmed our faith in it. Professor Park had been lamed by the kick of a horse, but he insisted on going to the new building, and Dr. Hamlin had him hauled up the hill in a Turkish cart drawn by two buffaloes. Those who remember Professor Park can imagine how he looked and the play of humor between him and Professor Hitchcock.

On Sunday, June 5, 1870, Constantinople was visited by a

conflagration which destroyed a large part of the quarter of Pera, consuming over eight thousand houses, destroying at least one thousand lives and leaving some fifty thousand people homeless. Among the buildings destroyed was the palace of the English Embassy and many of the best houses in the city. No one ever attempted to estimate carefully the pecuniary loss. The homes of three of our students were burned and the parents of several others lost most of their property. Dr. Hamlin anticipated such a rise in the cost of material and in labor as would greatly increase the cost of his building, but the calamity was so great that the opposite result followed.

The year closed with only one graduate, an Armenian, but we put the Juniors all on the stage with orations and had a very successful Commencement. Dr. Hamlin left his work at Hissar to attend the examinations and wrote to Mr. Robert: "The examinations were good and gratifying. The progress of the year has been decided and hopeful for the future." The financial results of the year were equally satisfactory, as the income was sufficient to pay the expenses. But I called Mr. Robert's attention to the fact that this could only be hoped for so long as we had no permanent faculty and depended on cheap and transient tutors. Dr. Hamlin had encouraged Mr. Robert to believe that it was not only possible to make the College self-supporting, but that the profits would accumulate rapidly and furnish the means to erect additional buildings. He wrote to Mr. Robert that in the new building with 250 students, no more teachers would be needed than with 80 students, the number then in the College. It will be seen that this optimistic view has not been justified in our experience. A college without professors would be an anomaly anywhere, and to-day with 400 students we find 12 professors and 28 other teachers none too many for our work.

The eighth college year opened in the old building at Bebec in September, 1870, with 103 students, which increased during the year to 100 boarders and 35 day scholars, when we moved into the new building at Hissar. We had managed at the close of the previous year to organize another class so that we began with a regular programme of studies and Sophomore, Junior and Senior classes, the balance of students being more or less irregular.

Mr. and Mrs. Robert came to Constantinople in the middle of October and spent a month here. They went from here to Syria and visited the college which had been opened under the direction of Dr. Daniel Bliss at Beirut. The Beirut College interested Mr. Robert because it had been founded on somewhat different principles from that at Constantinople. It was closely connected with the Mission and was distinctively Protestant, taking the name Syrian Protestant College. It was largely under the control of a local board of managers. It had a medical department in view, which later became the most important branch of its work. The language of the college was Arabic, this being the common language of all nationalities in Syria, but after some years of experience this was changed to English. I regret that I have not in my possession and have never seen any of the letters written by Mr. Robert at the time of his visit to Constantinople and must depend upon my memory for everything connected with it. Mr. and Mrs. Robert spent most of the time that they were with us in the old mill house at Bebec, but Dr. Hamlin naturally saw much more of Mr. Robert than I did. He spent almost every day with Dr. Hamlin at Hissar and interested himself in all the details of the building, although he did not approve of the way in which Dr. Hamlin often exposed his life in various kinds of manual labor. It was not long after Mr. Robert left that he fell against a buzz saw and lost two of his fingers. However, Mr. Robert told me that he had never enjoyed anything more than these days spent at Hissar with Dr. Hamlin. He took time also to see everything at the College in Bebec — to make the acquaintance of the teachers and students and investigate every detail of every department. He did not hesitate to criticise and advise in regard to the work at Bebec or at Hissar, and so far as Bebec was concerned his criticisms were generally wise and timely, although it was sometimes impossible in our straitened circumstances to correct the deficiencies which he discovered. He also saw the missionaries and interested himself in them and their work, and drew out such criticisms of the College as they had to make.

The Grand Vizier, Aali Pasha, lived at Bebec and naturally knew of Mr. Robert's presence here. He informed the Sultan, who proposed to confer on Mr. Robert the decoration of the Medjidie, in diamonds. The Grand Vizier invited Mr. Robert to call on him and informed him of the will of the Sultan in most complimentary language. Mr. Robert expressed his high appreciation of the honor but declined to accept the decoration, as something altogether foreign to American ideas. The Grand Vizier took it very kindly, but there was a difference of opinion among friends of the College here as to the wisdom of his act. This official recognition of the College by the Sultan would have had its value in later years, and it is not exactly a gracious thing to refuse an honor of this sort, or a possible thing to make Turkish officials understand the motives of such a refusal. Still there is no evidence that any positive harm came of it in this case, and it would be difficult to imagine anything more incongruous than Mr. Robert wearing a Turkish decoration on his breast in a New York drawing-room.

There can be no doubt that this visit of Mr. and Mrs. Robert to Constantinople confirmed him in his determination to support the College to the utmost extent of his ability.

Not long after his departure we had a visit from General Sheridan, who was fresh from the great battlefields of France and enough of an American to interest himself in the peaceful work of an American college on the Bosphorus. He told me that, although he had seen the most bloody battles of the war, near Metz, he had seen no such desperate fighting as took place on several occasions during our Civil War in America.

After Mr. Robert left us we plunged into a sea of troubles, such as are incident to such an institution, but which were new to me. First came a most trying case of discipline involving two of the most prominent students, one English and one Persian, in a gross offense against morality. There was nothing to be done but to expel them both, although one belonged to a Christian family who were among our best friends. Later developments proved that this young man was a hopeless degenerate; but I felt then, as I have felt quite as strongly ever since, that to expel a student is a humiliating confession of failure on the part of the teacher and in some cases at least an evidence that the teacher has failed to do his duty.

Early in January we had an outbreak of typhoid fever in the College, due, as I believed, to the overcrowding of the old building at Bebec, although Dr. Hamlin was unwilling to admit this. Many were ill and there were four serious cases. The worst case was that of a young German boy from Trieste. We took him into our house, and Mrs. Washburn and I took care of him for many weeks. He sank so low that for two days he was unconscious and lay like dead, but he rallied again and finally recovered his health, to our great joy, as did all the rest of our patients. But for a time the College was a hospital, with no doctor within five miles of us and no trained nurses. It was a great strain on all the teachers.

It was partly on this account that Dr. Hamlin insisted upon moving into the new building at Hissar before it was finished. I think that no one else approved of it, but the result justified Dr. Hamlin's decision. There is a common proverb current here, "If you build a stone house, rent it to your enemy the first year, to your friend the second and live in it yourself the third." Every one prophesied evil of the dampness of the walls, and many would not send their sons on this account, but in fact the health of the College was perfect after our removal. The only inconvenience was the intolerable noise made by the forty or fifty workmen in the building. Dr. Hamlin's family moved into the building at the same time with the students. It was May 17, 1871, that the new building was occupied; and the change made in perfect weather from the narrow quarters in the midst of the village of Bebec to the hill-top at Hissar, the most beautiful site on the Bosphorus and one un- surpassed by any in the world, more than compensated for all the inconvenience of our unfinished building — and the bare, unim- proved grounds, cumbered with workshops and piles of rock and unprotected with walls. The number of students rose to 130 before the end of the year. The public opening was postponed to July 4, just two years from the laying of the corner stone. It so happened that Ex-Secretary Seward, on his way around the world, was in Constantinople at this time, and he came to the College to take the principal part in the opening exercises. Blacque Bey, who was the Turkish minister at Washington at the critical time when Mr. Morgan brought the college question before Mr. Seward with such success, was also there. Mr. Seward was a physical wreck, but he made a noble address, and his presence on this occasion impressed the Turkish government and all Constantinople with the idea that the College was under the special patronage as well as protection of the government of the United States. I suppose it was one of the happiest days in Dr. Hamlin's life — a day of triumph in what he believed to be a great and good cause and for which he had battled for ten years.

The Commencement exercises a month later were held in the study hall which occupied the northeast corner of the first story of the new building which I shall henceforth speak of as Hamlin Hall. Up to that time there had been 9 graduates, 2 in 1868, 6 in 1869, 1 in 1870,— 6 Bulgarians, 2 Armenians and 1 German. Mr. Petco

Gorbanoff remained several years in the College as instructor in Bulgarian and since that time has been a prominent citizen of Bulgaria, a lawyer by profession, and often a member of the National Assembly. Mr. Hagopos Djedjizian has been a Protestant preacher and an instructor or professor of Armenian in the College since 1869. Of the next class Mr. Jordan Economoff and Mr. Stephan Thomoff studied theology in Drew Theological Seminary in America and have since been Protestant clergymen in Bulgaria. Mr. Theodore Djabaroff has been a prominent official in Bulgaria. Mr. Peter Mattheoff has occupied high ministerial and diplomatic positions in the Bulgarian government after having been in the British postal service, and after having been engaged for the British Museum in explorations in Babylonia with George Smith. Mr. Diran Garabetian of 1870 has been an official of the Imperial Ottoman Bank ever since his graduation, and Mr. Naiden Nicoloff also a banker.

The class of 1871 were all Bulgarians, and no more distinguished class has ever been graduated from the College. Stephan Panaretoff has been instructor or professor of Bulgarian and Slavic in the College ever since his graduation, and Bulgaria has produced no more distinguished scholar and teacher. Mr. Stoiloff and Mr. Slaveikoff were both teachers in the College for a time. Constantine Stoiloff was the ablest statesman in Bulgaria until he died in 1901. Ivan Slaveikoff was one of the leading literary men in Bulgaria and held many high offices during his life until he died in 1901, as Minister of Public Instruction, Ivan S. Gueshoff is still a leading politician and just now diplomatic agent of Bulgaria in Constantinople, as he has been in Paris and Vienna. Petco Taptcheleshloff has been and is a merchant.

I was not present on July 4 nor at the Commencement. I had left for America June 20. The two years which I had agreed to give to Robert College while Dr. Hamlin was engaged in building had been completed and the building was occupied. Family affairs and other considerations made it necessary for me to go to America. But Mr. Robert and the trustees in New York and Dr. Hamlin in Constantinople urged me to accept a permanent position in the College, especially in view of the fact that it had been arranged for Dr. Hamlin to go to America in the autumn to raise an endowment for the College. Dr. Hamlin knew from two years' experience that I could never manage a college on his plan and declared often that he could never manage one on mine; but he thought that I had learned enough from him and had caught enough of his spirit, to make me the only possible candidate to fill his place while he was in America. I accepted the appointment after much hesitation, because I had become deeply interested in the College and because I believed, after two years of trial, that, in spite of our differences, we could work together in harmony — peacefully agreeing to differ as we always had. I did not forget that I had come to the College without any experience in teaching or in the administration of a school of any kind and that most of what I knew at the end of two years I had learned from Dr. Hamlin. Our differences grew out of our characters. He was an original genius, I was not. He abhorred all the trammels and details of systematic organization, which he declared belonged to Jesuits. To me such system seemed to be essential. We got on together because he tolerated my system and I was glad to have him work outside of it in any way he pleased.

CHAPTER IV
NINTH COLLEGE YEAR. 1871-1872

DR. HAMLIN left for America September 30, 1871, leaving his family in the house which I had occupied at Bebec, while I moved into Hamlin Hall, occupying the suite of rooms in the second story on the south side of the building, where we lived for twenty years.

A great change had taken place in the political situation at Constantinople due to the Franco-Prussian War. It was illustrated by a request made to me by an Armenian merchant at this time. "Please excuse my son from studying any more French, that is played out. Let him study the Prussian language instead." Since the Crimean War French influence, and under its protection Jesuit influence, had been supreme at Constantinople. Sultan Abdul-Aziz had visited Napoleon III at Paris, and the Empress, after opening the Suez Canal, had been entertained by the Sultan at Constantinople. The great Lycée of Galata Serai had been opened, with a staff furnished by the Emperor but supported by the Sultan, to compete with Robert College; and Dr. Hamlin had found all this influence arrayed against him when he was seeking permission to build at Hissar. All this was changed by the war and the fall of the empire. It was some years before Germany gained much influence here, but Russia came to the front and England regained much of her old prestige in the eyes of Turkish statesmen if not with Sultan Abdul-Aziz himself. The men who deposed him a few years later were in league with England. Russia took the place of France as the chief enemy of the College and used her influence to turn Bulgarian students from Robert College to Russia for their education. Unfortunately for Bulgaria she opened the way for a boy in Tirnova, where Dr. Long was a missionary, and a friend of this boy, whose name was Stambouloff, to go to Russia for a free education in a theological school. If he had come to Robert College he would have had other ideas of government than those which he learned in Russia. He was probably the strongest man that Bulgaria has produced and saved Bulgaria from Russian domination; but so far as the internal government of the country was concerned he too often fell back upon Russian methods. When a student he was expelled from Russia as a nihilist but secretly employed by the Russian Embassy as a sort of brigand revolutionist against the

Turks, before the massacres, and came to the front as a great leader after the fall of Prince Alexander.

The College opened September 15 with four college classes and a preparatory class, with but few students; but by the first of October there were 135 boarders and 30 day scholars. Mr. Grosvenor had left for America and in his place two new tutors, Mr. Forbes from Amherst College and Mr. Richardson from Hobart, had come, making with Mr. Anderson and Mr. Wetmore a most efficient staff of American teachers. We have never had better men and they have all distinguished themselves since. I can never forget what I owe and what the College owes to their devoted service.

The cause of so few students entering the College was the outbreak of an epidemic of cholera in the city. The horrors of the great epidemic of 1865 were fresh in the minds of all, and students were afraid to come. It was a wonder that we had so many. The first cases occurred before Dr. Hamlin left for America, and he hesitated about starting. It was while he was still detained in the quarantine at Trieste that I was roused from my bed by a messenger from Bebec, saying that Willie Hamlin had the cholera. It was a terribly stormy night, and it took me three quarters of an hour to reach them. I found the case far advanced, and no doctor could be found. Six years before in that very room my own son Harry had died of cholera in my arms. I fought the disease in this case until six o'clock in the morning, made all the arrangements for his immediate burial and disinfecting the house and came back to Hissar more dead than alive to go to bed and fight off an attack of cholera myself. Had I remained until the authorities knew of the case I should have been kept there some days in quarantine. It was a terrible shock to Mrs. Hamlin, but happily no other case occurred in the family. Within a few days I was called to three other cases in the families at Hissar. All died. There was something peculiar about this epidemic, unlike that of 1865. Nearly every case proved fatal, with treatment which in 1865 was generally successful. I had a second slight attack myself after one of these visits, and we had some three hundred cases of students with threatening premonitory symptoms, but every student was carefully watched, and we had no fully developed case of cholera in the College. Many thought that we ought to suspend and send the students home; but they and their parents had such faith in us that, so far as I can remember, only a single student was withdrawn. At one time Mr.

Wetmore had an attack when spending a night at Bebec, but I got to him at once and he recovered. Those were weeks when everything looked dark about us, but we put our trust in God and kept right on with the required routine of college work, and He did not fail us. The epidemic lasted about four months. There were about four thousand deaths in the city besides soldiers and sailors. The frantic attempts of the Turkish authorities to deal with the epidemic on modern principles frightened the people more than the disease itself. It was then that they first heard of microbes, and Turkish doctors stuffed chloride of lime into the mouths, noses and ears of their patients to keep the microbes from crawling out and attacking others.

Perhaps the most important event of the year was the purchase of the land between the College and the village of Hissar. It belonged to Achmet Vefik Pasha of whom Dr. Hamlin had bought the college lot of about six acres. This one contained about twelve acres, and included the well which was our only water supply, besides the cistern of Hamlin Hall. Dr. Hamlin had written at length to Mr. Robert urging him to authorize the purchase by telegraph. After Dr. Hamlin's departure a long letter came from Mr. Robert forbidding the purchase, but here appeared one of Mr. Robert's most admirable characteristics. Although the most positive of men in his judgments, he hesitated about imposing his authority upon us, even where it was a question of money which must come out of his pocket. He had held the letter over a day and then added a postscript which left the final decision to me.[1] I bought the land at once for thirteen thousand two hundred dollars. On this land to-day stand Theodorus Hall and six professors' houses. Achmet

---

1 In regard to this postscript Mr. Robert wrote to me October 30, 1871: "I think I see clearly the hand of God in suggesting those lines. I had conferred with Mr. Booth on the subject ... and we both decided it was not best to make the purchase. I went to Throgs Neck that evening feeling that we had done right, but thinking and praying over it, it occurred to me that I had never given Dr. Hamlin *positive* instruction as to anything, though I had several times differed from him, saying to myself why should I do so in this case. I name it because I have had the most pleasant emotions since reading your letter advising the purchase and cannot forbear expressing my feelings, for I have often during the past six weeks asked our Heavenly Father to guide all interested in the matter to such action as would be most for His glory, and my conviction is strong that in this thing we have all been directed by wisdom from above."

Vefik Pasha was in no special need of money at that time, but he was a warm friend of the College, and the price which he asked was very reasonable. He was the most interesting Turk whom I have ever known — a great linguist, familiar with sixteen languages and with the classic authors of all Europe, had held the highest offices in the government, was a great reformer and an honest man, — a very rare thing for a Turkish official; but his ideas of government were altogether oriental and I think that Haroon-al-Rashid was his ideal for a sovereign. He lived very near the College, and I spent many evenings with him. One I shall never forget. I found there a German savant, and they were discussing the inspiration of the Bible. I declined to take part and listened. The nominal Christian was denying it, and the Mohammedan defended it quite as though he had been a professor in a Protestant theological seminary. I was amazed, and the next day I went to ask him where he had studied theology. He laughed one of his hearty laughs and said, "Oh! When I was ambassador in Paris I lived next door to Renan, and we discussed religious questions almost every day." He died some years ago, a poor man; his family has disappeared, and the very house in which he lived has been pulled down and sold for firewood. His magnificent library, the best in Constantinople, was scattered, — partly stolen and partly sold to pay debts.

It is perhaps worth mentioning that in February, 1872, Nature favored us with an exhibition of the Aurora Borealis which surpassed everything that I have ever seen. For hours the heavens were as red as blood, great waves of light pouring down from a corona at the zenith and coming up from the horizon. It was the more remarkable as we seldom see anything of these displays here, and it made a great impression upon our students, as well as upon the superstitious people of the city.

We had some very interesting visitors during the year. First Professor North of Hamilton College, "the old Greek" as he was called by his students, and one who was greatly trusted by Mr. Robert. Many of our best tutors we owed to his recommendation. Three of them were here at the time of his visit. He was very enthusiastic about the College, and I have no doubt that his report of it was a great encouragement to Mr. Robert at a time when he specially needed it — when he was reluctantly giving up his school on Lookout Mountain that he might concentrate his efforts upon Robert College.

Later came General Sherman and Lieutenant, now General, Grant — Prince Grant as he was called by the Turkish newspapers, his father being at that time President of the United States. General Sherman was the guest of the Sultan, and he brought with him to the College the staff of pashas who were in attendance on him. He made an admirable address to the students and made it apparent to the Sultan and to all the city that Robert College was an institution honored by the government of the United States. Such support by such a man was invaluable to us. Later came Mr. Remington, of whom I shall write in connection with the Commencement exercises.

One of the questions brought up by Mr. Robert during this year was that of corporal punishment, which he objected to. Dr. Hamlin had flogged students publicly for gross offenses and considered this a proper punishment, and I had been so far influenced by Dr. Hamlin's example that in the earlier years of my administration I did sometimes resort to forcible measures in extreme cases even with older students, and some amusing stories are current among the alumni of my punishments. For a man as big and strong as I was it was not unnatural to meet resistance sometimes with force. I did once throw a Turk down stairs, who had intruded into a dormitory after having been ordered out of the building, and some students did feel the weight of my heavy oak cane when they were riotous. Looking back upon it now, I am inclined to feel that in those earlier years something of this kind was necessary; but as the College came to be a recognized power in the world its moral influence increased so much, that physical force was no longer needed to maintain discipline. In later years I never resorted to it with college students. But I have always believed that whipping was a punishment well fitted for the younger boys in the Preparatory Department in a certain class of offenses. Only I insisted that it should be administered by the president in private, not publicly nor by any other teacher, and solemnly. There were ten cases during this college year where such punishment was administered. In the later years I found that a public reprimand at morning prayers was one of the most effective of punishments, only it was necessary to resort to this as a rare punishment, and for serious offenses. If it had been common it would have been useless. The most difficult cases to manage were those in which I had to settle quarrels between students, especially when they were of different nationalities, to be an absolutely just judge between them, and to so far satisfy both

GEORGE WASHBURN

parties that there would be no further trouble.

In May, 1872, I was appointed by the trustees Director of the College, which did not disturb the position of Dr. Hamlin as president, and was equivalent to the position of vice-president, giving me full authority during his absence. The title of director was chosen as one that would be better understood in Constantinople.

Dr. Hamlin reached Constantinople June 17 on his return from America. His special purpose in returning was to erect a study hall building and two professors' houses. He was greatly impressed by the enthusiastic reception which was given to him by the College. He writes to Mr. Robert, "It was a most unexpected and enthusiastic affair." A week later he writes in regard to his eight months in America: "I have been able, some way or other, to secure a good hearing, but in the very crisis of the work, the getting of the money, I have failed. I have learned some things I never dreamed of as possible, and now it remains to be seen what success God will give to another year's deliberate and consecutive effort. If I can raise an endowment of thirty thousand dollars a year I am willing to give four years to it."

Dr. Hamlin's failure to get money is a mystery to me.[2] Since that day I have had long and repeated experiences in raising money for the College and ought to understand the business, but I cannot understand why Dr. Hamlin failed. I have never done such grand work or created any such enthusiasm as he did. He worked day and night. He had a great number of very successful public

---

2 In a letter to me Mr. Robert gives the following reasons for Dr. Hamlin's failure. 1st. The low state of religion in the churches. 2d. Humanitarian efforts. These were stimulated by the war and since then the sympathies of benevolent men have run in this direction. 3d. Denominational zeal. Ministers try to turn all gifts into denominational enterprises. 4th. For two years several of the largest denominations have been getting up "memorial funds." 5th. The Chicago fire. 6th. "Charity begins at home," the common excuse for not giving to anything foreign. My impression is that he might have added another more important one.

Both he and Dr. Hamlin thought that their strongest argument was to say that the College was and would be *self-supporting*. I have always used the opposite argument. Without an endowment the College could not live. There is a pleasure in starting a good thing which will go on by itself, but where is there a genuine college which is progressing without an endowment? According to Mr. Robert's books the College was self-supporting the fifth, seventh, eighth and ninth years, years when there were no professors. The other years there was a loss of more than two thousand dollars a year. It has never been self-supporting since the tenth year.

meetings, attended by the élite of America, and he diligently followed them up by personal interviews. No missionary has ever been more honored. No college president ever worked harder. But he got very little money. The great Chicago fire which took place while he was on the way to America may have had some influence, and in New York City the fact that Mr. Robert's name had been given to the College furnished some with an excuse for not giving. No man in New York was more highly or more universally respected than Mr. Robert, but he was not a popular man. There was no more liberal or conscientious giver in New York, but he carried out the injunction not to let his left hand know what his right hand gave, and few knew how generous he was. It is not surprising that Dr. Hamlin found difficulties in New York City, but I never found Mr. Robert's name or character an obstacle in other places, where most of Dr. Hamlin's work was done. I cannot account for his failure. It was a terrible disappointment both to him and to Mr. Robert, and in April Mr. Robert had written to me that Dr. Hamlin feared that I was dooming the College "to financial ruin" by insisting upon the appointment of professors and perfecting our equipment. He seemed to share this feeling. Under these trying circumstances nothing in the history of the College is more remarkable than the way in which Mr. Robert's faith and courage rose above it all to meet the emergency. He not only consented to everything which I had asked for, but sent Dr. Hamlin back to put up three new buildings.

It was during this college year and the next that Mr. Forbes and I made a careful geological survey of the Bosphorus region, extending back some twenty miles on each side of the Strait. Educated at Amherst under President Hitchcock, I had at one time thought of giving my life to geology. Mr. Forbes was also an Amherst man and had interested himself in this subject, and he joined in this work most heartily. I probably owe my long life to the fact that for some two years Mr. Forbes and I devoted all the time that we could get to this out-of-door work, and there is no part of my life here that I look back upon with more pleasure. It was a field which had hardly been worked at all, and we made many interesting discoveries. We settled the age of the different formations in this vicinity and learned much of its geological history. One incident brought our work to the knowledge of the scientific world. Much was made just at this time of the discovery of evidence of the existence of man in the Miocene period, based on the discovery by Mr. Calvert of fossil bones in Miocene strata eight hundred feet below the surface which were "covered with pictures which must have been made by human hands." The locality of the discovery was near the shore of the Dardanelles just on the edge of the Troad. Mr. Forbes and I went down there to investigate, and Mr. Calvert very kindly showed us the bones and informed us exactly where they had been found. We found the place, and the formation was undoubtedly Miocene. We found plenty of fossil bones of that period, some with similar marks on them, but we were able to demonstrate the fact that no human hands ever had anything to do with making these marks to the satisfaction of the scientific world. We afterward visited Hissarlik and were entertained there royally by Mr. Schliemann and his beautiful wife. The world is generally agreed now that this is the site of ancient Troy; but we came to the conclusion, after visiting all the supposed sites, that there is no place in the Troad which answers to all the demands, of the Iliad.

The college year closed with 210 students, and Dr. Hamlin wrote to Mr. Robert of the Commencement exercises, July 25, 1872: "Yesterday was a great day and a high day at Robert College. It was the best of all our Commencements. It crowned them all, and in all respects the exercises of the graduating class were excellent, not merely satisfactory, but positively gratifying, solid, thoughtful, clear, no flash, no 'hi-falutin,' but noble, manly and elevated. Music introduced for the first time and good. Speeches by Mr. Boker, American minister, Mr. Francis, our minister to Athens, Mr. Remington" and others. Mr. Remington helped to celebrate the day by giving five thousand dollars, the income of which was to be used for general purposes until it might seem wise to use the principal to start a museum of useful arts. We had already commenced a zoölogical museum, by the purchase of a unique collection of Turkish birds, which is still, I think, the only one in the city.

The graduates numbered 8, — 6 Bulgarians, 1 Greek and 1 English. Andrew C. Zenos, the Greek, has been for many years a very distinguished professor in American theological seminaries, now at McCormick Seminary in Chicago. Edward Binns, the Englishman, was thrown from a horse and killed in 1876. Of the Bulgarians the one to whom their country owes the most is Peter Dimitroff. He had paid his way through college by teaching Turkish and remained a teacher for several years after graduating. From the time of the Bulgarian massacres to the present day he has been one of the wisest, best and most devoted servants of his country. Constantine Calchof is now a wealthy banker and has occupied many important positions in the government of Eastern Roumelia and Bulgaria. Dimitry Economoff and Ivan D. Gueshoff have done good service in high official positions. Stephan M. Camburoff entered the army and died in 1882.

CHAPTER V
DEVELOPMENT OF THE COLLEGE. 1872-1873

THIS year marks an era in the history of the College. We crossed the Rubicon. We settled the question that this should be a college and not a high school, and that we would trust in God to raise up friends to support it. If Mr. Robert had not been a man of great faith, who lived very near to God, this decision would never have been made. I can never recall this decision on his part without a feeling of profound reverence for the man. Up to this time he had cherished the idea that the College might be self-supporting, and Dr. Hamlin had used this as one of his chief arguments in his campaign in America to raise funds. In fact during the last three years it had been self- supporting so far as current expenses were concerned, and the failure to raise money for endowment must have been a cogent reason in Mr. Robert's mind to avoid additional expenses, especially as we had managed to do some very good work under the existing system of having only one permanent teacher. Dr. Hamlin was a college in himself, as President Garfield said of Dr. Hopkins; but it must be remembered Garfield had in view that there should be only one student, "Dr. Hopkins on one end of the log, he on the other." During the ninth year there had been over two hundred students in the College. I was acting president, I was the Faculty, I was the college preacher, I was professor of Philosophy and Political Economy. I taught English, I was treasurer, I was dean, I managed the boarding department, I was secretary and had all the correspondence and the direction of fifteen temporary instructors of eight different nationalities; and I was *not* Dr. Hamlin. It would have been ridiculous to call such an institution a college except for the one fact that it was in Turkey and that there was no other school in the empire in those early years to equal it. On the same plan it might have continued to exist as a self-supporting high school, but it could never have been a college and never have attained the commanding position which it has held since 1872. Two professors were appointed and one adjunct professor. I was furnished with a secretary and Dr. Hamlin had returned from America. We had a Faculty. Rev. Albert L. Long, D.D., was appointed Professor of Natural Science, Edwin A. Grosvenor, Professor of Latin and History, Hagopos Djedjizian Adjunct Professor of Ancient and Modern Armenian. Dr. Long was a rare man, of distinguished ability and not quite forty years old. He had taught several years in America. He had been a missionary of the American Methodist Church in Bulgaria for some twelve years, where he had won the confidence and affection of the people and with Dr. Riggs had translated the Bible into Bulgarian. It was through his influence that Bulgarians first came to the College. No college president ever had a more devoted and efficient associate, and he was a tower of strength in the College until he died in 1901, mourned by all Bulgaria and by every student who had been under him. He had been beloved as a brother by all his associates. Professor Grosvenor had been a tutor in the College for three years and had proved so efficient that we were glad to persuade him to return as a professor. He came back as an ordained minister. He filled the place with distinguished ability until he resigned in 1890 to go to America and accept a professorship in Amherst College. Professor Djedjizian was a graduate of the College in 1868 and had been an instructor ever since. He already had the reputation among the Armenians of being a very eloquent preacher and orator, as well as an Armenian scholar. His appointment as adjunct professor was a reversal of the former policy of the College, in which policy I had fully agreed with Mr. Robert, that we should appoint no natives of the country to permanent positions in the College. We all agreed in 1872 that this was a mistake, and our experience ever since has fully justified this conclusion. My secretary, Mr. Robert Thomson, who remained with me five years, was a young Scotchman who had been a student in the College. He was an ideal secretary, and after leaving me he went to America and studied theology and has since been one of the best missionaries of the American Board in Bulgaria. In addition to these professors we began the year with four American tutors, Messrs. Richardson, Forbes, Arthur Hoyt and Woodbridge, eight other instructors and an English lady, Mrs. Dick, as matron. Our salary account for the year was increased about four thousand dollars over the previous year. The increase in our permanent staff enabled us to revise and improve our curriculum of studies, one thing Mr. Robert had constantly impressed upon us from the beginning. He often wrote about it. Dr. Hamlin's letters to him reëchoed the same thought, and we all fully realized the fact that progress, development in the College, was essential to life. No one realized it more strongly than I did, and it has been my principle of action always. But progress means more men and more money. Our progress has never caught up with our desires. We had made progress before 1872. To move from the old house in Bebec to Hamlin Hall at Hissar was an evidence of progress which deeply impressed all Constantinople. And we had done what we could from the first to improve our organization, our equipment and our course of study. We had been very fortunate in many of our tutors and instructors; but although we did our best with the men and the means which we had, the establishment of Robert College had already led to the establishment of the Galata Serai Lycée and several other national schools which in their equipment were in advance of us. Our superiority lay altogether in the moral and religious influences which went to the building up of character. Now with a live Faculty and Mr. Robert's determination to press forward, we were in a position to keep in advance of all rivals, and at the same time to bid them God-speed in their work.

One of our most pressing wants was a material one. Our study halls and recitation rooms were absurdly inadequate to the number of our students, and Dr. Hamlin had returned expressly to erect a new building to meet this want. He trusted perhaps too much to the good will of the Turkish government and commenced work without waiting for any permission, but Aali Pasha had passed away and the Grand Vizier was the tool of Russia. Perhaps it was our fault in having failed to give a *back-sheesh* to the inspector who came to see what was going on. At any rate, the work was stopped, and it was some months before Mr. Boker, the American minister, succeeded in getting an *iradé* for it. He could not get permission to erect professors' houses, and Dr. Hamlin returned to America without erecting them; but meanwhile he purchased the house in the village of Hissar in which I am now writing. Dr. Long moved into it at that time. The study hall building was a large one-story building behind Hamlin Hall, made with dry stone walls plastered without and within, containing two study rooms and recitation rooms in the roof, a temporary structure which cost about ten thousand dollars. Dr. Hamlin was probably joking when he wrote of it as "adding to the magnificence of the College." It was an ugly building externally, but it answered its purpose admirably for thirty years, when it was pulled down, and at the time when it was built it added greatly to the efficient working of the College.

After investing so much capital in land and buildings and authorizing this increase in current expenses, Mr. Robert's faith was to be severely tried up to the time of his death, but he never expressed to me any regret at what he had done. The year had hardly opened when the news of the great fire in Boston put an end to the hopes that he had had of help from there, and the great financial crisis of 1873 was not only discouraging in a general way, but it seriously reduced his own income. Much of his property was in real estate in the city of New York, and the value of this was steadily declining. Still he firmly believed that, in His own good time, God would provide for the College, as He has. His faith was not in vain.

The number of students registered this year was 257, of whom 68 were day scholars and 189 boarders, but the number present at any one time was never more than 170 boarders and 45 day scholars. There were some troubles during the year which led to the expulsion of 6 students. The number of Greeks in the College had increased to 48, and the great conflict of the Greeks and Bulgarians over the church question had lately been decided by the Turks in favor of the Bulgarians, in view of which the Greek Patriarch had excommunicated the Bulgarian nation as schismatics. The intensely bitter feeling between the two nationalities was political as well as religious, for this recognition of the Bulgarians as a separate nationality put an end to long cherished hopes of a restoration of the Greek Empire at Constantinople. It revealed to the world that the Christians of European Turkey were mostly Slavs and not Greeks. It was inevitable that our Bulgarian and Greek students should share in the general excitement, and on one occasion we escaped a general battle at the evening surveillance only because I happened to be within a hundred feet of the study hall. The Bulgarian instructor was in charge of the study hall, and I found him closed with a big Greek, while every student was on his feet just rushing to the fray. I sent the Greek to my office and had no difficulty in restoring order in the hall, but it was a narrow escape from a great calamity. It is to the credit of both the Greeks and Bulgarians that after this they respected the neutral territory of the College so far as not to have any more serious conflicts. But it was years before the better class of Greeks began to come in any number to what they often complained to me was a Bulgarian college. At this time, however, the Armenians had rather suddenly taken up the College and outnumbered any other nationality, which caused a combination against us of their national schools and attacks upon us in their newspapers, which culminated in the difficulties of the following year.

I had to go to America on important business in the summer, and as the president was here and Professor Grosvenor was living in Hamlin Hall I was able to get away a month before the close of the year. Nothing really serious happened in my absence; but with Armenians, Bulgarians and Greeks all in rather an excited state, it was natural that after my departure they should try the metal of the modified administration and see what they could do, especially as Dr. Hamlin was not living in the College. There was some rioting in the building at the close of the year, after Commencement, but nothing more serious than often takes place in American schools. Dr. Hamlin made little of it. His great trial was with a case of drunkenness. He thrashed two students publicly and expelled the third. This last was a curious case. The boy had given me endless trouble. Much of the time he was not an unattractive boy, but at intervals his behavior was such that it seemed to me like the cases reported in the New Testament of demoniacs. He seemed to be literally possessed of an evil spirit whom I could not cast out so that he should not return. I never heard of him after his expulsion until the time of my giving up the work here in 1904, when the old students raised a fund to found a scholarship in my name, when the committee showed me a most complimentary letter from him with a contribution of twenty francs for the testimonial, and then I learned that he was a most estimable man of very modest means, who wished to testify to the good that he had got in the College. Evidently Dr. Hamlin's discipline cast out the devil.

Our Turkish neighbors in Hissar were in general rather fanatical and sometimes made things unpleasant for us and our students, but we took as little notice of it as possible, hoping that as they came to know us better they would become friendly. They occasionally stoned us, sometimes spat on us and generally made use of their rich vocabulary of vituperation to abuse us. This year for some reason these manifestations increased so that we had to apply to our Legation for protection. It took six months of negotiations with the Sublime Porte to bring the affair to an end. The following year, under similar circumstances, when a lot of boys from the village molested us, I sent for the chief of the police, gave him a backsheesh and asked him to settle the matter, which he did by arresting the boys and thrashing them. We have not troubled our

Legation with such matters since. The leader in these attacks was the wife of the village imam, a remarkable woman who for many years ruled this quarter of the village, a virago whom I do not care to describe, for we have been good friends for many years. I think it was Dr. Long who first won her over, when he lived just opposite to her in the house where I am writing. It was hard for any one to withstand his kindness. It was some years later that she came to my house and one day begged me to understand that the trouble she made us in those early years was all a mistake. "We thought," she said, "that you were bad people and would corrupt our village and we determined to drive you away, but we have found out that you are much better people than we are and we are very sorry for what we did."

After the purchase of the house in Hissar Dr. Hamlin in some way got the idea that I intended to leave Hamlin Hall and move into this house. In fact I had never thought of doing so, but he wrote to Mr. Robert a solemn and rather violent protest against this. One paragraph may be quoted. "This measure would be revolutionary. Its ultimate moral result would be bad. It would end in failure. Should the measure ever be proposed and acceded to what course should I feel impelled to pursue? ... I will never assent to it, I will die first. Such a revolutionary measure would necessarily dissolve my connection, whether nominal or real, with the College and with its endowment." I lived in Hamlin Hall twenty years and only left it when forced to do so by my health; and when Professor Anderson and his family took our place, I still lived on the college grounds in Kennedy Lodge. I mention this matter here to record my absolute agreement with Dr. Hamlin's feeling, which prompted his protest. I believe that the work which Mrs. Washburn and I did in those twenty years was the best work we have ever done, that our influence over the teachers and the students was far greater and better than it has ever been since, even though we were living within a stone's throw of the College. So long as Professor Anderson lived in Hamlin Hall it was no great loss to the College, but it was a loss to me and Mrs. Washburn.

In the end, after some ten years, he also was forced to give it up. Our personal influence over the students while we lived in Hamlin Hall was worth more to them than the instruction they received in my classes.

One interesting episode of the year was a challenge to a cricket

HAMLIN HALL IN 1873

match sent to our students by the officers of the British gunboat *Antelope*. They anticipated an easy victory, but they were ignominiously beaten by our boys, and the same thing happened on the return match played a week later. They could not understand how Bulgarians, Armenians and Greeks in an American college could beat Englishmen at their national game, but they took it very good-naturedly.

Among other interesting visitors during the year were Mr. Bancroft, the historian, then American minister at Berlin, and Bevan Braithwait, one of the leading Friends in England. Mr. Bancroft was greatly interested in the College and was one of our best friends in America until his death. I took him to call on Achmet Vefik Pasha, who was as entertaining as usual, and made a great impression on Mr. Bancroft. He was just then Minister of Public Instruction, and he assured Mr. Bancroft that he had established forty thousand schools in the empire. Perhaps he had — on paper. Mr. Braithwait is still one of our warm friends in England and has visited us several times. "The Lord has always moved him" to address the students, and his addresses have been admirable.

We had only one graduate at the end of this year, and he had gone over the studies of the Senior year a second time, having failed to pass his examinations the year before. He was a Bulgarian, John J. Sitchanoff, and he has been one of the most useful of our graduates. He has been for many years the pastor of the Protestant church in Philippopolis, the most important in Bulgaria, and is held in high esteem by all classes in the city.

It will seem strange that the tenth year of the College, with more than 200 students, we had no Senior class. This resulted in part from the enlargement of our course of study, but chiefly from another cause. Of the 257 students registered the tenth year, only 54 ever graduated. This number would have been somewhat larger, but for the Armenian troubles the following year. Still it represents an important fact. If we take the whole number of students who have entered the College since its foundation, not more than one in six has completed the course and graduated. The primary reason for this is that when the College was founded the only idea that the people of Turkey had of education was the acquiring a practical knowledge of three or four languages, and this idea is still very common. Then again the majority of our students come to the College to be prepared for business and are always ready to leave when their parents find a promising opening for them. Many are too poor to complete their education. Again in Turkey proper there are very few openings for Christians in professional life or in government offices, so that the need of a college education is not apparent. Many fall out because they are dropped from their classes for failure to pass examinations and from other personal reasons. During the tenth year 24 students left either from illness or because their families were leaving Turkey.

But we have never measured the value of our work by the number of our graduates. The average length of time spent in the College by those who have not graduated is more than three years. We do what we can to induce those who are of more than ordinary ability to finish their course, whatever career they may have in view, because there is great need of such men to become leaders of their people; but many of our old students who did not complete the course have done more honor to the College and shown more affection for it than some of those who have graduated.

CHAPTER VI
RELIGIOUS QUESTIONS. 1873-1874

DR. HAMLIN left Constantinople September 26 with his family to renew his efforts to raise an endowment, honored and beloved by men of many races, but most of all by those who had been under his instruction in the Bebec Seminary and in Robert College. He never returned. On the twenty-fifth anniversary of the opening of the College every effort was made to induce him to come to Constantinople, at our expense, but he replied that if he could be sure that he would die there he would go. He could not again go through the trial of leaving.

I have postponed any extended statement in regard to the religious work of the College until this time, because it will be better understood in connection with the Armenian difficulties, which had been threatening for some months and culminated early in this college year. I cannot present it more clearly than by giving some of the letters which were written at the time to Mr. Robert. It should be said in advance that this is the only conflict that we have ever had with any of the old Christian churches of the East, and that for many years the highest authorities in the Armenian as well as the Greek and Bulgarian churches have been our warmest supporters and have recognized the fact that our religious efforts are directed to making Christians rather than Protestants — that it is not our purpose to destroy these churches, but to strengthen their spiritual life and their moral influence.

"October 2, 1873.

"There is good reason to believe that we are just now entering upon one of the most trying experiences of our college life. I have already informed you that the College has been made the object of a series of bitter attacks in the Armenian newspapers of the city. The *nominal* cause of this was a case of discipline which occurred while I was in America near the end of the year. In fact, however, this was only a pretense. The real cause came out in various letters published in these papers. 'Why,' they say, 'should Armenians patronize foreigners and heretics when we have such fine schools of our own and such distinguished instructors?' I saw a result of these attacks at the commencement of the term. No new Armenian students came. A number had been registered but have not come. Almost every one who was here last year came back this year, but on one pretense or another they have put off paying their bills, not all but most of them. . . . On Sunday last I received a letter signed by eleven Armenian students of which the following is a copy:

"'Considering that the commentaries on the Bible will not be in direct and strict conformance with the especial doctrines of the Armenian Church, considering that we are required by our religious officers as well as by our parents to be taught in religious matters by them, as they are exclusively acknowledged by the Armenian Church, we confess ourselves not authorized to conform to your summons concerning the Bible class, unless the permission of our parents be procured by an especial correspondence.'

"I let the matter rest a day or two, and last evening I called these boys and had a two hours' talk with them. At first they declined to say anything but that this letter expressed the will of their parents. I cut them off from that tack and finally led them into a frank, full confession of their plans and ideas. They assured me that they had nothing special to complain of in the Bible classes, that they and their religion had always been treated with respect. They confessed that what they intended to demand and insist upon was 'the *absolute abolition of all religious teaching in the College.* Only on this condition could they consent to remain. No one was authorized to give them religious instruction except the priests of their church, and as they did not understand the grounds on which their own faith was based, they feared that they might lose faith altogether in it. They and their parents were constantly abused and annoyed by other Armenians for patronizing a Protestant school and listening to heresy,' etc. I reasoned with them in the most kind, considerate and friendly manner, and the whole interview was very pleasant. Not one angry or excited word was spoken. But it was evident all through that they had not originated this scheme and were not their own masters, that they were simply a skirmishing party thrown out 'to feel the enemy.' It is not necessary for me to report my part of the conversation any farther than to say that I explained to them that you founded this College for the one object of giving a Christian education to the people of Turkey, that you regarded education without religion as more a curse than a blessing, that if I yielded to their demands you would remove me at once from my position as director. Moreover that I fully sympathized with your views, as we all do, that much as we might wish to retain the favor of the Armenians we regarded the favor of God as infinitely more important, that this was a matter upon which there could be no compromise and no hesitation.

"This morning five of them went to town to report and get further instructions from headquarters. What I anticipate is that they will do nothing until Sunday and then stay away from all the religious exercises, leaving it to me to punish them and thus give them a pretext for raising the cry of persecution. This would be the shrewdest course for them to take. [They did *not* do it, but attended the services.] I do not think that there is a chance of their giving up the battle without a sharp fight.

"I have looked back carefully over the past ten years in the light of this difficulty and I can see nothing to regret, nothing that I would wish undone in the course we have taken as to religious instruction. We have never attacked the faith of any of our students. We have had no controversy with them, but we have preached and urged upon them constantly the simple, practical truths of the New Testament, principles recognized by all Christian churches. We have never concealed from any parent, Christian, Jew or Mohammedan, the fact that we should teach their sons these things. On the contrary we have made it a point to explain it to them, that they might have no cause of complaint afterwards. I believe that this attack does not originate with the boys or their parents, but they are driven up to it by outside influence."

"Saturday, October 5, 1873.

"An Armenian newspaper of yesterday had a letter and an editorial on this subject in which it was said among other things that 'the director of the College was formerly engaged in paying Armenians to become Protestants, but now he had devised a plan by which he made them pay forty-four pounds for the privilege.' [This referred to my having been treasurer of the Mission Board.] This morning I called the leading Armenian students and told them that neither they nor we wished to have any conflict or any break in the uniform friendliness of our intercourse, that their plan of presenting me their parents' protest to-night and their refusing to attend the services to-morrow would inevitably bring on such a conflict and that, if they could not attend the services, it was better for them to go home for the Sabbath and return Monday morning. About twenty went home. As next week is the monthly vacation this will give us two weeks' time to settle the controversy. Their plan was to push things to a final crisis to-morrow and carry it through under excitement. They had made great efforts to induce the Greeks and Bulgarians to unite with them, but they failed utterly."

"Monday Evening, October 7.

"The Armenians returned and presented me with the following ultimatum signed by thirteen persons representing twenty-three boarding students:

"'SIR: Considering that the Protestant church ceremonies and Bible classes have become obligatory: considering that we have sent our boys simply to receive instruction in languages and in science, we beg of you by this present document that you would free our boys from attending the religious services and Bible classes, or if that is wholly contrary to the principles of your College you will please inform our boys that they may at once withdraw from the College.'

"To-morrow I shall give them this reply:

"'GENTLEMEN: I have the honor to inform you that no new regulations have been made in Robert College with regard to religious instruction of the students, and that the instruction has been simply such as is considered in all Christian colleges essential to good order and to the development of the moral character of the students. We have highly valued your favorable opinion and we shall regret to lose your patronage, but we cannot accede to your request to excuse your sons from attendance on religious services. Should we do so we must extend this permission to all students of all nationalities, which would involve the cessation of all moral instruction in the College, without which we believe no institution of learning can secure the favor of God or man.'"

"October 13, 1873.

"Tuesday morning I called these students together at half past eight o'clock and gave them the reply with some additional explanations. I then sent them home, having posted two or three teachers in such places that no disturbance could be made and they all went off in school hours as quietly as possible. They collected, however, in the field outside the college grounds and marched in a body through the village of Hissar, singing Armenian national songs and making other demonstrations. Twenty-three left on Tuesday, 1 on Wednesday, and 1 on Thursday, 1 later, 26 in all, of whom 9 afterward returned. Others would have been sent back by their parents but the boys declared that they could not stand the merciless ridicule which would be heaped upon them by the Greeks and Bulgarians."

The following year we had only 32 Armenian boarders in place of 70 the year before these troubles. This was not the end of the controversy. It was continued for months by the Armenian newspapers, with the result that for two or three years very few new Armenian students were sent to the College.

The following is a translation of a letter published in the Armenian papers after the students had left. It is signed by two of the best Armenian students in the College, who were leaders in this affair and did not return.

"We have recently seen several articles in the Armenian papers in regard to the religious instruction given to the students of Robert College. Since there are some who do not believe these statements, we as students of the College feel obliged to state publicly what the real facts are. It has always been obligatory on the students to attend the religious services and Bible classes, but we and other students have attended them without realizing the consequences of so unjust a regulation or giving any information to our parents. We attended them at first mechanically, but we unconsciously came under the influence of this indirect preaching about the different doctrines of the Christian Church and the Bible exercises. The consequence was that we lost our faith in the Orthodox Armenian Church. For this reason we have been obliged to guard against the probable and necessary result that we should become Protestants. We first informed the director about this state of things and asked him to excuse us from attending these religious services. We did not expect that he would refuse so just a request. It was impossible for us to believe that a celebrated American institution in Turkey would ever be the means of violating the freedom of conscience. The object of this institution, as it is expressed in the programme, being 'the highest mental and moral training of the students,' we wished to make another effort, so we presented the following document signed by our parents. [For this and my reply see previous page.] The consequence of this reply of the director

was the withdrawal from the College of the sons of those persons who had signed the paper, but it is to be regretted that there are still about thirty Armenians in the College. We hope that those who feel any interest in their own religion will remove their sons to our national schools. Finally we advise our people not to be deceived by the programme of the College, and assure them that if they send their sons there they will be the means of making them Protestants.
(Signed) HAGOPIAN AND CAPAMADJIAN."

Later, one of the prominent Armenians, who kept his son in the College, said to me with tears in his eyes: "The one thing that I desire for my son is that he should be a good man. I belong to the Orthodox Armenian Church and so have my ancestors for hundreds of years. It would be a grief to me if my son should become a Protestant, but if he cannot be made a good man without that then let him be a Protestant."

Some time after this the Hagopian who signed the above letter sent the following to the papers:

"There is one thing that, up to this time, I have kept secret. Mr. Washburn, when we went to be excused from religious exercises, said to us: 'We are no longer in the dark ages. This is the nineteenth century. It is an age of light. Men do not now cover their eyes and stop their ears from fear of learning something different from what they have believed before. Men do not accept blindly everything they are told by their priests, but investigate and judge for themselves. We do not ask you to accept what we say because we say it, but to judge it and see if it is true. You expect to be educated men, to be the leaders of your people. You can only be so by becoming thinking men, willing and anxious to know the truth.'

"He also said that Mr. Robert would rather cut off his right hand than abolish all religious instruction in the College."

The Mr. Hagopian who wrote these letters has been for many years one of the leading Armenians in Constantinople and one of the most faithful and devoted friends of Robert College.

I should add a brief statement of exactly what was required of our students at that time in the way of religious services. It has been modified since 1902 in some details, but is essentially unchanged.

All students are required to attend morning prayers at 8.15 every day except Sunday. At these the Scriptures are read and prayer offered. Sometimes there is a very brief application made of the Scripture passage. On the Sabbath we have a preaching service at 11 o'clock; at 3 P.M. we have Bible classes, with a general exercise of half an hour under the direction of the president at the opening, prayer, singing and a brief address either historical or exegetical. At 7.30 P.M. an informal service, where a great variety of subjects are treated. All students who do not live at home are required to attend these Sabbath services. At that period I preached half of the time, Dr. Long and Professor Grosvenor the other half. The evening services were conducted by the tutors and instructors and often in the native languages or in French. At these services it is intended that the teaching shall not be polemical and shall not touch on points at issue between the churches. No attack is ever made upon any religion, but the essential and practical teachings of the New Testament are presented as clearly as possible. It is no doubt true that this religious instruction has an influence upon the students. If we thought that it did not we should give it up. The old Christian churches have long since come to appreciate its value, and I believe that it is the religious and moral influence of the College which, more than anything else, leads parents to send their sons here. Even the Turks appreciate this and they have sometimes said to me, "I send my son here that he may be brought up with English morality," English in this case meaning Protestant.

The long continued and violent attacks upon the College in the Armenian papers probably had some influence in stirring up the Turkish government to adopt hostile measures. The Grand Vizier told Mr. Boker, the American minister, that the government had determined to prohibit the circulation of the Bible in any language and that they would not allow that Protestant college to put up the houses we had asked for. He told Sir Henry Elliott that they had determined to oppose Protestantism with all their might as a matter of patriotism. This Grand Vizier was a tool of Russia and no doubt this also accounts in some measure for his opposition to England and to Protestantism. He was the same man who, during the Crimean War, as Turkish commander at Kars, is said to have sold the place to Russia.

Other interesting events of the year can only be noticed very briefly. In February and March we had great snow-storms and cold which paralyzed the city and threatened us with starvation at the College. Men were killed and eaten by wolves within sight of the College. Wild boars were shot on the shores of the Bosphorus. There were remnants of these snow-banks on the hills near us two months later.

In the summer of 1873 Dr. Long had gone at Mr. Robert's request to Paris and Vienna to purchase the apparatus needed in his department. This came early in the year and attracted much attention, bringing us many visitors of different nationalities, including Turkish pashas, who were much impressed by the experiments which they saw.

April 1 we had our first Junior exhibition, under the direction of Professor Grosvenor. The new study hall was crowded with guests, and the orations, ten in number, were remarkably good. The moral and religious tone breathing through them impressed the audience most favorably.

Aside from the Armenian troubles the year was a peaceful one, although two students had to be expelled for engaging in a diabolical plot against one of their companions. The health of the students after the great storm was unusually bad, and I had to send my son to America in May with Mrs. Washburn as he was threatened with tuberculosis. Happily he recovered. We were greatly distressed also by hearing of the illness of Dr. Hamlin.

The number of students present at the close of the year was 178, of whom 47 were day scholars, 31 less boarders than at the end of the previous year, representing a loss in tuition of some five thousand dollars. It is not strange that this unhappy experience impressed upon us and upon Mr. Robert the absolute necessity of an endowment. Dr. Long wrote to Mr. Robert: "To secure the permanence of the College it must be sufficiently endowed to enable it to tide over just such difficulties as this, even if they should take away four-fifths of our students. Those who know the character of the nationalities of the East, know that a popular tumult is very easily raised and a storm is liable to arise at any time, when we shall be in danger of going down so long as we are pecuniarily dependent on their patronage. The life of so noble an institution as this must not be contingent upon the favor of a fickle populace," — or, he would have added a few years later, of political disturbances and revolutions.

The Commencement exercises were about as well attended as the year before and five students were graduated, all Bulgarians. One of these died a few years later. The other four have all distinguished themselves in the government of Bulgaria, and are still living.

CHAPTER VII
VISIT OF MR. ROBERT. 1874-1875

IT was evident, even at the opening of the college year, that storms were gathering about us in the political world which might seriously affect our work. The Eastern question had reached a critical period when some form of European intervention seemed probable, but which form it would take could not be foreseen. In Constantinople Russia, under the lead of General Ignatieff, and England, represented by Sir Henry Elliott, were both playing a dangerous game, which ended in massacres, revolution, war and the dismemberment of European Turkey. While the College had nothing to do with these political intrigues we felt the influence of them in many ways. Constantinople was in a ferment; there was a vague fear of what might happen which kept away some students and naturally excited those who came. We, who knew what was going on, could not but feel some anxiety. It was not diminished by a visit which I paid to Bulgaria in the Easter vacation with Mr. Panaretoff. I had never before had any conception of the suffering of the Christians under Turkish rule, but I saw things there which filled me with horror, which were not so much direct acts of the government as the results of a general policy — the tyranny of the armed Turkish minority over the unarmed and helpless Christian majority. It was not so bad in the towns where the well-to-do Bulgarians kept the Turkish officials in their pay, but the peasants were practically serfs with no rights. I accidentally met one young man who confessed that he belonged to a company which was planning a rebellion against the government, and I spent an hour in trying to convince him of the utter folly of such an attempt, which was certain to fail and could only add to the suffering of the people. Such outbreaks had taken place near the Danube, under the secret patronage of Russia, but were easily put down.

Notwithstanding these political troubles the year opened and passed away without any disturbance of the peace of the College. Our staff consisted of the director, Professors Long, Grosvenor and Djedjizian. Mr. Panaretoff was also appointed adjunct professor of Slavic and Bulgarian. Our tutors were Messrs. Arthur Hoyt, Webber, Savage and Webster. There were seven other teachers. Mr. Hoyt lost his health and very nearly his life from malaria resulting from a summer excursion through Bulgaria, and to our great regret was obliged to return to America, where in time he recovered, to become a distinguished professor in Auburn Theological Seminary. Mr. Webber had charge of the Preparatory Department. Miss Haynes came as matron in November.

The whole number of students registered during the year was 208. The number present at the close of the year was 176.

Boarders 144
Day scholars 32-176

As all of the Bulgarians were boarders, they were more numerous than any other nationality in Hamlin Hall.

The nationalities represented were as follows:

Armenians 55
Greeks 48
Bulgarians 45
English 21
Americans 8
Turks 6
Jews 6
Germans 6
Italians 4
Dalmatians 2
French 2
Austrians 2
Dutch 1
Russian 1
Pole 1-208

The most interesting event during the year was the visit of Mr. Robert, who reached the College June 12, 1875, and lived in Hamlin Hall until after the Commencement exercises, just six weeks. At the time of his first visit we were still in Bebec. It has been said many times that Robert College was the product of Dr. Hamlin's brains and Mr. Robert's money. Dr. Hamlin never said this, and it is no disparagement of him to say that Mr. Robert not only gave his money and his heart to the College, but that every step that was taken from the first conception of the College to the time of his death was fully discussed with him and largely influenced by his judgment. It was to his credit that when an agreement could not be reached with Dr. Hamlin or with me he never used his authority to override our judgment, but left the final decision with us. His two visits to the College were devoted to the most careful study of existing conditions and future development — to getting light on everything connected with the work. He talked with all the teachers, made the acquaintance of students and their parents, consulted the missionaries and other foreign residents and listened to everything that any one wished to say about the College. He investigated every department of work, and this not as a matter of curiosity or a question of expense, but that he might be able to give more intelligent advice in what was the one thing that he was always insisting upon — the necessity of steady growth. He gave us the best he had of brain work as well as of money.

He entered heartily into the social life of the College and the city, and he told me after his departure that he had never spent six happier weeks in his life. He greatly enjoyed a grand picnic that he gave to the teachers and students of the College. He chartered a steamboat and made an excursion up to the Black Sea, returning to Hunkiar Iskelessi, where we had our dinner under the trees, with speeches and sports afterwards, getting back to the College in the evening. He also gave a breakfast to the missionaries and their wives at Buyukdere. He found them more friendly to the College than they had been five years before. His addresses to the students were very practical, and they were greatly interested in what he told them of his own early life and the lessons that he had learned from the Book of Proverbs. He gave each student a copy of the book, and I have often had occasion since to quote his authority, in addition to that of Solomon, as to how a young man was to win success in life.

In those early years he was a subject of much discussion among the people of the country, who could not understand what motive prompted him to found the College. I have often heard it discussed on the Bosphorus steamers. Mr. Hanson, the English banker, told me that he heard this conversation between two Turkish gentlemen. "Do you see that College?" "Yes." "Well, in my opinion it is the greatest disgrace to the Turks of anything in Constantinople." "Why so, I never thought of that. It is a fine building." "So it is, but what does it mean? Here was a stranger, an American gentleman, who came to Constantinople for a few days and was so impressed with the necessities of our people, with their ignorance and their need of education, that he took his own money and built this splendid College and endowed it for the good of those who were strangers to him. We have hundreds of rich pashas, some of the richest living in sight of this College. Which of them ever saw or cared for the wants of the people or gave a piaster of his money to educate them? This College is a shame and disgrace to us." The native Christians often said, "He did it for his soul," i. e. to purchase a high seat for himself in heaven. There were many, however, who had a sufficient appreciation of his motives and of the advantages the College had brought to them to express, and I have no doubt to feel, gratitude — and now I seldom hear any other comment.

One important subject of discussion when Mr. Robert was here was the question of the title to the land which we had bought since the first purchase, which was made secure by the *iradé*. The other land was held by a legal fiction — in the name of "Mariam bint Toma" which was Mrs. Hamlin, who had been registered under that name as a Turkish subject. English and other foreign institutions held their property in the name of the consulates or embassies; but the United States government refused to allow this, and for a long time refused to sign the protocol allowing Americans to hold property in their own names. It was temporarily transferred to me as director of the College, and a few months ago (1906) the greater part of it, after all these years of negotiation, was secured to the College by *iradé* — which reminds me that it took thirty years to get permission to build, at our own expense, a sewer from the College to the Bosphorus. These delays to which we are always subject do not come from any hostility to the College on the part of the government, but from the nature of the government itself, and are the common experience of all, natives and foreigners. Much also depends upon the character and spirit of the minister who represents the United States government here. We were particularly fortunate at this time in the appointment of Horace Maynard, who arrived here in May, 1875, who was not only a statesman of great ability, but an earnest Christian in full sympathy with our work. Many of the ministers sent here to represent the United States have had no interest whatever in the Americans resident in Turkey and have had as little to do with them as possible. Personally I have never had occasion to complain of any one of them. For many I have had the highest respect; but there have been times when if it had not been for our intimate relations with the British Embassy, the College would have fared very badly. It has generally, not always, been true that the English government has shown much greater interest in the College than the government at Washington. A distinguished Englishman who visited Washington when Mr. Bayard was Secretary of State was amazed to find that he had never heard of Robert College. I suppose that Mr. Bayard was equally astonished to learn that this Englishman thought that the founding of Robert College was the most important thing that America had done in Europe. Mr. Hay was the best friend that we have ever had in the State Department. Mr. Blaine was also very friendly. No President has shown more interest in the College than Mr. Roosevelt. Some of the distinguished ministers who have been here have been warm friends, and all of them have been ready to preside at our Commencement exercises and thus give their official sanction to the College.

Among them all we have had no better minister than Horace Maynard and none to whom the College owes more. I do not think that any minister here has ever won the confidence and respect of the Turkish government so fully as he did. The famous editor of the *Louisville Courier-Journal* told me, some years after the war, that he considered Mr. Maynard the greatest man in the South who remained loyal to the government. He was rather a singular looking man, and it was said at the time that the Sultan, after his presentation, inquired whether he was an American dervish. But he soon acquired great influence, by his straightforward integrity and the skill with which he defended every American interest, while carefully abstaining from all association with the great political intrigues which were going on at the time.

The class work of the College went on very satisfactorily during the year. We had settled down upon a programme of studies for the four college classes which was based upon what was generally adopted at that time in New England colleges, but modified to adapt it to the practical wants of our students. The great practical difficulty which we had to meet was the multiplicity of languages. There was no escape to giving a prominent place to English. That was the language of the College. If we did not require Latin the European universities would not recognize our diplomas. Every student wished to study French. Armenians, Bulgarians, Greeks and Turks must have thorough instruction in their own languages and in the ancient languages from which these were derived, or they could never hold their places among their own people. This meant that each student must study at least five languages — probably Turkish also for Turkish subjects. As there was no escape from all this linguistic work, the question was how to find time for anything else. We have since added a year to the college course and put four years into the Preparatory Department, but in 1875 this was not practicable. It did not trouble us that we had to depart from American standards, for it was our duty to adapt the College to the circumstances of the East, but we had to learn from experience that the study of modern European languages and an introduction to their literature was worth quite as much to our students as the study of Latin and Greek had been to us. We give more time to the native languages now than we did then.

At that time we took our students through Algebra, Geometry, Trigonometry, Surveying, Analytical Geometry, and Conic Sections, giving six hours a week to these mathematical studies. In Science they had Zoölogy, Physics, Physiology, Chemistry, Botany, Geology and Mineralogy, and Astronomy, in this order, an average of five hours a week. History three hours a week, Political Economy, Rhetoric, Parliamentary Law, Physical Geography, Psychology, Ethics, History of Philosophy, History of Civilization, International Law, each five or six hours a week for one term. There were no optional studies in the course, but some students did get additional work in some branches. This course of study was quite equal to that of any American College fifty years ago, and there was no school in this country which at that time even professed to equal it. To most people here it seemed unnecessarily extended. They would have been quite contented with the languages, arithmetic and a little science, the latter just for the name of it. It is due to those who were teachers in the College at that time to say that so far as it went the instruction in all these branches was honest and thorough. There was no pretense or humbug about it.

The number of graduates in 1875 was 11, 7 Bulgarians, 3 Armenians and 1 Greek, all but 2 of whom are still living (1907). The Armenians and the Greek are all merchants, one of the Bulgarians was a distinguished teacher, one has been Prime Minister, one has been several times a minister, one was private secretary of Prince Alexander and later of Prince Ferdinand, and the others have occupied important positions in Bulgaria.

Commencement in those early years of the College was in

some respects a more important and more interesting affair than it has been since 1894. There was a freedom of speech which has not been possible of late years. Our audiences were necessarily limited by the size of the study hall, which however was always crowded, with more or less Turkish women looking in at the windows. One afternoon was devoted to prize speaking, and that evening in 1875 was occupied by an English spelling match. Sometimes it was a prize debate between two classes. On Commencement Day only invited guests were admitted, and after the orations of the graduating class in various languages, addresses were made by the distinguished official guests who occupied the places of honor on the platform. In 1875 the principal speakers were Mr. Maynard and Mr. Robert. It was on this occasion also that prizes were announced and given out for the prize speaking, for the highest rank in scholarship in the different classes and for special work in certain departments. At the close of the exercises the guests were entertained at lunch in the college dining room.

That year Mrs. Washburn, who had returned from America in November, and I spent the summer vacation in Switzerland, and Mr. Robert went with us as far as Zurich, where we met our son returning in good health from America.

CHAPTER VIII
POLITICAL CRISIS IN TURKEY. 1875-1876

THIS is in no sense a history of Turkey, but it is impossible to write a history of the College at this period without some reference to our environment, and an explanation of our relations to what was taking place about us, and it should be made clear at the outset that Dr. Long and I were personally responsible for the attitude of the College at this time. Dr. Hamlin was so violently anti-Russian in his sympathies that he was the principal advocate of Turkey in the United States and was officially thanked for this by the Turkish government. Mr. Robert had always forbidden all meddling with political affairs, and he was right. This has always been the policy of the College. It was mine and Dr. Long's. The College has always used all its influence to keep the students out of politics and to make them realize the folly of rebellion against the government. We have always recognized our duty to respect the laws of the country, and no official complaint has ever been made against us by the Turkish government, nor was any complaint ever made against Dr. Long or me as individuals, although it is true that great political changes were brought about in some measure by our personal influence. We did our best to prevent the outbreak in Bulgaria which was the excuse for the massacre which followed; but when it was a question of the massacre of thousands of innocent and unarmed Bulgarians, men, women and children, we did everything in our power to put a stop to it. We saw then, what the Turks see now, that this massacre was one of the greatest blunders that they have ever made. We did our best through the British Embassy to make them see it at that time. Whatever we did we reported to Mr. Robert from week to week, and in the end we had his full approval.

When the College opened in September, 1875, the situation of political affairs in Constantinople was alarming and complicated. There was a Turkish conspiracy, supported by England, secretly working against Sultan Abd-ul-Aziz, who was defended by Russia; and a serious insurrection against the Turks had broken out in Herzegovina, also one of little importance in Bulgaria. The Grand Vizier, Mahmoud Nedim Pasha, who lived just below the College, was the tool of Russia, and there is evidence that he had arranged for the sending of Russian troops to Constantinople to defend the Sultan. The alarm and excitement in the city was increased by his communication to the embassies that he had discovered a plot for the massacre of Christians and foreigners, and by his stopping the payment of interest on the national debt and seizing all the hypothecated revenues. Mr. Robert was so much alarmed by the news that he proposed to send us a consignment of rifles to defend the College, which we declined. As time went on Servia and Montenegro threatened war and aided the revolutionists in Bosnia and Herzegovina, while the European Powers prepared to intervene. This resulted in the "Andrassy Note," which was a demand for certain reforms in the insurgent provinces. The Sultan tried to forestall this by issuing an iradé decreeing general reforms in the empire. The Powers regarded this as so much waste paper. Nothing came of either the iradé or the note, except more general discontent and excitement. Thus ended the year 1875.

Meanwhile the College had opened with 137 boarders, of whom 33 were Bulgarians, and 30 day scholars — 167 students in all, only 9 less than at the close of the previous year, which was evidence that the public regarded the College as a safe refuge. We had one new tutor, Mr. McLean from Hamilton College, whose health gave out so that he left before the end of the year. Some friends — missionaries in Persia — came in September to spend the night with us, and that night one of the children came down with what proved to be typhoid fever. It was nine weeks before they could leave us, happily all well. It was during this autumn that began the stream of distinguished English visitors to the College, which continued for twenty-five years, bringing us into acquaintance with many of the leading statesmen and philanthropists of England. Lord Campbell and Lady Strangford were among the first. She was especially interested in the people of the Balkan Peninsula, and the College was already known in Europe for its connection with the Bulgarians. The winter passed quietly at the College, although every one saw that a storm was gathering all about us which would bring changes of some kind, either for good or evil, and there was a constant exchange of notes between the Powers, which came to nothing.

May 2, 1876, there was an insurrection in the mountain towns not far from Philippopolis in Bulgaria. It had been planned for several months, and the Turkish government was fully informed of the details of the plan and of those engaged in it. The Turkish governor at Philippopolis had implored the government at Constantinople to allow him to put a stop to it, and had promised to guarantee absolute quiet, if a single regiment of troops were sent to him. But the Turks anticipated a war with Servia and wished to find a pretext to terrorize this part of Bulgaria, which commanded the road to Servia, before the war broke out, so they had quietly fostered this revolutionary movement which was too insignificant to constitute any real danger. They had withdrawn their troops, but the whole Turkish population was armed, while the Christians were unarmed, and all arrangements had been made to give over the Christian population to the tender mercies of the Turkish militia (Bashibozooks), having first, as far as possible, cut off all communication between Bulgaria and the outside world. The results are too well known to be detailed here. In these first massacres and the reign of terror which followed fifty or sixty thousand men, women and children were massacred in cold blood, sold as slaves or judicially murdered. It was the most natural thing in the world that in their terror and helplessness the Bulgarians should have thought of us, who had no political interests at stake, as friends whom they could trust to help them, and they found means to communicate to us the details of what was going on from week to week. At the outset we alone had these details, and what we did with them is no secret. It was no secret at the time that we first of all gave them to Sir Henry Elliott, the British ambassador, who was a warm personal friend of ours and who represented a government which was at that time the chief supporter of Turkey in Europe. We did this in the hope that he could make the Turks see that they were making a terrible mistake. We also communicated the facts to powerful friends in England and to our friends Mr. Pears, correspondent of the *Daily News*, and Mr. Galenga, the correspondent of the *London Times*. Could we have done less or acted more honorably? It will be seen later on that Sir Henry Elliott was at this time engaged in a conspiracy which he regarded as likely to change the whole face of affairs in Turkey.

The day after the outbreak in Bulgaria, of which the world knew nothing, all Europe was startled by the murder of the French and German consuls at Salonica by a fanatical Mohammedan mob. This increased the excitement in Constantinople, which was already at fever heat, and when, a week later, a mob of thousands

SULTAN ABD-UL-AZIZ

of Moslem theological students (*softas*) rushed through the streets of Stamboul on their way to the palace to demand the dismissal of the Grand Vizier and the Sheik-ul-Islam, the whole city realized that it was at the mercy of revolutionists. The Sultan yielded to the demands of the mob, and another near neighbor of ours was made Grand Vizier in place of Mahmoud Nedim. A little more than two weeks after this (May 30) the city was roused in the morning by the roar of cannon which announced the advent of a new Sultan, Murad. Abd-ul-Aziz had been dethroned in the night. This was the outcome of the conspiracy to which I have referred. The real leader in this was the Minister of War, Hussein Avni Pasha, supported by the new Grand Vizier, Mahomet Ruchdi Pasha, and the new Sheik-ul-Islam, who had given a *fetva* (decision) authorizing the act. Kaisarli Achmet Pasha, the Minister of Marine, who controlled the ironclads anchored before the palace, joined them. The supposed leader was Midhat Pasha, and it was through him that Sir Henry Elliott was brought into the plot and the support of England secured. Her Mediterranean fleet arrived off the Dardanelles the day before the act and was ready to come to Constantinople in case of need. Murad, the new Sultan, who lived in the palace with his uncle, had not been forewarned; and, when he was taken by armed men, he believed that he was to be put to death. He never recovered from the shock sufficiently to assume any control of the government. The week which followed was one of wild excitement in the city, at first of joy and satisfaction, but as the days went on there was a decided reaction against the revolution among the Turks in favor of the old Sultan. At the close of the week it was suddenly announced that Abd-ul-Aziz had committed suicide. Nobody believed it at the time; and after hearing all the evidence my own belief is that he was murdered by order of the new administration through fear of a counter-revolution, though Queen Victoria had telegraphed to Sir Henry Elliott to protect his life.

This was not the end of the tragedy. A few days later there was a council of ministers at the house of Midhat Pasha. A Circassian officer, whose sister had been a favorite of Sultan Abd-ul-Aziz, obtained admission to the house, entered the chamber and shot Hussein Avni Pasha and the Minister of Foreign Affairs, very nearly killed the Minister of Marine and killed several of the attendants before he was captured. As the house had been left unguarded and no attack was made upon Midhat Pasha, it was suspected at the time that he might have had knowledge of this attack, the result of which was to make him the principal power in the state. The officer was hanged without examination or trial. This new shock still further demoralized the Sultan and incapacitated him for all business. At the end of August, 1876, he also was deposed and his brother made Sultan. In this change also Sir Henry Elliott took the lead, and Abd-ul-Hamid became Sultan. His brother was kept a close prisoner until he died some thirty years later. Meanwhile Servia and Montenegro had declared war against Turkey in July, and the story of the Bulgarian massacres had roused no little excitement in the Christian world, especially in England, where it was felt that the English government was largely responsible for existing conditions in Turkey, — which, as we have seen, was true.

During the spring and summer, while these events were taking place, there was a general feeling of insecurity in Constantinople, and unpleasant incidents were very frequent. We did not know what to expect from one day to another, as the city was filled with half savage irregular troops who were under very little control. We were always on the watch, and one day the alarm was given that a large armed band was coming down upon the College from the hill above us. Happily the students were all in the building, and having given orders that no one should be seen at the windows and that all doors should be closed, Dr. Long and I went out unarmed to face the mob, who were already entering our grounds. They were Turks, mostly young, who had come several miles from the Arsenal on the Golden Horn to make an end of the Bulgarians. It was a trying quarter of an hour that we had, not to be forgotten; but they were evidently puzzled by finding no one but two foreigners, who met them without any appearance of fear and quietly explained to them that they were trespassing on our ground. If they had had an enterprising and fearless leader I do not know what would have happened, but it was a mob without leaders; and when they came to face us and our authority, their courage failed them, and in the course of half an hour we had won the day. Extraordinary stories are current in America of the devices which we resorted to in defense of the College during this and the following year, such as that we met a night attack by parading a skeleton rubbed with phosphorus. There is no truth in this or any of these stories. Another incident, which was characteristic of the unsettled conditions of the time, occurred in June, 1876. I was sitting in my office one evening when a servant came to say that a Turkish pasha begged to see me. He had just arrived on horseback. I invited him in. He proved to be a fine looking, well-dressed gentleman, perhaps fifty years old. He introduced himself as Ibrahim Pasha, and after the usual exchange of compliments he told me that he had just escaped assassination and come to take refuge in the College. Would I protect him? I bid him welcome, gave him dinner and a bed, but I reminded him that, although this was American territory, the authorities could apply to the American minister and he would have to give him up. I excused myself and went over to see Achmet Vefik Pasha, to see what he knew of the man and what he would advise me to do. He knew all about the man and advised me to send him to take refuge in the British Embassy at Therapia. I proposed this to Ibrahim Pasha, and he agreed to do it; so I gave him a letter to the ambassador and he started in the early morning, but he never reached the Embassy, and I could never find out what became of him. Probably the authorities were on the watch for him. It is not uncommon for people to disappear in Constantinople.

While these things were happening in Constantinople the reign of terror continued in Bulgaria, and we communicated information about it to Sir Henry Elliott and to our friends in England. The Turkish government denied the truth of these statements to Sir Henry, and, in the confusion which prevailed here at that time, it is very likely that the government really knew very little of what was going on in Bulgaria. It was under Abd-ul-Aziz that the massacres were planned and commenced. But we had to face a more serious difficulty. It was to be expected that the Turks would deny everything; but Mr. Disraeli, the English Prime Minister, declared in Parliament that the reports, for some of which we were responsible and which he must have known came from us, were "mere coffee house babble" and without any foundation — that he had official information to this effect. We begged Sir Henry Elliott to send one of his own secretaries to Bulgaria to investigate and report to him. After excusing himself for some time he sent for me one day and told me that he had at last received orders to do so, and that he would send Mr. Baring down to see me before he started, which he did. But before that I had learned from Sir Henry himself that he was not only sending his youngest secretary, who knew but little of the country and none of the languages, without any interpreter who knew Bulgarian, but that he was to get his information from the Turkish authorities and to be in the country only two or three days. I protested in vain, although Mr. Baring agreed with me. Sir Henry told me that he was acting under instructions from home. This made it clear that there was to be no real investigation, and what was wanted by Mr. Disraeli was an official report to confirm his statements that nothing serious had happened in Bulgaria. There was nothing left for us to do but to defend our honor and our veracity as best we could. I went at once to Mr. Maynard, explained the situation to him and begged him to send Mr. Schuyler, who had just arrived in Constantinople as secretary of the Legation and consul general, to make an independent and impartial investigation of the situation in Bulgaria with proper interpreters for Turkish, Bulgarian and Greek. He said that he had no authority to do this, but that, if I could persuade Mr. Schuyler to go, he would find a way to send him. I found it easy to persuade Mr. Schuyler, and he left Constantinople with his interpreters the day after Mr. Baring, overtaking him at Adrianople. Mr. Baring was an honest man, and I do not think that he was sorry to find himself checkmated at the beginning of the game. He saw at once that Mr. Schuyler's report would be accepted and believed by all the world. I do not know what report Mr. Disraeli got. He did not publish it; but the first result of Mr. Schuyler's preliminary report, made in ten days, was to convert Mr. Gladstone and make him the leader in the great agitation which finally overthrew the Disraeli government, and which before that led to the Conference of Constantinople. Mr. Baring went with Mr. Schuyler to Batak, and saw with his own eyes the unburied bodies of some five thousand men, women and children who had been slaughtered in this one town, far from the seat of the insurrection. Our graduate Mr. Peter Dimitroff went with Mr. Schuyler as his Bulgarian interpreter. Could we have done less than this under the circumstances? It did not in any way interrupt our friendly relations with Sir Henry Elliott, who never charged us with having any political aims in view. In the summer vacation Mrs. Washburn and I went to the Engadine to recruit my health, and Professor Panaretoff, who was with us, improved the opportunity to go to England and see our friends there. He was in the Speaker's Gallery in the House of Commons and heard the last speech made by Mr. Disraeli, before his promotion to the House of Lords. It was on the question of the Bulgarian massacres.

I do not think that the Turkish authorities ever thought of the

College in those troublous times, although Mahomet Ruchdi Pasha, the Grand Vizier, was our near neighbor, and Midhat Pasha was often at his house. Dr. Long had known the latter very well when he was in Bulgaria, and Midhat was himself a Bulgarian by race and birth, but a *Pomak* or Mohammedan Bulgarian. Sir Henry Elliott's faith in him was absolute, and it is true that he had been remarkably successful as a provincial governor in Bulgaria and in Bagdad. I once spent two days with him on an Austrian steamer, and we discussed Turkey most of the time. He was a very remarkable conversationalist, and his head was full of schemes of reform. I am free to confess that he captivated me; but Dr. Long did not believe in his capacity to reform the empire. He certainly failed, and, at the time of his greatest power, he failed to organize any party to support him and failed to get the confidence of the Sultan whom he had put on the throne. He was finally exiled to Arabia and assassinated.

To return to what is more strictly the history of the College. Mr. Robert remained in Europe until the end of October, 1875. Very soon after his return to America it was evident from his letters that he was very much tried by the financial conditions there, as well as by the political situation at Constantinople. His letters were full of exhortations to economy and to caution about mixing in political affairs. His advice was good, and we did our best to follow it. Some of the things which we did in the spring alarmed him, and he was evidently in doubt whether to adopt Dr. Hamlin's opinions or ours about Turkish affairs. We told him everything, and, in the end, he thanked God that we had been able to do something for the Bulgarians, of a sort which the founders of the College had never dreamed of. In the spring of 1876 we had a visit from Rev. Dr. David B. Coe, one of the trustees, who had been the secretary of the Board from the beginning, and who was the chief support of the College after Mr. Robert's death — a man of admirable spirit and great practical wisdom. One of the amusing incidents of the year was the arrival of a consignment of codfish from New York. Mr. Robert had interested himself while here in the students' table and it appears had concluded that Yankee codfish balls ought to be an acceptable addition to their diet. Mrs. Washburn superintended the Armenian cook so that we produced the genuine article, and I made a speech at the table in honor of Mr. Robert and the dish; but, alas! we discovered that early education was necessary to an appreciation of this national dainty — and most of the codfish was disposed of to American families.

One of the most welcome results of the political troubles here was the arrival of American war vessels, sent here by our government for the protection of its Legation. At different times the Vandalia, the Quinnebaug, the Gettysburg, the Wyoming, the Despatch, the Marion, were here, sometimes two or three at once. Their presence here was an assurance of protection, and it was a joy to see the American flag on the Bosphorus. We were not so proud of the ships as we were of the officers. We saw much of them. Like our great generals who have visited Constantinople, and unlike some of our civil representatives, they were interested in us because we were Americans, and I have been a firm believer in the navy ever since. To many of them we were under special obligations.

As the year went on and the political troubles increased the number of our students diminished. At the end of the year the number of boarders had fallen from 137 to 111. One hundred and forty in all were present at the close. Some of the Bulgarians were unable to return home on account of the state of the country, and we had to keep and protect ten or twelve of them at the College during the long summer vacation. As we could not suddenly reduce our expenses to any great extent, the loss on the current expense account was heavier than for any previous year, amounting here and in America to sixty-five hundred dollars. As Mr. Robert's private income had been seriously reduced during the year, this must have been a severe trial to him, but he did not complain. He exhorted us to have faith in the future. We arranged to reduce our expenses for the following year by taking Dr. Long and his family to live with us in the College, while Professor Grosvenor moved into the house in Hissar belonging to us. The change was made in July, so that Dr. Long looked after the College and the students remaining there during the vacation, while I was in Switzerland. Mr. Robert had insisted on my taking this trip and had sent me the money for my expenses.

The Senior class held together to the end of the year, and there were 15 graduates, the largest number since the opening of the College. One of them took the degree of B.S.; 7 were Bulgarians, 7 Armenians, and 1 Greek. Twelve of them are still living (1907). All of the Bulgarians became distinguished men, four of them as soldiers. Two of them commanded regiments in the famous battle of Slivnitza, one of whom was killed. His name was Marinoff, one of the most attractive men who ever graduated at the College. The other died in 1902 as Minister of Public Works in Bulgaria. The other two are among the best officers in the Bulgarian army to-day, one of them a general. Of the others one is a physician, one is judge of the Court of Appeals at Sophia and one was secretary of the same court. The Greek is a successful physician in Constantinople. Of the Armenians three are merchants, one in Chicago, one in England and one in Constantinople. One is the head of the Society for Ethical Culture in Chicago, one is a clergyman, and two are physicians. One of them is one of the leaders of his profession in Constantinople.

CHAPTER IX
THE RUSSO-TURKISH WAR. 1876-1877

WHEN I returned from Switzerland in September, 1876, I found a new Sultan on the throne. Murad had been deposed and his brother Abd-ul-Hamid installed in his place chiefly through the influence of Midhat Pasha and Sir Henry Elliott. Very little was known about him even by the Turks, but he was supposed to be a quiet, unobtrusive man with little knowledge of political affairs, who would be a tool in the hands of the conspirators who had deposed his uncle and his brother. It was not long before they and the world were undeceived.

The College opened with 83 boarders, 27 of whom were Bulgarians, and 27 day scholars, 110 in all. Ten more Bulgarians came later, but other students left so that the number at the end of the year was still 110, in place of 140 at the close of the preceding year. It was much better than we had feared. We were not able to make any essential reductions in our staff of teachers. Professor Panaretoff returned with us, and, although his presence in London had attracted some attention and had alarmed Mr. Robert, nothing was ever said to us about it here. The Turks were too much taken up with their own affairs to trouble themselves about him. One of the most serious of their troubles was financial. They had destroyed their credit by going into practical bankruptcy and could borrow no money and were forced to resort to the issue of an irredeemable paper currency (*caimé*). It was the financial condition of the country, even more than the unsettled political condition, which reduced the number of our students, for people generally regarded Robert College as about the safest place in Constantinople. The Turks set traps for us now and then, during this and the following years, to test our loyalty; but, as we never walked into them, they found nothing to complain of.

In the war with Servia the Turks were successful in spite of the fact that a large number of Russian officers and soldiers had been allowed by their government to go to aid the Servians. The Turkish armies were arrested only by the direct intervention of Russia and the threat of war. The Great Powers finally agreed to call a European conference to meet at Constantinople to consider the situation and induce the Turkish government to agree to such reforms as would satisfy the people of European Turkey and prevent a war, which might involve all Europe.

This conference was for many reasons a matter of the greatest interest to the College. If successful it would insure a long period of peace to Turkey and quiet and prosperity to the European provinces. It would check any advance of Russia, and give the Bulgarians a chance to educate the nation. We were brought into somewhat intimate relations with it by the fact that England had been a leader in the plan of the Conference and that her representatives believed that we knew more of the people and the situation in Bulgaria than any one else in Constantinople. Lord Salisbury and Sir Henry Elliott were the English delegates, and two of the men who came with Lord Salisbury were in later years ambassadors here, Lord Curry and Sir William White. Admiral Sir John Hay was also here. The delegates gathered here early in December, 1876, and had a number of informal sessions, to see if they could come to an agreement among themselves before meeting with the Turkish delegates. The anticipated antagonism between Lord Salisbury and General Ignatieff, the Russian delegate, did not appear. They worked together all through the Conference, and reached a plan which, if it had been accepted by the Turks, would have brought peace and prosperity to the empire. Unhappily Sir Henry Elliott did not agree with Lord Salisbury, as he told me himself, and, perhaps unconsciously, he encouraged the Turks to resist. The full Conference met December 23. Midhat Pasha had prepared a *coup de théâtre* for the occasion. The Conference was formally opened and discussions about to begin when it was interrupted by the roar of cannon; and the Turkish president of the Conference, Safvet Pasha, rose and declared that "these guns announced the promulgation of a constitution, a change in a form of government which had lasted six hundred years and inaugurated a new era of prosperity for the Ottoman people." There was no longer any need of a conference. All the people of Turkey were to enjoy far more than the Conference was prepared to ask for the European provinces. The Conference did not accept this view because it offered no guarantee for the carrying out of reforms.

The session continued, and the delegates gave up one demand after another until the scheme was of little account, but the Turks refused to accept anything; the Conference adjourned, and all the Great Powers recalled their ambassadors and broke off relations

SULTAN ABD-UL-HAMID

with the Sultan. The Turks, before the final refusal to accept, went through the farce of calling an assembly of the Turkish notables and the heads of the Christian communities to express an opinion. The Bulgarian Exarch refused to attend on the ground that he was ill. The Vekil of the Protestant community was the only one present who dared to speak of the danger of refusal and to advise caution. The man in the street, whether Turk or Christian or Jew, was equally careful to express nothing but joy at the new Constitution.

The Constitution was full of sonorous words and phrases, borrowed from similar documents, but was altogether worthless as a charter of liberty and not adapted to the conditions of the country. Only six weeks after its promulgation Midhat Pasha was summoned to the Palace in the middle of the night, seized there, put on board of a steamer and shipped out of the country in disgrace, to Brindisi in Italy, nominally under a provision of his own constitution. However, the promised Parliament — a Senate appointed by the Sultan and a House of Deputies chosen in various fashions in different provinces by the people — did meet six weeks after the exile of Midhat and was opened by the Sultan in person, March 19, 1877. Our friend Achmet Vefik Pasha was chosen president of the lower house, and there were a number of members whose independence and good sense astonished every one, but it was a unique assembly. I attended one of the sessions. Among other incidents a green-turbaned descendant of the Prophet interrupted a speaker and was called to order twice, with no result. When Achmet Vefik Pasha roared at him, "Sous eshek" (Shut up, you donkey), he dropped into his seat as though he had been shot. The Parliament was altogether too independent and was dissolved June 28, 1877. Another was chosen six months later which made itself still more disagreeable, and that was the end. The failure of the Conference was a disappointment to us at the College, and, as we believed, a misfortune for Turkey. We also believed that it would be better for the Bulgarians to be gradually emancipated. I am of the same opinion to-day. Whatever influence we had at the Conference was exerted with this in view. All that we did was in the interest of peace. The failure of the Conference meant war. A distinguished member of the Ulema explained to me at the time that the difficulty was that the government had stirred up the fanaticism of the people and had found it impossible to explain to the rank and file the necessity of yielding to the demands of infidel Europe.

Painful negotiations between the Powers followed the failure of the Conference, and war was not declared by Russia until April 29, 1877. The English government was unwilling to permit Russia to act in the spirit of the Conference and coerce the Turks; but the Bulgarian massacres had roused public opinion in England to such a pitch of hostility to Turkey that the government did not dare to protect her openly. Austria also had to be bought over to the side of Russia by the promise of Bosnia and Herzegovina. England and Austria both stipulated that Russia should not occupy Constantinople.

It does not come within the scope of this history to narrate the events of the Russo-Turkish War. At the outset the Turks had the advantage, and, if the Sultan had not attempted to direct the armies from his palace and had given the supreme command to any one of two or three of his generals, the Russians would have been miserably defeated, the first year at least; but Suleiman Pasha with the best of the Turkish troops was kept in Montenegro to be beaten by those mountaineers, while the troops who should have united against the Russians in Bulgaria were commanded by generals who did not work in harmony. The Russians were altogether unprepared for war, and the government had been forced into it by public opinion. The excitement in Constantinople during the spring and summer was intense, and the whole Mohammedan population of the empire was roused to defend the faith against their old enemy. The Christians did not know which to fear most, a great defeat or a great victory for the Turks. Our students shared in this excitement, especially as nearly half of our boarders were Bulgarians; but the College was never molested in any way, and we did our best to keep the students occupied with their studies.

At one time there were reports of a great Russian victory, and there was great alarm among the more ignorant Turks in the city. One day the wife of the *imam* of the quarter next the College came to me in great excitement and told me that the Russians were coming and would certainly murder them all. She came in the name of the women of Hissar to know if we would take them all into the College and protect them against the Russians. I told her that we would, and that she would find the American flag a sure protection. She went away comforted. It was very fortunate for us during the excitement of the war that our neighbors were friendly. At one time they took pains to warn us that it would be dangerous for a few days for our Bulgarian students to leave the college grounds.

We were greatly indebted to the officers of the Vandalia for the interest which they took in the College at this time. Their frequent visits were a boon to us in many ways. One evening Lieutenant Danenhower brought up some twenty sailors, who gave the students a negro minstrel concert, closing with a tableau of the Goddess of Liberty supported by the army and navy. It was a great success, and the sailors spent the night at the College. Another day they came up for a baseball match. These things were a great relief to the strain under which the students lived. The College was also a centre to which all visitors, English and American, to Constantinople came for information. Mr. Maynard, Mr. Schuyler and Mr. Tuckerman, minister to Greece, were also constant visitors, and they gave lectures to the students on various subjects.

The fall of Midhat Pasha made it impossible for Sir Henry Elliott to return to the British Embassy here, and Sir A. Henry Layard was sent to take his place. He had been here in the time of Lord Stratford, before he became famous for his work in Babylonia, and he was welcomed by the Turks as an old friend and a well-known Turcophile. He was also a devoted friend of ours, which at that time was most fortunate for us. Dr. Long and I continued to conduct the Sunday services at the British Embassy in Therapia as we had done for several years in the summer months under Sir Henry Elliott. A good many Turks at that time gave us the credit of having brought on the war, and Sir Henry Layard improved a favorable opportunity to ask the Sultan and the Grand Vizier whether they had any complaints to make of Robert College. Both of them assured him that they were perfectly satisfied that neither the College nor any of its students had ever done anything to encourage rebellion in Bulgaria. This was the simple truth. It was a relief to know that it was acknowledged to be true by the Sultan. Sir Henry Layard represented here the pro-Turkish and anti-Russian policy of Lord Beaconsfield, and his relations with the Sultan were more intimate than those of any other ambassador before or since. He was consequently in a position to mitigate, in some measure, the severity of the treatment of the Bulgarians by the Turkish authorities. We were able through his influence to save some lives in Bulgaria of old students and others. In one important case, however, we had an illustration of the difficulty of accomplishing anything under the Turkish administration. There were some fifty Bulgarians, some of them educated gentlemen and friends of ours, who were in imprisonment or exile, mostly in Mesopotamia and Syria. Some had been there for years. They had never been tried, but had been arrested and sent off on suspicion, simply because they were more intelligent than others. They had never been told what their offense was supposed to be. Before the Russians crossed the Danube it was a time when it was the policy of the Turks to conciliate the Bulgarians, and we represented the case of these Bulgarians to Mr. Layard, giving a detailed statement of each case. He saw the point and took our paper to the Sultan, who also saw the point and in Mr. Layard's presence ordered the immediate release of these men. Nothing was done, and Mr. Layard again spoke to the Sultan. He immediately summoned the officer to whom he had given orders and asked why his orders had not been carried out. It was said that they had not yet verified the statements in our paper. Again he gave orders and again nothing was done. A third time Mr. Layard called the Sultan's attention to the matter. He got this answer, "Have I not given you my word?" Nothing was ever done until the Russians at San Stefano secured their release.

We had troubles of our own in the College during the year, two cases of scarlet fever and a case of chicken pox, and at that time we had no doctor within five miles and no trained nurse or proper hospital. It was due to the devotion of the teachers and one of the students that we escaped an epidemic. In June Dr. Long had to go to America to bring home his eldest daughter, who was seriously ill. Professor Grosvenor was ill for some time, and I was not in good health at any time during the year. Then we were perplexed as to what policy we ought to pursue in regard to the College. The Lycée of Galata Serai and the national schools in Constantinople were closed soon after the outbreak of war. For a time Mr. Robert was in favor of closing, and the question came up as to what would be done with the building in that case. Could it be used as a hospital? Would the United States minister be willing to occupy it officially, or the consul general? It was our opinion that we should not close the College, whatever might happen, unless forced to do so by the Turkish government, a contingency which we had no reason to anticipate. Mr. Robert finally accepted this view, although it seemed very doubtful whether we should have many students. Another important question was brought up during the year by Professor Grosvenor. He was an enthusiastic Greek scholar and more interested in the Greeks than the Bulgarians. He wrote very strongly to Mr. Robert as to the weakness of our Greek Department and attributed to this the small number of our Greek students. We had only seven Greek boarders and four day scholars. His criticism of the department was just. We had one Greek professor, learned, but a poor teacher, who was of very little use to the students. We dismissed him at the end of the year and found it very difficult to get another. In fact the Greeks who were here did not come here for Greek, but for English and for a general education, and objected to studying Greek. The real reason why we had so few was that Robert College was looked upon by the Greeks as a Bulgarian college and they detested the Bulgarians. I was often told this in so many words. Still Professor Grosvenor was right in principle, and we never reached the Greeks to any extent until we found our present Greek professor, Professor Eliou, and through him were able to make this department equal to a Greek gymnasium. We now have six Greek teachers. The trouble in 1877 was that we had no money to expend in experiments.

Our Commencement exercises at the close of the year were an agreeable disappointment to us. It seemed doubtful whether, in the existing state of feeling in the city, it would be wise to have public exercises and whether any one would come if we did. The prize speaking on Wednesday and the public debate in the evening brought together large audiences, although the day was very hot and sultry. The debate on the question, "Has war produced more good than evil in the world?" interested the students very much and justified their choice of this subject. Thursday was a beautiful day, and the study hall was crowded to its utmost capacity with a distinguished audience. The orations were good and the speeches made by our guests excellent, as well as judicious, which was very important at that time. The Turkish representative of the government, a member of the Council of Public Instruction, declared that they held the College in the highest esteem and wished it all possible success. After the exercises we gave a luncheon to two hundred of the guests.

The graduating class numbered 14, of whom 10 are now living (1907). Five were Bulgarians, 6 Armenians, 2 Greeks, and 1 was an Englishman. Two of the Bulgarians have occupied high official positions, 2 have been teachers and literary men, 1 a successful merchant; 3 of the Armenians, the Englishman and the Greeks have been merchants; 1 of the Armenians is now a professor in Robert College, 1 died soon after graduation.

Many of our Bulgarians could not go home or even leave the college grounds. The feeling against them was more bitter than ever. General Gourco's foolish, unsupported raid across the Balkans and occupation of Eski Zagra, with the atrocities committed on the Turks there, had been terribly revenged by Suleiman Pasha, who had been recalled from Montenegro, with thousands of Bulgarians slaughtered and the town destroyed. Both events had increased the desire for vengeance among the Turks here. So Mrs. Washburn and I spent the summer in the College to protect the students who remained there. It was well for us that we had American men of war in the harbor, and that the officers and Mr. Maynard were frequent visitors at the College. As it was we had no serious difficulties of any kind. Dr. Long's wife and daughters lived with us. The deficit for the year on the current expense account here and in America was eighty-six hundred and twenty dollars, two thousand dollars more than the preceding year.

CHAPTER X
THE RUSSIANS AT SAN STEFANO. 1877-1878

THE College opened September 18, 1877, with 69 boarders and 26 day scholars. Thirty-nine of the boarders were Bulgarians. At the close of this year there were 80 boarders, of whom 44 were Bulgarians and 28 day scholars. Dr. Long returned from America September 21 and was in charge of the College as acting director during the year. Mrs. Washburn and I left for America September 26, my health having given out. I was suffering from nervous prostration. Professor Panaretoff had gone to Europe for the summer vacation and could not return on account of the violent persecution of all Bulgarians who came within the reach of the Turkish authorities here. The arrival of the Russians at San Stefano in March put an end to this, and Professor Panaretoff returned for the rest of the year. Mr. Slaveikoff had done his work up to this time, when he left the College and accepted a place on the staff of one of the Russian generals. Similar positions were already filled by several of our former students. Mr. Ludskanoff of the class of 1875 had greatly distinguished himself on the staff of General Skobeleff, who spoke of him to me in the highest terms. The necessity of such appointments grew out of the ignorance of the language of the country by the Russians, and the presence of a large number of Bulgarian volunteers in the Russian army. Two new tutors arrived in September, Messrs. Truax and Nash, both of whom in later years distinguished themselves in America, the first as a lawyer in New York and the second as a theological professor in California.

It was near the beginning of this year that the prospects of the war began to change in favor of the Russians both in Europe and Asia. The condition of the Russian armies had steadily improved, and the Roumanians had joined them in Bulgaria, while the Turkish armies were steadily deteriorating, through the weakness of the government at Constantinople. We cannot follow the course of the war in the field. We have only to do with events at Constantinople. After the fall of Plevna, the terrible winter passage of the Balkans and the rout of the Turkish army in the bloody battle of Shenova, the Russians pressed on to Constantinople, sweeping everything before them. The Turkish population of the country fled in terror, believing that the Russians and Bulgarians would avenge the massacre of the Bulgarians by a general slaughter of the Turks. It would require the pen of a De Quincey to picture the horrors of that winter exodus. I have heard the number of those who died on the road and in the streets of Constantinople estimated at a hundred thousand, but no one will ever know whether it was more or less. General Skobeleff, who commanded the advance guard of the Russians, related to me one incident of his own experience which may illustrate faintly the nature of this flight. It was between Philippopolis and Adrianople that he unexpectedly heard the sound of guns and hastened to the front. It was at a place where two rivers came together, and crowded in between them were an immense number of carts and some thousands of Turks, men, women and children. He ordered his troops to retire and rode forward himself to assure the refugees that they had nothing to fear; but he could not approach them as they persistently fired upon him, so he waited until they could get away. When he finally started at the head of a regiment of Cossacks he soon saw a baby by the roadside. He ordered a soldier to pick it up, and before he reached the next town nearly every soldier in the regiment had a child in his arms, which had been thrown away by its parents in their mad flight. At this town he seized a sufficient number of carts to carry these children to a Turkish village in the mountains where there was hope that the people might feed them. What their fate was he could not tell. It was reported from other sources that some two thousand children were thrown by their parents into the rivers, and that their bodies actually dammed the streams. It was said that the whole line of the railway from Adrianople was marked by the corpses of those who had fallen from the trains, too nearly frozen to keep their hold on the tops and sides of the cars. Great numbers starved to death with cold and hunger on the roads through the desolate country this side of Adrianople. Including the disbanded troops it was estimated that some three hundred thousand reached Constantinople in such a piteous state that, instead of plundering the unprotected city, they lay down and died in the streets and mosques. Typhus fever and smallpox raged among them and infected the city. There was a scarcity of food and of places to shelter them. It was altogether the most terrible experience that Constantinople had witnessed since the Turkish conquest. It was in the midst of these scenes that the new Parliament, chosen in some fashion, was holding its sessions, and it astonished every one by suddenly rousing itself and passing a vote of censure on the ministers. The ministers resigned, and the Sultan, without any apparent reason, abolished the office of Grand Vizier, appointed our friend Achmet Vefik Pasha Prime Minister, and ordered him to form a homogeneous ministry. Three months later, after he had been ignominiously dismissed, he told me many things in regard to his experiences. He found it almost impossible to transact business with the Sultan, and at times for two or three days together he seemed to be out of his mind. He trusted no one and really allowed the ministers no initiative in any business. But one thing Achmet Vefik Pasha accomplished with the aid of Sir Henry Layard which was of vital importance. When the Russians approached Constantinople the Sultan determined to retire to Brousa, the old Turkish capital, and gave orders accordingly. If he had done so the probability is that he would never have returned. They finally persuaded him to abandon the project. The story is that Sir Henry literally went down on his knees to the Sultan, but I do not know whether this is true. Certainly he did metaphorically. The Parliament was dispersed, many of the members escaped from the country, others were imprisoned, and that was the end of the Constitution. It was never formally revoked, but died a natural death. It was originally decreed by absolute power, simply to checkmate the European Powers, not because it was demanded by the people or adapted to the wants of the country, and it had never in any way limited the autocracy of the Sultan. He had made the war of his own will and he made peace in his own way.

With the arrival of the Russian army came the English fleet, which had nominally forced the passage of the Dardanelles in defiance of treaties, and hoped to prevent the occupation of Constantinople by the Russians. It was not war but a threat of war. So far as the Turks were concerned there was nothing to prevent the Russians entering the city without firing a shot. General Grant, who was here a little later, was in St. Petersburg at this time, and he told this story on the authority of a high official there. "When the Grand Duke arrived at San Stefano he sent many telegrams to the Czar, among others this, 'We are in sight of St. Sophia. There are no troops between us and the city. Shall I enter and take possession?' All the other telegrams were answered at once. This one was not, in the full belief that the Grand Duke would understand that he was to take the responsibility himself and occupy the city. To the great disappointment of the Czar he did not." General Grant added that this seemed to him the greatest mistake the Russians had made.

March 3, 1878, a treaty of peace was signed between Russia and Turkey at San Stefano which would have been final but for the attitude of England and Austria. For some time it looked as though war would result from this intervention, and during these months we received many visits from English and Russian officers, which puzzled us at first, but we soon discovered that it was a question of whether Russian batteries on the grounds of Robert College could prevent the British fleet from ascending the Bosphorus and entering the Black Sea to cut off the communication of the Russian armies. Dr. Long had information that a large force with heavy guns was not far away, and for a time was quite anxious about it. Happily we escaped this danger. The only occasion that we ever had to complain of the Russians grew out of what they had learned of Robert College in Bulgaria. All the forces that returned to Russia were brought to Constantinople and sent home by sea, so that every transport passed the College, and when opposite us, if there was a band on board, it struck up some American tune and the men gave three cheers. We had to explain to General Skobeleff that while we were grateful for the interest they had in us, this manifestation of it was not likely to improve our relations with the Turks, and we begged that it might be dispensed with. The streets of Constantinople were full of Russian officers and soldiers as long as they were at San Stefano, and we never heard of any conflicts between them and the Turks.

The treaty of San Stefano was of course a hard one for Turkey, but it would have been better for England and for all the people of European Turkey if it had been allowed to stand, and far better for the Armenians of Asia. The Sultan himself had no reason to thank England or Austria for their intervention. The secret convention by which England acquired Cyprus was little better than a theatrical trick of Lord Beaconsfield's. It interested the College only in that the British government asked us to furnish them with officials from among our graduates. The treaty of Berlin, which was signed July 13, 1878, was one of the most important events of the nineteenth century in European history, but it was not made in the interest of any one in the Turkish Empire. I do not know that it professed to be, although Lord Beaconsfield congratulated himself on having "consolidated" the empire, an euphemism for having reduced the size of it. Each Power sought only to further its own interests and ambitions; and for the people chiefly concerned the result has been a succession of wars, revolutions and massacres down to the present day. This is not the place to discuss this treaty, but we may take a single illustration from the people in whom the College was most interested at that time, the Bulgarians. The treaty of San Stefano had created a Bulgaria essentially on the lines agreed to by the Powers at the Conference of Constantinople. The treaty of Berlin divided the Bulgarians into *five* sections, giving one part to Servia, one to Roumania, one to an autonomous province called Eastern Roumelia, one to Turkey and one to constitute the Principality of Bulgaria under the suzerainty of the Sultan; and it was England especially that insisted upon this and also upon the right of Turkey to occupy and fortify the range of the Balkans, all with the object of making it impossible for the Bulgarians to form a viable state, which might be friendly to Russia. The Englishmen who knew Bulgaria, all our friends, understood the folly and wickedness of this at the time. All England has learned it since. Thus far the results have been the revolution of 1885, which resulted in the union of Bulgaria and Eastern Roumelia, the war with Servia, the insurrection in Macedonia and the province of Adrianople, and all the massacres and unspeakable horrors of the last thirty-nine years in Macedonia, to say nothing of what Bulgaria has suffered from the intrigues of foreign Powers ever since the treaty of Berlin. The awful massacres and persecutions from which the Armenians have suffered since 1886 have been equally the result of this treaty.

At the time, however, the advent of peace was a great boon to Constantinople and to the College, although we were brought into direct relations with an amount of human suffering on the part of the Turkish refugees from Bulgaria which was very distressing, and we found ourselves feeding and clothing some of the very people who had massacred the Bulgarians two years before. There were many of them quartered near the College, and a few remain to this day (1907) still recipients of our charity. Some of them suffered great remorse for what they had done and felt that their present suffering was a just judgment of God, and most of those near us have proved to be very decent though very ignorant people. Some have returned to Bulgaria.

There was a severe shock of earthquake in Constantinople April 19, which alarmed the city and shook Hamlin Hall vigorously, but without doing any injury to the building or causing any loss of life in the city. People's minds were so much occupied with the political disturbances that the earthquake excited very little attention.

Dr. Long proved himself a very efficient director of the College and a very wise representative of its interests in these troublous times, with our neighbors the Turks as well as at the embassies and with the government. It was due largely to him that the peace of the College was never disturbed and that none of our Bulgarian students were molested.

I spent the year in America, and so far as my health permitted I devoted myself to raising money to aid those students who had been left in poverty by the massacres and the war in Bulgaria. Thanks to the kindness of many friends, especially in Boston and vicinity, I raised five thousand dollars for this purpose. We also received some money from friends in England. I often saw Mr. Robert during the year. He was in feeble health, and the doctors sent him to Europe in June, 1878; but his interest in the College never flagged, and his inability to sufficiently endow it was a constant burden on his mind. The last time that we spoke about it the tears ran down his cheeks as he talked, but he had great faith in its future. I also visited Dr. Hamlin in Bangor. His heart was still in the College, but he altogether disapproved of everything which the College had done in connection with the Bulgarians, and thought that Dr. Long and I had very nearly, if not quite, put an end to its usefulness. I did not succeed in convincing him that times had changed since he left Constantinople. All the same, I had a very pleasant visit and, in spite of what he said, had very little doubt but that if he had been in our place he would have done very much the things that we did.

The Commencement exercises took place in the middle of July, a few days after the signing of the treaty of Berlin, when the city was rejoicing in peace, and brought together quite a distinguished assembly. Mr. Maynard, the American minister, presided; Sir Henry Layard, the British ambassador, made a speech; the Turkish government was represented by an officer who spoke in praise of the College; and the Armenian Patriarch sent his vicar to present his salutations and best wishes. It was a happy end of a very trying year, and all our students were able to return in peace to their homes.

There were 8 in the graduating class, of whom 3 were Bulgarians, 3 Armenians, 1 a Greek and 1 an Englishman. Only three of this class are still living (1907), two of them in Constantinople and one in New York. One of the Bulgarians was distinguished as a jurist and a diplomatist, the other two were officers in the Bulgarian army. Of the others, two were in the civil service of the British government, one is a banker, one a merchant in Constantinople, and one an official in New York.

CHAPTER XI
MR. ROBERT'S DEATH. 1878-1879

THIS year marks the beginning of a new era in the history of the College. Mr. Robert died suddenly in Paris, October 27, 1878. He had been in feeble health for some months, but his death was unexpected. He had written me a long letter on the 25th and was about to return to America. His death left the College to stand or fall on its own merits. Up to this time he had controlled and supported it. Nothing had been done in the College without his knowledge and approval. In addition to weekly letters, monthly reports were made to him of every detail of expenditure and of every student in the College, and in return we received advice or instructions from him in regard to everything. It is true that we did not always follow his advice or even obey his instructions; but in such cases we never failed to explain and justify our action by a full statement of our reasons, which he generally accepted as satisfactory and always with a recognition of the fact that he might be mistaken. The trustees in New York naturally left everything to him. We had no correspondence with them, and except Mr. Booth and Dr. Coe he seldom consulted them. They knew very little about the College. Whatever money was expended during these fifteen years for building, current expenses or any other purpose, he furnished. How much it amounted to I do not know, but it could not have been less than two hundred and fifty thousand dollars. This was not an ideal arrangement, and Mr. Robert's death left the College in a precarious position. But in reading the correspondence of those fifteen years I have been deeply impressed with its revelation of Mr. Robert's character, as a man whose chief end in life was to understand and do the will of God. He loved the College and cared for it as a shepherd might love and care for his master's flock, but it was not as his College. It was the Master's. He did not look upon those who were at work in the College as his servants, but with him fellow-servants of the Master. His experience in connection with the College seemed to develop a spirit of humility rather than pride and self-satisfaction, and as the years went on it was more and more a work of faith rather than self-confidence. It was God's work, and it would prosper. It should be remembered that he solemnly protested against having his name given to the College, and that he did everything in his power to induce others to share his interest and responsibility. He realized as fully as we did the dangers of the situation in which we might be left. He never drew upon the money invested for endowment to meet expenses, and he set apart a contingent fund himself which the trustees might use to meet any emergency in case of his death. Nothing tried his faith so sorely as Dr. Hamlin's failure to interest others in the College. He never blamed him, but he felt it to be a mysterious dispensation of Providence, which he could not understand, but which he must not allow to disturb his faith.

When he died we found ourselves in possession of property in Constantinople valued at $150,000
    Endowment raised by Dr. Hamlin and
        invested 12,000
    Endowment given by Mr. Remington
        and invested 5,000
    Contingent Fund — invested 10,000

    Total $177,000

In his will he left the College the real estate that he owned at Lookout Mountain, where he had opened a school after the war, which we sold some years later for forty thousand dollars, and also one-fifth of his general estate. His will was contested by some members of his family, but finally, some years later, it was decided in favor of the College, and we received about one hundred thousand dollars as our one-fifth.

The trustees to whom we were responsible were William A. Booth, President, Rev. Dr. D. B. Coe, Secretary, J. D. Vermilye, Treasurer, W. G. Lambert, A. S. Barnes and E. A. Brinkerhoff. Except the first two we had at this time no acquaintance with them, and they knew but little of us or our work. Mr. Merriman, who had been for some years Mr. Robert's private secretary, was the only other person in New York who had any personal knowledge of the details of college affairs, and he continued to assist the treasurer for many years, being at the same time in the service of Mr. Robert's eldest son, who was the executor of his father's will and united with the College in defending it.

It was of course impossible for the trustees to assume any such supervision of the College as Mr. Robert had carried on, but they realized their responsibility for the property and legal status of the institution and did what they could to carry out the wishes of the Faculty; but we were made to understand that henceforth the fate of the College depended upon us and not upon them. They had appointed me president June 6, 1878, just before Mr. Robert left for Europe, and at our request Dr. Long was appointed vice-president. I find in the correspondence that they also appointed an advisory committee in Constantinople, consisting of the American minister, the American consul general and half a dozen missionaries, nominated by us; but I have no recollection of ever having called this committee together, and I suspect that it was even more short-lived than Dr. Hamlin's advisory committee, although we often had occasion to seek the advice of individual members.

Probably the most important act of the trustees during the year was the appointment of Rev. Alexander van Millingen as professor. He has been one of the main pillars of the College ever since. Born in Constantinople, educated in Scotland and a minister of the Free Church, the son of a distinguished English physician, who was one of the most noteworthy men in Constantinople during a long period of years, he has rendered invaluable service to the College and is recognized as the highest authority on the archæology of Constantinople. Although appointed during this year, he did not enter upon his work until the beginning of the next, having in the meantime married one of the most brilliant and attractive ladies in New Haven, Conn.

The fact that Professor van Millingen's appointment was made at the request of the Faculty is evidence that we had not lost our faith in the future of the College. In fact we felt that there was nothing for us to do but to go forward, trusting in God, and to make the College worthy of support. That meant progress and development. To remain stationary meant failure, for the influence of the College had already created a demand for a higher and better education than any one in Turkey had thought of fifteen years before, and the new Bulgaria was crying out for thoroughly educated young men. We could not diminish our expenditure. We prepared to increase it. Only, as president of the College, I determined that we should keep out of debt and never spend money which was not in sight. We adhered to this principle, although we often had occasion to mourn over lost opportunities, or what seemed to be such, but I believe in the principle to-day as firmly as I did thirty years ago. I have always looked upon this as God's work and felt that, if we did our duty in it. He would give us the means to carry it forward just as fast as He saw it to be best.

When the College opened in September, 1878, the treaty of Berlin had been signed, but the condition of things in Constantinople and in the provinces was far from satisfactory. The Russian armies still occupied Bulgaria and were still encamped at San Stefano. The Turkish government was bankrupt and disorganized, the city was still full of starving refugees, and the irredeemable paper money was our only currency, so that business was stagnant. We could not hope for any immediate increase in the number of our students. The year opened with 96 boarders and 38 day scholars, 134 in all, against 108 at the close of the preceding year, which, all things considered, was encouraging. At the close of the year there were 103 boarders and 43 day scholars present.

It was during this year that we published the first catalogue of the College. It was in the English language and designed for circulation in America rather than in Turkey. Statements in regard to the College for use in this country had to be published in five different languages. This catalogue shows that at that time there were five professors (not including Professor van Millingen), three American tutors, one French, one German, one Italian, one Greek, one Turkish and one Armenian instructors, besides a teacher of music and the president's secretary. It gives a detailed account of the 76 graduates of the College, and shows that up to that time there had been 912 different students in the College. It gives the names, nationality and residence of 11 Seniors, 9 Juniors, 19 Sophomores, 14 Freshmen, 22 Sub-Freshmen and 76 preparatory students, 151 in all registered during the year, together with all necessary information in regard to the course of study, the terms of admission, and, in general, of the objects of the College. It is a pamphlet of twenty-eight pages, printed in Constantinople by an Armenian who learned his trade in Andover, Mass.

Looking over the list of instructors reminds me of my experience with the German instructor. He was a brilliant and accomplished young man of one of the best families in the kingdom of Hanover, and the leading German pastor in New York city gave him the highest recommendations; but he turned out to be a thoroughgoing vagabond, who had run away from Hanover to escape from military service. When we found him out we had to expel him from the College, and for many years he used to send me, every few months, from different parts of the world, abusive postal cards, informing me of his intention to come to Constantinople to kill me or to horsewhip me in the streets, or some other threat. It is some years now since I have heard of him, and I have no doubt that he is dead. The story of my experience with him from first to last would furnish material for the stage of a Bowery theatre.

The American tutors this year were Mr. Nash, of whom I have already spoken, Mr. Porter, who was here only one year, and Edward M. Vittum, who is now (1907) president of a College in North Dakota.

I returned from America in September, 1878, in better health, traveling by way of England, where Mrs. Washburn and I stopped to visit Mr. William E. Forster, the famous English statesman, at his home in the English Lake Country. Mrs. Forster was the daughter of Dr. Arnold of Rugby, and we saw much of Matthew Arnold, who was visiting his mother at this time. Mr. Forster had been for several years one of our most trusted and most influential friends in England and was so as long as he lived. He was one of England's ablest statesmen. The misfortune of his life was his appointment as Irish Secretary. I visited him in London soon after his appointment, and I know that he accepted the office out of pure benevolence, with the one thought of conciliation and with full faith that the Irish people would trust his justice and goodwill. In the time of the great famine he had gone with his father to the rescue of the sufferers in Ireland and had never lost the sympathy for them which had its origin in that visit. He was of an old Quaker family and a man of very tender heart. I was walking with him one day over the hills near his house when we started several hares. I asked him if he ever indulged in shooting. He answered, "I never shed the blood of any fellow creature." It was in this spirit that he went to Ireland and there escaped assassination only by an accident. I asked him once what he thought of Matthew Arnold as a philosopher. He said, "I have often told Matthew that he ought to make up his own mind before undertaking to instruct the world." We found Matthew Arnold a most interesting conversationalist, and, as we went to church together one Sunday, I found him apparently one of the most devout worshipers in the congregation.

The next time that I visited Mr. Forster was in the summer of 1880, when he had just carried through the House of Commons a bill designed to conciliate the people of Ireland. I was in London when it came before the House of Lords, and the Marquis of Bath secured from the Lord Chancellor an invitation for me to a seat on the steps of the throne, where I had the Prince of Wales, Mr. Forster and other distinguished men for company. It was one of those rare occasions when the Lords muster in full force to resist a Liberal government. They were all there that night, and they rejected Mr. Forster's bill by an overwhelming majority. This was a foregone conclusion, and the debate was not of a high order. Beaconsfield, who led, was dull. The only eloquence was on the Liberal side. What impressed me most was that the Lords were not an intellectual looking set of men. There were great men there, but the majority looked as though they neither knew nor cared anything about the questions — old men with one foot in the grave, young fellows who looked excessively bored and men with no gleam of intelligence in their faces. I lost my faith in the House of Lords that night.

On our arrival at Constantinople after a year's absence we found Dr. Long very anxious as to the health of his daughter; and, not long after, Mrs. Long and his daughter went to southern France in the hope that a change of climate might restore her health, but before the end of the year he found it necessary to go to Montpellier and bring his family back. His daughter died at the College, August 3, 1879, after which the family went to live at the house belonging to the College in Hissar. In the intimate relations in which we lived, the whole College in Hamlin Hall, we all shared in the trial through which Dr. Long and his family were passing.

While I was in America my attention was called to the fact that a young Armenian, who had come to America and graduated at Bowdoin College, was raising money to found a university at Constantinople, under the patronage, as he claimed, of the President of the United States and other distinguished officials and philanthropists, in opposition to Robert College. I was requested by some persons to whom he had applied for money to investigate the matter in America and in Constantinople. I was told in America that he claimed to be sure of a very large sum of money — as much as a million, it was said; but Peter Cooper, whom he claimed as one of the largest givers, declared that he had never promised to give anything. He had secured, however, some money and the patronage of a number of distinguished men and women, including one or two personal acquaintances of mine. One of the best-known clergymen in New York roundly abused me and called me hard names for the inquiries that I made. In Constantinople I could find no one who knew anything of this projected university. The young man came to Constantinople with some money and was said to have bought a house for himself in Scutari. That is the last that I have heard of him. I have nothing to say of this young man's honesty or good intentions. He had been a long time absent from Turkey and perhaps did not know that his scheme was an absurd and impossible one. What interested me in the matter was this: Dr. Hamlin, whom everybody had professed to honor, had been trying for years to raise money for Robert College; and many of the very people, the best of people too, who had honored him but given him no money, were ready to take up, champion and support a young man, a foreigner, just out of college, in founding a university in Constantinople in opposition to Robert College, without even taking the trouble to inquire whether his scheme was a practicable one or not. I record the story here because it is one of the mysteries of American benevolence, of which this is not the only illustration that has come to my notice.

The political event of the year which most interested us at Robert College was the national convention which met at Tirnova in April, 1879, to adopt a constitution and choose a prince of Bulgaria, under the supervision of a Russian general. All Europe looked on with interest, and all Europe was astonished at the result. It was natural enough that the favorite cousin of the Czar, Prince Alexander of Battenberg, should be chosen prince, with the consent of the Powers. It was most unexpected that the constitution adopted should be one of the most democratic in Europe, and that Russia made no objection to it. The assembly itself was unique, made up largely of peasants, many of them in their sheepskin clothes, and I think that there was no one in the assembly who knew anything about parliamentary law except the old students of Robert College, who were in force. There was not a member who had had any personal experience in civil government. One of the acts of the assembly was to pass a resolution of gratitude to Dr. Long and myself for what we had done for the elevation and independence of Bulgaria. Similar resolutions of thanks to Mr. Gladstone and Mr. Schuyler were adopted. Prince Alexander himself was a young man without experience, and for his private secretary he chose Mr. Stoiloff, a graduate of the class of 1871, who became his most intimate friend and counsellor.

The other Bulgarian province of Eastern Roumelia was also organized by a European commission, and a Bulgarian, who had been in the Turkish service, appointed governor. Austria secured Bosnia and Herzegovina only by conquest after a long and fierce conflict with the inhabitants. Servia, Roumania and Montenegro became independent states, but other provisions of the Treaty of Berlin, as to Greece, Macedonia and Montenegro, were not carried out.

The class which graduated in July, 1879, numbered 11, — 6 Bulgarians and 5 Armenians, 6 of whom are still living (1907). Of the Bulgarians one became a teacher, two lawyers, of whom one is a distinguished judge, one an officer in the Bulgarian army, two are dead. Of the Armenians one became a physician, one a teacher and clergyman, the others merchants.

CHAPTER XII
AFTER THE WAR. 1879-1880

IN the summer vacation of 1879 Mr. Maynard invited Professor Panaretoff, who knew both Turkish and Russian, and me to go with him on a trip around the Black Sea in the United States corvette Wyoming, commanded by Captain Watson. It was the first time that an American war vessel had been seen in the Black Sea, and we visited all the principal Turkish and Russian ports, and were received everywhere with the highest honors by the authorities and with enthusiasm by the people. The Wyoming itself was a sad specimen of the decay of the American navy. Her boilers leaked so that she could not make more than six or seven knots an hour, and her guns were in such a damaged condition that it was not safe to fire them; but her officers and men were an honor to the country, and, when she was lying in a harbor, she was not a bad looking ship. What most interested us in Russia was that it was an Empire of Discontent. High or low, official or unofficial, it made no difference; every one talked of the unsatisfactory condition of the country — even General Todleben, the hero of Sevastopol and Plevna, who was then the governor-general of Odessa. It was a result of the Russo-Turkish War — a foretaste of what was to follow the war with Japan, and, but for the assassination of the Czar, it might have led to such changes as would have saved Russia from the calamities of the last few years. It is well known that at the time of his death he was on the point of giving a constitution to his people.

We returned to Constantinople in season for the opening of the College. The number of students was 130 boarders and 48 day scholars. At the close of the year it was 137 boarders and 56 day scholars. The whole number registered during the year was 209, — Bulgarians 77, Armenians 74, Greeks 27, other nationalities 31, a decided advance over the previous year. Professor Grosvenor was absent during the year on account of the health of his family. Professor van Millingen joined us, and Miss Susan Farley, a niece of Dr. Hamlin, came out as matron. During the year we lost Mr. Maynard, who was recalled to be Postmaster-General. To him and to his family the College owes a debt of gratitude which no one connected with us at the time can ever forget, and the United States has never been more worthily represented in Constantinople than by them. He was followed by General Longstreet, who found himself out of his sphere and remained here less than a year.

The inner life of the College during this year was uneventful, but the work done was most satisfactory. Everything was harmonious, and the students not only did good work in their classes, but encouraged us to feel that we were really moulding their characters and fitting them for a higher life. We have always felt that the religious side of our work was the most important part of it — the only reason for our being here at all; but it is very difficult to tabulate or even to describe the nature or the results of it. The Sunday services and the daily religious exercises which all the students are required to attend are very important, but I have always felt that our direct personal influence and the incidental religious teaching in the classroom were more important. I have just read a letter from one of the most distinguished of our earlier graduates which was written in 1880, in which he says, "My interior and religious convictions show me only one principle of life and that is duty towards God and duty towards my fellow men," and he thinks that the government of Bulgaria should send young men to Robert College as the one place where this lesson can be learned. We have been disappointed in some of our students, but it is a fact that many of them have illustrated this principle in their lives, and it is also true that the high reputation of the College all over this part of the world is due to the personal character of our graduates. A tree is known by its fruit and a college by its graduates.

While it was always our purpose to keep politics out of the College, we could not but feel an intense interest in the course of events about us, and this year everything seemed to be going wrong. Whatever personal influence I had I used in the various complications which arose, without in any way compromising the College, in the interest of peace and progress. To begin with Bulgaria, Mr. Stoiloff was the private secretary of Prince Alexander and Mr. Dimitroff was chief of the Chancellery of Aleko Pasha, the Governor-General of Eastern Roumelia, so that I was in intimate relations with both; and in the spring of 1880 I visited Eastern Roumelia. Prince Alexander had loyally undertaken to organize the government of the Principality of Bulgaria under its democratic constitution, but the result was discouraging and threatened anarchy and a new Russian intervention. There were parties in Bulgaria calling themselves conservative and liberal, but there were no leaders who had any experience in government, and the National Assembly chosen by the people was hopelessly ignorant and unmanageable. I suppose that nothing better could reasonably have been expected of a people suddenly emancipated from Turkish rule, but it was a great disappointment to us as well as to Prince Alexander.

In Eastern Roumelia Robert College men were more numerous and the administration better organized, but the people resented their separation from Bulgaria and the constant intervention of the Turks in their affairs, and were encouraged by Russia to hope for union with the Principality. They were more interested in revolutionary plots than in the existing government. This was an inevitable result of the treaty of Berlin, but unfortunate for the people of Eastern Roumelia. While I sympathized heartily with their desire for union, it did not seem to me that it could best be brought about by these revolutionary methods. It was sure to come in time in a peaceful way.

In Asiatic Turkey the situation was more discouraging than in Bulgaria. We naturally felt a deep interest in the Armenians, and England, by her action at Berlin in regard to the treaty of San Stefano, and by the Cyprus treaty, had made herself responsible for such reforms in Turkey as would secure their well-being. The Patriarch Nerses, a noble Christian man, was a friend of mine and was the embodiment of the hopes of his people, but in no sense a revolutionist. He had great faith in England, and when he lost it he died of a broken heart.

To a certain extent the government of Lord Beaconsfield had realized its responsibility, and Sir Henry Layard had pressed the matter here, with the result that there was much talk about reforms and an *iradé* issued which professed to ordain "such reforms as would secure equal rights to all his Majesty's beloved subjects." As it was only a reform on paper it did not matter much that it was far less liberal than some previous ones. The condition of the Armenians in the provinces meanwhile was growing steadily worse, especially where the Kurds were given a free hand to plunder them. Sir Henry Layard gave up all hope of accomplishing anything, and when Mr. Gladstone came into power he was replaced by Mr. Goschen, who came out on a special mission to bring the Sultan to terms, and failed. We not only regretted this failure from our sympathy with the Armenians, but because it seemed to us that the Sultan had made a mistake which might lead to serious consequences. It is clear now that he had a better knowledge of the possibilities before him than we had, and he has maintained the same policy successfully to this day (1907) — of resisting foreign intervention and restricting the influence of his non-Mohammedan subjects.

The situation in Constantinople was not much better than in the interior. The Sultan had already concentrated the administration of the government in the palace and begun to gather around him the sort of adventurers who have since been the great curse of the empire. For a time a Tunisian statesman, Khairadin Pasha, had been Grand Vizier and had excited the hopes of the people, but he was summarily dismissed. The spirit of the palace was illustrated by the assassination of the military attaché of the Russian Embassy, as he was riding along the public street, by one of the Sultan's servants. This man intended to murder the *chargé d'affaires*, but mistook the military man for him. All the influence of all the embassies was not sufficient to secure the punishment of the assassin.

The insecurity of the city was brought home to us by the murder of Haritoon, the Armenian steward of the College, who had been for many years Dr. Hamlin's right-hand man and most trusted assistant in everything mechanical, as well as in the management of the boarding department. He was murdered by two hired assassins at midday within a stone's throw of the College, and these assassins were employed by an officer of the palace, who had attempted to abduct the two attractive daughters of Haritoon, but had failed, as their father had succeeded in getting them out of the country. Nothing could be done to secure the punishment of the officer or of the murderers, although the whole story was known by everybody in the vicinity, and told pretty fully in the Turkish newspapers.

Some two years later an attempt was made to murder me at exactly the same place, but I think that, in this case, the object was robbery. The man had crept up behind me and was just in the act of throwing a girdle around my neck to strangle me when some unconscious mental activity led me to suddenly turn round face to face with the assassin; and this unexpected movement so startled him that he jumped back, and finally fled, believing no doubt that I was armed.

One of the curious incidents of this year in which we were interested was the effort made by Mr. Spanoudis, a Greek gentleman, to rescue the Bulgarian women and children who had been captured during the war and were held as slaves in Constantinople and the vicinity, by the Turks. He undertook the task as a Christian duty and had many extraordinary adventures. He came to us that we might secure for him the support of the British Embassy, which we did. He was the means of rescuing a large number, who were sent back to their homes. Of this there is no doubt, although I must confess that some of the adventures which he related sounded very much like fairy tales and certainly could not have been true, even in Constantinople, in ordinary times; but it was a period of uncertainty, before the Sultan had established his authority. Other extraordinary things were taking place, and the Turks knew that, in the eyes of the world, they had no right to hold these Bulgarians as slaves. Mr. Spanoudis had the moral support of the Russian and British embassies. No one dared to challenge or resist the authority which he assumed. An English society, *The Aborigines Protection Society*, also interested itself in this matter, but there is no doubt that a very large number of Christian women and children were held in slavery in other places where they could not be reached.

The question came up during the year of the possibility of Dr. Hamlin's return to the College, and the Faculty unanimously voted to request the trustees to propose this to him; but, after due consideration, the trustees decided that under the circumstances this was not practicable. About the same time they began to insist upon the necessity of my going to America to raise money for the endowment of the College, as nothing could be expected from Mr. Robert's estate for some years, even if the decision of the highest courts should finally be in our favor, and our means of support would soon be exhausted. Before the end of the year it was decided that I must come during the summer and undertake this work. It appeared to me almost a hopeless task; but, as it seemed to be a matter of life or death for the College, and there was no one else to go, I consented, left Constantinople in July and was absent two years, Dr. Long acting as president in my absence.

At the close of the year Professor Panaretoff was sent to London by Prince Alexander on a special mission to the British government. As there was no conflict with the Turkish government involved we made no objections.

The Commencement exercises passed off as successfully as could be expected in the old study hall, which was the only room that we had for religious services or public occasions. It was a wonder that guests came to be packed in among the desks and benches in discomfort for two hours; but we did our best to hide our nakedness with flags, flowers and green leaves, making it appear a special favor to allow them to come by admitting only those who had cards of invitation. The crowd came as usual, the distinguished and official guests occupying the platform, and I suppose what really brought them was the prevalent idea that Robert College was a centre of influence unsurpassed by any other in Constantinople, in spite of its meagre appointments. In fact, we had no official position, no army behind us, no selfish ambitions to gratify, nothing but goodwill to all and the desire to lend a helping hand wherever we could.

There were 7 graduates that year, all of whom are still living (1907), 4 Bulgarians and 3 Armenians. All the Bulgarians have occupied important official positions and two of them have been distinguished as teachers. One of the Armenians is the first secretary of the Persian Legation in Washington and two are honored merchants in London and New York.

CHAPTER XIII
TWO YEARS IN AMERICA. 1880-1882

I LEFT Constantinople in July, 1880, to raise money for the College in America and did not return until August, 1882. During my absence Dr. Long was acting president of the College, so that I was never disturbed by any anxiety as to what might happen here. Dr. Long was by choice a scholar and teacher and shrank from the responsibilities of administration; but when called to this work he never spared himself, and he made an admirable president. He understood the students, he loved them, and his personal influence over them was one of the best things in the College to the day of his death. The eighteenth year the Faculty consisted of Professors Grosvenor, van Millingen, Hagopos, Panaretoff and Vittum, with Messrs. Orville Reed and Charles Hoyt as American tutors, and seven other instructors. The nineteenth year Mr. Vittum had returned to America and Messrs. Beckwith and Haynes had come to the College as additional tutors.

In 1881 Professor van Millingen built a house for himself on the college grounds, for his own use while he lives and then to be the property of the College.

The number of students registered the eighteenth year was 232, of whom 74 were day scholars. There were 89 Bulgarians, 85 Armenians, 28 Greeks, 7 Turks and 23 others. The nineteenth year the number registered was 259, of whom 86 were day scholars. There were 105 Bulgarians, 94 Armenians, 24 Greeks, 12 Turks, and 25 others. The building was overcrowded and the staff of teachers too few for the work, and Dr. Long wrote to me in October, 1881, "We must have a new building or decline." Nothing saved us at that time from a serious loss in the number of our students but the fact that Bulgaria had not yet organized her school system and that there was no other institution in Constantinople which attracted either Bulgarians or Armenians, and they believed in Robert College. The Greeks were not unfriendly to us, but they did what they could to keep their students in Greek schools, and we were too poor to organize a Greek department which would attract them.

In December, 1881, we were distressed by the failure of our bankers, Messrs. Charles S. Hanson & Co., not so much by the loss of money, as we had only about twelve hundred dollars on deposit

ALBERT L. LONG

at the time, as by the misfortune which had befallen a family which had been for almost fifty years the leading English family in Constantinople and had been the most trusted and devoted friends of the College in the city. Mr. C. S. Hanson had died not long before. He and Mrs. Hanson were the best specimens I have ever known of the ideal English gentleman and lady of the first half of the nineteenth century. Lord Lyons, when he was ambassador here, said the same thing to me about them. Their sons, with their families, were equally warm friends of the College, and their failure was a decided loss for us, as well as to the English-speaking colony generally.

The political situation in Turkey and Bulgaria during these two years was even more discouraging than in the previous year, and a cause of anxiety to Dr. Long, although the consequences of it were not apparent at that time in the College, which was more prosperous than ever before. The Sultan had fairly inaugurated the policy which has characterized his reign, of resisting to the utmost all foreign influences in the Empire and reducing the number and influence of his Christian subjects, while at the same time building up and strengthening the Mohammedan population and reviving the old spirit of Islam. I do not know that we have any right to blame the Caliph of the Mohammedan world for adopting this policy, if he believed that, as Sultan of Turkey, he could put it in execution without endangering the existence of the empire or violating treaty obligations. At the time of which I am writing he was interested in encouraging a panislamic movement in Syria, Egypt and northern Africa, which finally led to the English occupation of Egypt. He had commenced his work of putting down the Armenians, of limiting the rights of foreign and native Christian schools and of the Christian religious organizations generally. He was successfully resisting the decisions of the Congress of Berlin, in favor of Greece, Montenegro and Macedonia, and had refused to recognize the right of England, under the Cyprus treaty, to interfere in the government of his Asiatic provinces. He had made it clear that no Mohammedan would be allowed to change his religion and that no criticism of Islam would be tolerated. The general censorship of the press had commenced. Although none of these things directly affected us, except the school regulations, which were never enforced against Robert College, the general outlook was discouraging, not only here, but for me in America, where there was a natural hesitation about investing money in Turkey.

We were also very anxious about the state of things in Bulgaria, where, in May, 1881, Prince Alexander, with the approval of the Czar, suspended the Constitution for seven years, and brought in Russian officials to govern the country. He was supported in this by the so-called conservative party, which was in the minority in the country. It looked as though Bulgaria had been freed from Turkey only to fall under the equally bad rule of Russia, especially after the assassination of the Czar and the accession of Alexander III, who had hated Prince Alexander of Bulgaria ever since they were boys together. The Russian officials now took their orders from St. Petersburg and treated the prince with contempt. They undertook the Russification of everything, and if they had been men of a different stamp they might have won the people over to their side; but they treated the Bulgarians as a conquered people, like the tribes of Central Asia, alienated their sympathies and really prepared the way for Prince Alexander's *coup d'état* of 1883, when he restored the Constitution and cleared them out. But in 1882 there was no such change in view, and we felt as though we were to be disappointed of all our hopes for this people of whom we had expected so much. There was little that we could do for them beyond the influence that we had over our present and former students and over the policy of the British government through our friends in the ministry and at the Embassy here. Things were somewhat better in Eastern Roumelia, but here two Russian consuls were doing what they could to create trouble and foment discontent. There was nothing promising improvement in the condition of Macedonia or of the Armenians in the Asiatic provinces, but rather a foretaste of what was to come in later years.

The conflict of interests among the European Powers made it impossible for them to intervene, and gave the Sultan a free hand to carry out his own plans. England was the only Power that had the interests of the people of the East at heart. At this time, under Mr. Gladstone, she did what she could, but she was in danger of war with Russia. France was unfriendly and Germany doing what she could to create difficulties. She already had her eyes on Asia Minor as her share of the Ottoman Empire when the empire went to pieces, and had begun her exploitation of it under the pretense of friendship for the Sultan. I happen to know that the English Liberal ministry did not look upon such a scheme with disfavor. Russia was the power which they feared, and Asia Minor in the hands of Germany would be a barrier to her advance and also make it necessary for Germany, with her small navy, to keep on good terms with England. England at that time did not want any more territory on the Mediterranean. Bismarck, after the Franco-Prussian War, had urged upon her the occupation of Egypt, but no statesman whom I knew of either party was in favor of it.

I find nothing in the records of the Faculty during the two years of my absence of general interest, beyond the evidence which they give of the hard work that was done by all the teachers and the constant effort to advance, to do better work in every department and to bring the students up to a higher standard of life. I have no account of the Commencement exercises in 1882, but a letter from Dr. Long gives a detailed account of those of 1881. On July 13 there were prize declamations in the afternoon and a prize debate in the evening between the Sophomore and Freshman classes on the question whether a state owes more to her literary men than to her inventors. There were good audiences, and the students acquitted themselves with honor. But the great day was July 14, which brought out the usual crowd of many nationalities, and the orations of the graduating class were in English, French, Armenian and Bulgarian. The subjects are worth recording, when it is remembered that these orations were delivered in Constantinople by Armenians, Greeks and Bulgarians, — True Education, Christianity and Patriotism, The Dark Ages, The Influence of the Fine Arts, Man and Nature, Free Thought, Representative Government, Violation of Popular Rights, The Destiny of States and Nations, The New Sovereign (*i. e.* the People), Fall of the City of Constantine, and Political Parties. There was certainly no other place in Constantinople where such subjects could have been publicly discussed, although there was nothing seditious in any one of them. They were new subjects of thought for the young men of the East and for a Constantinople audience.

Among the distinguished guests present were the Persian Ambassador, Lord Dufferin the English Ambassador, and the Marquis of Bath. The two latter made very interesting addresses, after the orations, and were warm friends of the College all their lives.

In 1881 there were 12 graduates, of whom 8 are still living; 9 were Bulgarians, 2 Armenians and 1 Greek. Six of the Bulgarians were teachers for a time and one an editor. One has been for many years in the diplomatic service. Four have occupied important official positions. Two are merchants. One of the Armenians is a distinguished teacher, the other studied medicine. The Greek is in business.

In 1882 there were 9 graduates, of whom 8 are living (1907); 5 were Bulgarians, 4 Armenians. Two of the Bulgarians were teachers and one an editor. Two are now judges and one has been Minister of Public Instruction. One is a merchant. One of the Armenians is an official of the Turkish government. The others are in business.

My work in America during these two years was one for which I am sure that I was never fitted. I never had any difficulty in interesting people in Robert College, and they were often enthusiastic in their sympathy. I can never forget all the kindness and goodwill which I met with — the delightful homes that were opened to me and the friends that I made; but I lacked altogether that sort of persuasive power which I have seen in many other beggars, and could never argue the question with one who declined to give. I had many bitter disappointments, but when the two years were over I had the satisfaction of knowing that whatever money I had collected had been given heartily, not under pressure of any kind, but only because God had put it into the hearts of the donors to lend a hand in what they saw to be a good work. In many cases it was without my ever directly asking for it. Nearly all of these benefactors of the College have passed away to a higher life, but their memory is very precious. The following is a list of the principal donors. In Boston, William Endicott, Jr., Mrs. V. G. Stone, William S. Houghton, H. P. Kidder, S. D. Warren, W. O. Grover, Ezra Farnsworth, Henry Woods, Miss E. F. Mason, J. N. Dennison, R. C. Greenleaf, Frederick Ayer, J. L. Brewer, Elisha Mulford, Phillips Brooks, B. H. Nash, William Claflin, Mrs. Hemenway, T. G. Appleton, E. P. Beebe. In New York: William E. Dodge, William E. Dodge, Jr., M. K. Jesup, D. Willis James, A. J. Barnes, John Taylor Johnson. In other places, C. P. Whitin and Mrs. John Whitin of Whitinsville, P. L. Moen and Stephen Salisbury of Worcester, George H. Corliss of Providence, Mrs. M. B. Young of Fall River, S. M. Edgell of St. Louis. The whole sum contributed was sixty-one thousand eight hundred and fifty-four dollars.

There were many others who were like the Apostles Peter and John. Silver and gold they had none, but such as they had they freely gave, — their sympathy, their counsel, their influence, —

Edward Everett Hale, President Eliot, Rev. Dr. N. G. Clark, Mrs. Julia Ward Howe, the ministers and editors generally in Boston. Other college presidents and ministers in New England and New York were equally in sympathy with the College; but most of my time, when I was well enough to do any work, was spent in Boston and vicinity, where I was at home. I was a stranger then in other parts of the country except in New York City. I visited other cities and met with a hearty reception in many homes, but got no money. The first gift that I received came unsolicited from a very poor man, a good minister. It was two silver half dollars. I replaced them and keep them still as a memento and shall have them framed and put in the College Museum.

I have just gone through the long list of the names of those upon whom I called, from most of whom I got nothing, and I do not recall anything unpleasant in connection with any one of them. Only one man ever treated me uncivilly and ordered me out of his office, and he repented and did works meet for repentance — gave me the largest gift that I received. I do not regret the experience of these two years or of those which I have had since in this work. They have brought me friends whom I should not have known otherwise, whose friendship has been one of the chief joys of my life, and given me strength and courage for my work in Constantinople. I have no complaint to make of those who might have given money to the College and did not. I have come to feel a deep sympathy for all those who are known to be givers, and to marvel at the patience with which they listen to endless applications for money for every conceivable scheme, good, bad and indifferent. They are right in declining to give to anything which they do not approve or do not understand, and they must choose among the things which they recognize as good. No man can give to everything. Robert College was far away. It did not appeal to any national, denominational or party interest. There were but few who had ever visited Constantinople or realized its importance as a centre of influence, and few who could understand the power of a Christian college to influence the destiny of a nation. Those who gave were those who were already interested in foreign missions and who had some knowledge of what Robert College was doing. Some who began to be interested at that time kept up this interest, learned more about it and gave liberally in later years.

CHAPTER XIV
THE COLLEGE AT THE END OF TWENTY YEARS.
1882-1884

ON my return from America in the summer of 1882, I spent some days in London and visited my old friends Mr. William E. Forster and Mr. Bryce1 — as well as other influential men. Lord Granville was the Minister of Foreign Affairs, and he invited me to call on him at the Foreign Office, as he wished to talk with me about affairs in the East. I found him one of the most agreeable of men and well informed in regard to the state of affairs in Turkey, The question of Egypt was then approaching the crisis which resulted in the bombardment of Alexandria, the outbreak of fanaticism which followed and the English occupation of the country. He had a keen appreciation of the dangers resulting from the state of excitement in Egypt and Syria, connected with the revolutionary movement of Arabi Pasha, and the intrigues of the Sultan, who sought to take advantage of this to bring about a panislamic revival. He told me that he wished to avoid armed intervention, especially by England alone, and considered it impossible for England to occupy Egypt for any length of time. I saw no one in London who did not share his opinions. If Arabi Pasha had yielded to the demands of the British admiral at Alexandria, which were very reasonable, I do not believe that England would have occupied Egypt. On the other hand, it was the general opinion of foreigners living in Egypt and Syria that if this movement were not checked in some way it would result in a general rising of the Mohammedans in Syria, Arabia and northern Africa against Christian and European influence. It was this and the importance of the Suez Canal which led the government of Mr. Gladstone to run the risk of presenting an ultimatum at Alexandria, and the obstinacy of Arabi Pasha which determined the measures which followed.

After I reached Constantinople General Lew Wallace, who was the American minister here, told me that at the request of the Sultan he had telegraphed to Washington a request for our govern-

---

1 No English statesman has followed events in the nearer East so carefully and sympathetically for the last thirty years as Mr. Bryce, and no one has been a more devoted friend of Robert College.

ment to intervene and mediate between England and Turkey, to which our government had replied that, if England also wished it, we might do so, and he thought that it was the knowledge of this which decided England to act at Alexandria to forestall any such proposition; but he had no evidence of this beyond the coincidence of time.

General Wallace was a special favorite of the Sultan, more so than any other minister or ambassador here, and after his return to America he was his eulogist. He was always ready to take up his defense and say a good word for him, but I do not know that he ever told in public the story of one tragic incident connected with this same Egyptian question. There was a time when it was a question of the joint occupation of Egypt by England and Turkey, and Lord Dufferin was doing his best to persuade the Sultan to agree to this. France and Russia, who did not wish to see England's occupation legalized, advised against it and represented that the plan proposed would make England dominant there, while the Turkish forces would be a mere side show. The Sultan sent for General Wallace to ask for his advice. General Wallace very properly told him that this was an affair in which the United States minister could not possibly take any part. The Sultan told him that he had not sent for the United States minister and did not wish the opinion of the United States government, but that he had sent for his personal friend General Wallace and wished his personal opinion. After vainly endeavoring to evade the question, General Wallace said, "If you really wish to know what I would do if I were in your place I will tell you." The Sultan insisted, and General Wallace said: "If I were in your place I would get my troops ready, embark them and *go with them* to Egypt. Once there no one can question your supremacy and you have the game in your own hands." The interpreter had hardly finished the translation of this when the Sultan gave a groan and fell forward in a fainting fit. He saw the point of General Wallace's advice and knew that he did not dare to follow it. General Wallace was hurried out into an antechamber and left in suspense as to his own fate for a couple of hours. Finally a chamberlain came with the Sultan's regret that he had an ill turn and could not continue the conversation. The subject was never alluded to again. General Wallace told me this story himself. It was generally believed in Europe that England did not desire a joint occupation of Egypt and that Lord Dufferin was really "riding for a fall" — to have the credit of wishing a joint occupation, but pressing it in such a way as to secure a refusal, and he got great credit in diplomatic circles for his skill in playing this double game. Just before he left Constantinople he assured me confidentially that this was all a mistake — that in fact he had been in dead earnest and that his mission here had been a failure.

We greatly enjoyed General and Mrs. Wallace during the four years of his stay here. They were warm friends of the College, and a great addition to our social life. The most curious incident of his life here was the declaration of a Presbyterian minister in Missouri that he had been in Constantinople and had seen and handled in the library of the Mosque of St. Sophia the original manuscript from which General Wallace had borrowed his story of "Ben Hur." This absurd tale gained such currency in America that General Wallace obtained the Sultan's permission for Dr. Riggs and me to investigate the matter in the library itself. I happened to be ill, and Dr. Long went in my place. It proved that, except two European princes, no foreigner had visited this library for many years, and it goes without saying that no manuscript having any relation to "Ben Hur" existed there. The most remarkable thing about this masterpiece is that when General Wallace wrote it he had never been out of America, and yet the book breathes the spirit of the East and of the age which it represents.

We had another interesting experience which grew out of the discovery of the "Didache" or "Teaching of the Twelve Apostles" by the Greek Bishop Bryennios in the library of the Jerusalem Monastery at Constantinople. It at once excited the attention of the Christian world, and Dr. Schaff of Union Theological Seminary wrote to me asking me to see if I could get a photograph of the manuscript. I went to see Bishop Bryennios and met with a cordial reception. He promised me all that I asked, and I arranged for Dr. Long to go down and take the photograph. Dr. Long went, but found the monks in charge of the library anything but cordial. After much delay they allowed him to take a photograph of what they declared to be the last page of the "Teaching." When he got home and printed the photograph he found that, while it was the last page of the manuscript, it did not contain a word of the "Teaching," which was not the last document in the manuscript. It was valuable as it gave the name of the copyist and the place and date of the writing (1056), but it was not the "Teaching." A few weeks later Bishop Bryennios was exiled to Nicomedia by the new Patriarch.

The College had no direct interest in Egyptian affairs, but the air in Constantinople was charged with political electricity, and this naturally influenced our course of thought during the year. It was the situation in Bulgaria and Eastern Roumelia which chiefly interested us. We had a larger number of Bulgarian students than ever before, but until Prince Alexander's *coup d'état* in 1883 the condition of things there seemed more hopeless than ever, and then this revolt of the prince against Russian dictation gave new strength to the party in Russia which was determined to make his rule impossible. The Russian papers attributed this anti-Russian feeling in Bulgaria to the influence of Robert College, and one of them declared that I had expended half a million dollars of British money to bring about this result. It was no doubt true that the general influence of Robert College was a factor in leading the Bulgarians to resent Russian methods, but there were Robert College graduates and students in all the various parties in Bulgaria. I do not think that any of them favored the absorption of Bulgaria into the Russian Empire, but there were those who felt that the independence of all Bulgaria could be secured only by the help of Russia, and that it was necessary to conciliate the Czar at any cost, even by the sacrifice of Prince Alexander, whom he hated. As to money influence, I never had a dollar to spend in Bulgaria or anywhere else for political purposes; and I happen to know that the British government failed to supply its own diplomatic agency at Sofia with money even to obtain information, which it ought to have had, at a critical moment. It was the Russian agents themselves whose high-handed abuse of power changed the universal gratitude of the Bulgarians into fear and dislike.

The twentieth and twenty-first years of Robert College represent a period when it had reached the greatest development possible with the means at its disposition and under the conditions in which it existed, and it is in place to give a picture of what it was at this time.

It occupied one building with a temporary annex which served as a study hall and room for the Sunday services and all general and public gatherings. Hamlin Hall, the main building, was occupied by dormitories, the boarding department, a hospital room, library, museum, laboratory, recitation rooms, tutors' rooms, servants' rooms, offices and the apartments of the president's family and the matron. Everything about this building, except its solid walls, and everything about the annex, their furniture and their conveniences, represented enforced economy and primitive conditions. We had no water supply except what we caught on the roof and stored in a cistern, and no drainage, except into a cesspool. The students slept in dormitories, fifteen to twenty in a room, which could not be heated or properly ventilated. We had not been able to build a wall around our grounds. When Hamlin Hall was built it was the finest school building in Turkey, and it certainly occupied the finest site in Turkey, if not in the world; but the founding and successful development of Robert College had roused the government and the various nationalities to the necessity and the power of education. The Sultan had determined to do for the Turks what he believed that Robert College had done for the Bulgarians; and the Bulgarians so fully appreciated the importance of education that they had already begun to establish colleges and schools of all grades in Bulgaria and Eastern Roumelia. The Greeks and Armenians in Turkey were also doing what they could. Robert College found itself in competition with all these rival institutions, and some of them were far better equipped than it was. Our deficiencies became apparent to all, although it cannot be said that our general influence had diminished or that our reputation had suffered. It would have done so very soon if we had not shown evidence of progress.

In the crowded and inadequate quarters which I have described we had, the twentieth year, 243 students on our registers, 165 of whom were boarders: 110 Bulgarians, 83 Armenians, 26 Greeks, 11 Turks, 13 others. The twenty-first year 215 registered, of whom 142 were boarders: 91 Bulgarians, 82 Armenians, 29 Greeks, 5 Turks, 8 others.

The rising bell rang at 6.30 o'clock. Breakfast for the tutors and students in the basement dining-room at 7, and prayers at the commencement of study hours at 8.20. All the students were required to be present. Then came classes until 12.30. Lunch, classes again from 2 until 4.30. Dinner at 6 and study hours in the evening from 7.30 until 9. All in bed at 10. Wednesday P.M. declamations at 1.30 was the only college exercise. Saturday afternoon was free. Sunday at 10.45 religious services, preaching by president, Professor van Millingen, Dr. Long or Professor Grosvenor. Bible classes in the afternoon after a general meeting at 2.30 under the direction of the president, occupying an hour in all. Meeting in the evening generally under the direction of tutors. All boarding students were required to attend all of these. During the recreation hours there were games, walks, etc., when the weather permitted. The students had an average of twenty-five classes a week and each teacher from twenty to twenty-five classes, besides his other duties. We had an interesting museum, a library of about five thousand volumes and a very fair supply of apparatus. We had no doctor within six miles of us and no proper hospital. Dr. Long, Mrs. Washburn and I had some knowledge of the care of the sick and of what needed to be done in case of accidents; and no small amount of work of this kind fell upon us, which brought us into the most intimate and friendly relations with the students. Mrs. Washburn knew the other languages and had learned Bulgarian that she might get nearer to the boys when they were ill. I am not sure that we did any more profitable work than this. We had a number of small boys in the Preparatory Department at that time who lived in Hamlin Hall, occupying two dormitories on the same story with the president's rooms, who needed special care. Miss Farley and Mrs. Washburn gave a good deal of attention to them.

The most important characteristic of the College was that the professors and their families and all the teachers who lived in Hamlin Hall were inspired with the idea that we were making men who in turn were to be the leaders of their people to a higher life. Giving instruction in various branches of learning was not the end for which we were working, but only a means to a real end which we had in view. To attain this end was the one thought of our lives, and no one counted it a sacrifice to do anything which would help on this work. We did not doubt that it was an essential part of it to discipline the intellectual powers of our students, to teach them to think for themselves, and we never neglected our classes. That we were reasonably successful is proved by the fact that the universities of Europe recognized our diplomas, and that many of our graduates distinguished themselves in their professional studies. We naturally rejoiced in this, but it was not the secret of our success, or of the harmony and enthusiasm with which we worked together, or of our intimate relations with the students, who thoroughly appreciated the fact that there was nothing perfunctory about our work, but that we were doing our best to make men of them — that we were living for them and not for ourselves; that whatever concerned them interested us, to whatever race or nationality they might belong.

The class which graduated in 1883 numbered 10, of whom 7 are living — 5 Bulgarians, 4 Armenians and 1 Greek. Of the Bulgarians Mr. Voicoff has been ever since one of the most valued instructors in Robert College. Stoicoff is the principal naval officer in Bulgaria, Dimitroff is a banker, Djambazoff was a judge and Djabaroff a teacher. Of the Armenians Djiladjian is a chemist, Tashdjian was a lawyer, the others are merchants. The Greek was in business.

The class of 1884 numbered 22, of whom 19 are living. 14 were Bulgarians, 7 Armenians, 1 Greek. Of the Bulgarians, 4 were teachers, 4 merchants, 2 connected with the Ministry of War, 2 physicians, 1 major of cavalry, 1 in the diplomatic service. Of the Armenians 3 are merchants, 1 teacher, 1 dentist in New York, 1 was private secretary and 1 in publication department of the American Mission. The Greek is a steamship agent.

Many of those who were students in the College during these two years but did not graduate have held honorable positions in various walks of life. One of them is now Minister of Finance in Bulgaria.

One of the most important events of the twenty-first year was the coming of Mr. Louisos Eliou, Ph. D., a graduate of the University of Athens, to take charge of the Greek Department in the College. Up to this time we had never been able to do for the Greeks what we were doing for the Armenians and Bulgarians, as we had never found a satisfactory teacher to build it up. In Mr. Eliou we found the right man. He was appointed professor later on and has been one of our most honored colleagues ever since, honored alike by us and by the Greek nation.

CHAPTER XV
THE GREAT CRISIS IN BULGARIA. 1884-1886

PROFESSOR PANARETOFF was absent the twenty-second year on account of a very serious illness, which attacked him on the train when on his way to Vienna with my sister and son. He was in a hospital in Vienna for a long time and later at Meran, but at the end of the year returned in good health. Dr. Long was absent the twenty-third year, having been requested by the trustees to go to America to raise money for the College. He was a distinguished and highly honored minister of the Methodist Episcopal Church, which had a mission in Bulgaria, of which he had been the director before coming to the College. The trustees thought that he would be able to interest the Methodists as well as others in the College. He was in every way a most attractive man, and we also had faith in his success. It was a critical time for the College, when we must show some signs of progress or lose our influence. The number of our Bulgarian students had already fallen from 110 to 71, owing to the opening of similar institutions there. The whole number registered of all nationalities had fallen from 259 in 1881-1882 to 173 in 1884-1885. Unhappily we were all disappointed. He was well received everywhere and got plenty of sympathy, but no money. I believe that no 5 Methodist has ever given any money to Robert College, although the bishops of the church have been our good friends, and some of our graduates are Methodist ministers.

Miss Farley, the matron, was absent for two years in America on account of ill health.

Professor Ormiston came to the College in the summer of 1885 to take Dr. Long's place for one year, but remained as instructor and later as Professor of Chemistry, Geology and Mineralogy.

The number of students registered the twenty-second year was 173, of whom 115 were boarders. Seventy-one were Bulgarians, 63 Armenians, 28 Greeks, 2 Turks, others 9.

The twenty-third year the number registered was 182, of whom 120 were boarders. Seventy-one were Bulgarians, 64 Armenians, 37 Greeks, no Turks, 10 others.

The absence of Turkish students then and in the following years was due to the effort of the Sultan to prevent Turkish boys attending foreign schools rather than those which he had himself provided for their benefit, not to any special hostility to Robert College, although everything English, even the English language, was regarded with disfavor at this time on account of the occupation of Egypt by England.

In the summer of 1885 Mrs. Washburn and I spent two months in Eastern Roumelia and Bulgaria. We had received many pressing invitations to make this visit from our graduates who occupied important official positions in both these states, and the time seemed to us favorable, as there was no political controversy at that time between them and the Turkish government. We had long desired to visit our old students in their own homes and to see with our own eyes what they were doing for their country, and what progress had been made in the country itself.

We went by train to Philippopolis, which then took two days, as the trains did not run in the night or at any great speed in the day time. To our great surprise we were met at the station by the prefect of the province, the mayor of the city, the Bishop and a large number of other notables and escorted to the home of the prefect, our graduate Mr. Dimitroff, where we were entertained; and later on we found that we were the guests of the state as well as of the people and were received and entertained with great honor everywhere. It became a sort of triumphal journey through the country, in honor of Robert College. The details of that trip are not in place here. Mr. Shipkoff was with us for a part of the journey and Professor Panaretoff for the rest. From Philippopolis we made an excursion into the Rhodope Mountains with Mr. Dimitroff, and Mr. Stoiloff entertained us at Sofia. We traveled in a phaeton drawn by three horses abreast, and accompanied by an honorary guard. In some places we had to travel on horseback. We visited the most beautiful parts of the Rhodope and Balkan Mountains, crossed the Shipka pass to Tirnova, the ancient capital, spent some time in Sofia, the present capital, and some days in the famous Rilo Monastery in the mountains on the frontier of Macedonia, finally returning to Philippopolis. Aside from our relations with the people it was an ideal excursion, unsurpassed by any other in our experience; but after all, the chief interest of it was in the reception given us by our former students and the people generally, in their grateful recognition of what Robert College had done for them, and in our satisfaction at the influence of our students in the country. I also gained a knowledge of the real situation of affairs in both provinces, of the difficulties and dangers in view, and of the spirit of the people, which enabled me, in the trying times which soon followed, to be of greater service to them than I had ever been before.

It was made plain to me that, sooner or later, an attempt would be made to unite Eastern Roumelia and Bulgaria; but I was no less astonished than the rest of the world when the revolution broke out at Philippopolis, September 18, less than two weeks after our return to Constantinople. Meanwhile I had given Mr. Pears,1 the distinguished correspondent of the *London Daily News*, a long interview on the situation there; and his letter, embodying this, with my name, was published in London on the day when the telegraph announced the outbreak of the revolution. As it was the only news on the subject it was reproduced all over Europe, and it was generally believed that I had had some part in the plot. This was absolutely untrue. I know of only one Robert College student who was a leader in it, and, as it was absolutely necessary for it to be kept a secret from the prefect, with whom I was staying, this student told me nothing about it. It was only the general unrest which came to my knowledge, with the fact that Russia was interested in some such plan in the hope that it would lead to the overthrow of Prince Alexander, which was the chief end of Russian policy at that time. Prince Alexander himself had some knowledge of the plot, but before it came to a head he did what he could to prevent the outbreak; while the Russian consul at Philippopolis attended the meetings of the conspirators, and encouraged them, believing that Prince Alexander, who was then in Varna, was not in a position to profit by it. It was a bloodless revolution; the elaborate but artificial government of Eastern Roumelia went to pieces and disappeared without a struggle, and the people cried out for Prince Alexander. He came, knowing very well that he did so at risk of his throne and probably of his life. There is nothing more pathetic in the history of Europe and nothing more diabolical in the history of Russia than the story of the events in Bulgaria which followed this Philippopo-

---

1 Edwin Pears, Esq., was not only the correspondent of the *London Daily News*, but was and still is the leading English lawyer in Turkey. He is also the author of two of the most valuable historical works on Constantinople — *The Fall of Constantinople* and *The Destruction of the Greek Empire*. Through a long period of years he has been one of my most intimate personal friends and a devoted friend of the College, to whom we owe a great debt of gratitude.

lis revolution. The prince was sacrificed by Europe to the personal hatred of the Czar, and Bulgaria became a united state, in spite of Russia. The Turks had very little interest in the matter so long as their people in Eastern Roumelia were unmolested and Macedonia was not invaded; but Russia insisted on an immediate invasion of the country by the Turks and carried most of the Powers with her. Happily England was then represented here by my old friend Sir William White, who was not afraid to defy the world in a good cause, and who had the full confidence of Lord Salisbury. He alone saved the day by sheer force of will, and the Turks did not move. The Russians also attempted to destroy the power of Prince Alexander by suddenly recalling all the Russian officers from the Bulgarian army, which had up to that time been kept in their hands. The Minister of War and all officers above the rank of captain were Russians. Then, having failed to persuade the Turks to war, they encouraged Servia to attack Bulgaria. The result of their success in this was the utter defeat of the Servians, making Prince Alexander a hero in the eyes of the world, and rousing the sympathy of Europe for the Bulgarians; but no one who was not behind the scenes can know what a desperate struggle went on from day to day, before anything was settled. In Constantinople it was a conflict between Sir William White and the representatives of all the other Great Powers, led by Mr. Nelidoff, the Russian ambassador, whose object was to restore the *status quo ante* in Eastern Roumelia and thus prevent the union. The conflict here finally resulted in a compromise by which Prince Alexander was appointed Governor-General of Eastern Roumelia, which was a personal union, but which implied a separate administration under the old régime.

In Eastern Roumelia it was a conflict between Prince Alexander and his friends under the lead of Mr. Dimitroff, prefect of Philippopolis, with the agents of Russia and their adherents, including the consuls, except the English; and in this Prince Alexander won the day, for the old régime was never reëstablished and the union was perfected. No little credit is due to the Sultan for this result, for, while he kept up the appearance of following Russia in the exact execution of the treaty of Berlin, he refused to become so far her tool as to use force to prevent the union. The difficulties were unhappily complicated by the action of Greece, which threatened war if Eastern Roumelia were united to Bulgaria. As this did not suit the plans of Russia she joined the other Powers in keeping Greece quiet.

PRINCE ALEXANDER OF BULGARIA

The troubles of Prince Alexander did not end with the defeat of the Servians and his appointment as Governor-General of Eastern Roumelia. Russia was as determined as ever to destroy him, and spared no effort to stir up opposition among the Bulgarians, and even organized plots to kill him. The Bulgarians generally were devoted to him; but there were party leaders and army officers, I am sorry to say some graduates of Robert College, who allowed themselves to become the tools of Russia, some from the honest conviction that Bulgaria could not afford to antagonize Russia, others from purely selfish interests. As I was in correspondence with men of all parties, I did what little I could to keep the peace between them and strengthen the hands of Prince Alexander.

Meanwhile the Gladstone government had returned to power in England and Sir Edward Thornton replaced Sir William White at Constantinople. It was a sad mistake for all concerned, especially for Bulgaria. Sir Edward was a first-class ambassador of the stamp of Sir Henry Elliott, and the Gladstone government even more in sympathy with Bulgaria than Lord Salisbury; but Sir Edward was absolutely ignorant of everything connected with the political situation here, and Russia had the field to herself. He was recalled in a few months and Sir William White sent back, but not in season to save Prince Alexander. Lord Rosebery was responsible for this mistake, and bitterly regretted it before Sir Edward reached Constantinople. Personally I found Sir Edward a most intelligent and agreeable gentleman, and under ordinary circumstances he would have filled the post with honor. But England has had no representative here since Lord Stratford who can be compared with Sir William White. He had a more comprehensive and accurate knowledge of everything concerning the Eastern question than any other man living—and a better knowledge of all the men with whom he had to deal here and in Europe. Like Lord Stratford, too, he had unbounded faith in England and a lofty conception of her mission in the world. He felt that when he spoke it was England speaking, and he made those who heard him think so too. He was somewhat rough in his manners, like the typical English squire, and when he saw fit to be angry it was like the descent of a cyclone with plenty of thunder and lightning in his vocabulary. No man cared to experience it a second time. This was the Ambassador. Personally he was a man to be loved, of tender heart and deep religious feelings — a friend to be trusted to the death. He was a sincere Roman

Catholic, but he used to say that I was his father confessor, which meant simply that he enjoyed talking with me frankly about whatever was in his mind or heart, whether of the political situation or of his deepest religious feelings. He always did most of the talking, and I have never met a man to whom it was more profitable or more entertaining to listen.

The American minister here at that time was Hon. S. S. Cox, commonly known as Sunset Cox. He and Mrs. Cox were genuine Americans, who were more interested in their own people than in the foreign society of Pera. They were warm friends of the College, and we were indebted to them for many pleasant hours of social intercourse. I do not think that he enjoyed his position here, and he resigned it after two years; but he found time to write three very entertaining books, and the "Diversions of a Diplomat" show that he appreciated the humorous side of life here if he did not enjoy the tragic side of it, which he could not modify.

There was nothing special in the inner life of the College during these two years which needs to be mentioned. They were years of very hard work for all of us — of peace, harmony and progress within the College — of considerable anxiety as to our financial prospects, and of deep sympathy with the trials of our students in the political situation of their nationalities. It was a wonder to us that they could do such good work in their studies.

The graduating class in 1885 numbered 15, of whom 14 are living (1907). Nine were Bulgarians, 4 Armenians, 1 Greek, 1 Hebrew. Of the Bulgarians 3 are physicians, 2 merchants, 2 government officials, 1 lawyer, 1 professor of law in Sofia University. Of the Armenians 1 is a teacher, 1 a manufacturer, 1 is dead, 1 went to America, graduated at Massachusetts Agricultural School and is a practical farmer in the interior, making his farm a model for others. The Hebrew is a lawyer in Bulgaria, the Greek in business.

The class of 1886 numbered 20, of whom 16 are living. Twelve were Bulgarians, 8 were Armenians. Nine of the Bulgarians have been teachers at some time, 5 are so still, 2 army officers, 1 is a judge, 1 a merchant, 3 government officials. Of the Armenians 5 are merchants, 1 Protestant pastor, 2 died soon after graduating.

CHAPTER XVI
THE OVERTHROW OF PRINCE ALEXANDER. 1886-1888

AT the close of the twenty-third year the doctors sent me to Carlsbad for the cure there. When I reached Vienna on my return I heard from the British ambassador what was known of the kidnaping of Prince Alexander, and went at once to Bucharest to Sir William White, who had returned to his former post there, after leaving Constantinople. Prince Alexander had already passed on his return to Bulgaria, but his brother who had been with him was still with Sir William. From them I learned details, and to this day my blood boils with indignation whenever I recall them. For the Bulgarian officers who executed the will of the Czar there is this excuse. They had been educated in Russia — they were young and had grown up with no experience of a country of their own, towards whose sovereign they had any feeling of loyalty. They had just taken part in a revolution and evidently did not realize the infamous character of their treason, especially as they acted in the name of the Czar. But for the Czar, the cousin of Prince Alexander, the embodiment of the divine right of the sovereign, there is no excuse. He could not plead ignorance of the nature of the plot. He honored and rewarded his agents. He made no apology to the civilized world and pushed it to the bitter end, by making the peace of Europe depend upon the Powers uniting to drive Prince Alexander out of Bulgaria.

It was a military plot carefully elaborated and carried out by officers who had fought under Prince Alexander at Slivnitza. They broke into the palace, seized him in the night, and hurried him off by carriage to the Danube, where a steamer was waiting to take him to Russia. He was treated with the greatest indignity on the way and finally delivered over to Russian officials, who in turn transported him in the same fashion to the Austrian frontier town of Lemberg. Lemberg did not love Russia, and Prince Alexander was received there with enthusiastic demonstrations of welcome, after his five days of suffering every indignity, to learn that all Bulgaria had risen against the traitors and demanded his immediate return. He went back, and his journey through Austria, Roumania, and especially in Bulgaria was like a Roman triumph; but he went back to learn at Sofia that the enmity of the Czar was more bitter than ever, and to hear from the capitals of Europe, even from England, that the peace of Europe depended upon his abdication. He remained there only a few days,— long enough to restore order and establish a regency to take charge of the government, — abdicated and left the country, with great difficulty persuading the people not to prevent his departure by force. So far as Prince Alexander was concerned the Czar had won the day by base means to which no other sovereign in Europe would have descended. Even Prince Milan had never thought of such barbarism; he never paid agents to assassinate the prince. But the Czar had forgotten the people of Bulgaria, who boldly defied him and all his plots to the day of his death, secured the permanent union of Bulgaria and Eastern Roumelia, and won the confidence of all the rest of Europe, and to-day Prince Alexander is the hero of the Bulgarians. When he died his body was brought to Sofia, and his mausoleum is the most sacred place in the city. The father of the Czar, who freed Bulgaria, is equally honored; but the name of Alexander III is, as far as possible, forgotten. Prince Alexander came to Bulgaria a young man without experience and no doubt made many mistakes; but he identified himself with the people over whom he ruled, made every sacrifice for them, lived for them. He was a man of high character and very simple tastes, economical of the people's money and perfectly at home with the most humble of his subjects. As a ruler he developed rapidly, and had made great progress in educating the people in the science of self-government and in adapting the administration to their wants. His chief difficulties came from the constant intrigues of the Czar to make his position untenable. Bulgaria does well to cherish his memory.

It was at this time that Stambouloff came to the front as one of the regents appointed by Prince Alexander, and commenced that terrible struggle with Russia for the independence of Bulgaria, which lasted to the day when he was murdered in the streets of Sofia, after he had seen Prince Ferdinand firmly seated on the throne. The conflict began as soon as Prince Alexander had left the country, when General Kaulbars arrived as the representative of the Czar to get control of the government, and continued on the part of Russia until the death of Alexander III by such means as are supposed to be peculiar to anarchists, rather than to emperors. In this conflict the Turks had the good sense to sympathize with the Bulgarians rather than with Russia, and were supported by the

Western Powers, especially by England.

The Bulgarians sought everywhere to find a prince who would accept the place in face of Russian opposition, and finally chose Prince Ferdinand of Coburg, a grandson of King Louis Philippe, but a resident of Austria. He was a young man about twenty-six years old, of whom little was known, by religion a Roman Catholic, and supposed to be favorably regarded by the Austrian government — a very different man from Prince Alexander. He had the courage to accept the place and to hold it, although he was not officially recognized by any Power until after the death of Alexander III.

It was in the midst of this intense political excitement that the College opened in September, 1886. There was a general expectation of a European war and a general stagnation of business in Turkey and Bulgaria. In addition to this the Turks established a very strict quarantine against Bulgaria, partly for political reasons, but nominally because of an outbreak of cholera on the Danube. The outlook for students was not promising, but, in spite of all obstacles, we had more than during the previous year. The character of our Bulgarian students was well illustrated by their determination to reach the College. One party of twelve, from places only two or three days from Constantinople, were four weeks making the journey; having vainly tried two routes and spending a week in quarantine, they started anew and came over the mountains in carriages.

The whole number of students, the twenty-fourth year, was 182, of whom 130 were boarders. Seventy were Bulgarians, 53 Armenians, 36 Greeks; English and Americans 15, others 8. The first death in the College since my connection with it occurred this year — a most promising Bulgarian boy, who died in my arms after a painful illness of two weeks.

Professor van Millingen was absent during the year on leave in America, without salary. The Board of Instruction for the year consisted of the president, four professors and eleven other instructors — and too much cannot be said of their absolute devotion to the work of the College and the highest interests of the students. Much time was given during the year to a thorough revision of our course of study, to meet, as far as our means allowed, the increasing demands of our patrons. One year was added to the Preparatory Department and the requirements for admission to the college classes correspondingly raised. The necessity of at least one new building had become so pressing that we began to take steps for its erection, hoping that the money might be found when we had obtained the necessary permission from the Turkish government, the circumlocution offices of the Porte requiring from one to two years, under constant pressure from the American Legation, to bring the matter to the attention of the Sultan and secure his action. We have never failed to get permission for any building that we have asked for and have never had our work stopped, although in this and most cases the official *iradé* has not been received until after the building had been completed — which is a good proof of the friendly spirit of the Turkish officials. My personal relations with them have always been friendly.

I have rather a vague recollection of the Commencement exercises of twenty years ago and few records of anything except my baccalaureate sermon and the order of exercises for the day; but I have no trouble in recalling that of 1887, and what has fixed it in my mind was the closing prayer at the Commencement. It happened that Rev. Dr. Arthur Brooks of New York was one of the guests on that occasion. As he was an Episcopal clergyman accustomed to a formal service I hesitated about asking him to make an extemporaneous prayer, but he accepted the invitation at once, and such a prayer I have seldom heard. It was that of a man who lived in constant and intimate communion with God, and it brought us into His immediate presence in a way which I can never forget. The presiding officer that day was Mr. Oscar S. Straus, the American minister, who made an admirable address, and there were twelve orations in five different languages by the graduating class. An Armenian bishop made a most sympathetic and interesting address.

Immediately after the Commencement in June I went to America partly on private business necessitated by the death of my sister and partly to see the trustees in regard to the erection of a new building. Mrs. Washburn had gone to America two months before. The trustees approved of going on with preparations for a new building, but with the understanding that I should come to America in 1889 to raise money for it. We waited in America for the marriage of my son, and after visiting friends in England reached Constantinople early in November, to find the College going on as usual, but with a falling off in the number of boarders.

The whole number the twenty-fifth year was 170, of whom 113 were boarders. Sixty were Bulgarians, 55 Armenians, 33 Greeks, 19

English and Americans, 3 others.

Looking back upon it now, it would seem that the most important event of the year was the visit to the College of Mr. and Mrs. John S. Kennedy of New York in May, 1888. It was the beginning of an interest in the College on their part which has gone on deepening ever since, and been of incalculable value to us, and which is one of many illustrations of the way in which God has raised up friends for the College, when we most needed them, without any plan or forethought of ours. Such experiences as these have done more than anything else to sustain my faith in the College as really God's work and not ours. I believe that its success is due to the fact that from its foundation we have sought to make it first of all a Christian college. It is as such that God has blessed it. Our political influence has incidentally been very great. We have done our best to give our students a thorough and practical secular education, but I believe that the people of the East, of all religions, rate the moral and religious influence of the College as its most important work. In our summer in Bulgaria, I was struck with the fact that in all the addresses presented to me, the first thing spoken of was the religious influence of the College, and I believe that the same feeling exists among the Greeks and Armenians — to some extent at least among the Turks. They sometimes say, "Of course my son will not cease to be a Mohammedan, but I want him brought up with English morality."

Our most trying experience was in the spring of 1888, when Mrs. Washburn and Professor Panaretoff came down with scarlet fever at the same time, taken, in an act of charity, from a poor boy whom they brought across the Bosphorus in a caïque with them. Miss Farley, who was also in the boat, had had the scarlet fever before and was immune. In our crowded quarters there was nothing to be done but to cut off our apartment from the rest of the building, absolutely except for a dumb waiter which connected our dining-room with the kitchen, Mrs. Washburn in one room and Professor Panaretoff in another. From the 9th of April to the 13th of May I took the whole care of both of them, night and day, no other person but the doctor ever entering our apartment. Mrs. Washburn was very dangerously ill, but happily Professor Panaretoff's case was a mild one. In the end the whole apartment was thoroughly disinfected, and there has never been a case of scarlet fever in the College since. The College work went on as usual, under the direction of Dr. Long.

The last visitor whom I saw before going into quarantine was Mr. Walter, the proprietor of *The London Times*, whom I had met in England, when visiting at Newstead Abbey. I was sorry not to see more of him here, for the editors of *The Times* had long been among my good friends in England, and they were friends worth having.

Before the college year ended we were saddened by another death among our students, a German from Roumania, who died after a long illness of typhoid fever. It was a strange case. For several weeks until a few days before he died he would have gone to his classes if the thermometer had not shown that he had the typhoid fever and was growing steadily worse. He was the only child of a widow, and his mother, who had been ill herself, arrived here only just before his death.

As this was the twenty-fifth year of the College it seemed to us appropriate to inaugurate the annual celebration of Founder's Day, which we fixed for the 23d of March, Mr. Robert's birthday. It was made a holiday in the College, with a religious service at nine in the morning and a thanksgiving dinner for the students in the evening. It was not designed so much to glorify Mr. Robert as to have an appropriate occasion to make our students understand the object for which the College was founded, the motives of the founders and the principles which we were trying to act upon — our ideal of a Christian college. This day has been observed each year ever since and has served to keep fresh the memory of Mr. Robert, Dr. Hamlin, Dr. Long and others to whom our students are indebted for the privileges which they enjoy.

The class which graduated in 1887 numbered 26, of whom 23 are living (1907). Thirteen were Bulgarians, 10 Armenians and 3 Greeks. Of the Bulgarians 4 are government officials, 3 teachers, 3 physicians, 2 merchants, 1 a lawyer. Of the Armenians 7 are merchants, 1 a physician, 1 a publisher, 1 a civil engineer. Of the Greeks 1 studied medicine, 1 is a dentist and 1 a merchant.

The class which graduated in 1888 numbered 28, of whom 24 are living. Fifteen were Bulgarians, 12 Armenians, 1 Greek. Of the Bulgarians 3 are physicians, 3 teachers, 2 judges, 2 merchants, 1 a lawyer, 1 a government official, 1 a civil engineer, 1 died soon after graduation, 1 unknown. Of the Armenians 6 are merchants, 2 teachers, 2 government officials, 1 a civil engineer, 1 an agriculturist. The Greek, who is now in the office of the American Bible

Society, was sent to the Chicago Exposition in an official capacity in 1893 by the Turkish government.

The American minister, Mr. Oscar S. Straus, presided at the Commencement exercises in the old study hall on both these occasions. He was then and has been ever since a warm friend of the College.

CHAPTER XVII
ARMENIAN AND BULGARIAN TROUBLES. 1888-1890

IN the summer of 1888 the doctors sent me to Carlsbad again, and Mrs. Washburn went with me to recruit after the sickness and work of the previous year. We had a delightful summer, meeting many friends, and stopping at Sofia on our way home, where we had an enthusiastic reception. We came back early in September to arrange our apartment for a new order of things before the term opened.

During the previous year the Faculty had passed the following resolution: "*Resolved*, That with a view of relieving the president of all duties not properly connected with his office, the trustees of the College be requested to send out a man at the beginning of the next college year, if a proper person can be found, who shall live in the college building with his family, take charge of the boarding department and students' accounts, have a general supervision of the boarders out of study hours and aid in their physical and moral training." A full consideration of the subject satisfied the trustees that no one could take my place in Hamlin Hall who had not the rank and work of a professor, and after due deliberation they appointed Rev. Charles Anderson Professor of Ethics, Rhetoric, Oratory and Physical Culture, with the understanding that he should live in the College building and relieve me of the duties mentioned in the resolution. Mr. Anderson had been a tutor in the College for three years from 1869 to 1872, after which he graduated at Andover Theological Seminary and was at this time the pastor of a church in Woburn, Mass. His wife was a daughter of Dr. Hamlin. For a year we all lived together in Hamlin Hall until I went to America in the summer of 1889. I was very glad to welcome him as a colleague; but Mrs. Washburn and I have never ceased to regret that, with increasing years, our strength had so far failed that we had to give up this common life with the tutors and students in Hamlin Hall. When we returned from America we lived in Kennedy Lodge, the president's house on the college grounds, and so long as Professor Anderson lived in Hamlin Hall the College suffered no loss.

The number of students this year was somewhat less, owing to the unsettled state of affairs in Turkey and Bulgaria. The number registered was 158, of whom 104 were boarders. There were 52

Bulgarians, 43 Armenians, 33 Greeks, 20 English, 5 Americans, 3 Turks, 7 others.

The condition of the Armenians had grown steadily worse since the Berlin Congress, especially in the interior. The policy of England was largely responsible for this. She had undertaken to defend their rights and secure reforms in the Turkish administration and had encouraged them to look forward to the establishment of an autonomous province of Armenia, partly out of sympathy for this Christian race and still more in her own interest, as she believed that an autonomous Armenia would be a barrier against the farther advance of Russia. It was not an anti-Turkish policy, for England had no desire to acquire any of her Asiatic territory, and believed that the Turkish government would be strengthened by such changes. She utterly failed to convince the Sultan of this, and could not induce him to do anything to ameliorate the condition of his Christian subjects. Unhappily a certain number of Armenians conceived the idea that it would be possible to force the hand of England in the same way that the Russian government had been forced by popular excitement over the massacre of the Bulgarians to declare war against Turkey; and they organized secret revolutionary societies with the object of bringing about a crisis, which would result in such atrocities on the part of the Turks as had taken place in Bulgaria, but, as they believed, would force England and Europe generally to intervene in their behalf, and create an independent Armenia. I did not personally know any of these revolutionists, but I used whatever influence I had with the Armenians whom I knew to make them see that they had everything to lose and nothing to gain by such movements — that there was no similarity between the situation of the Armenians and the Bulgarians, and no hope of any European intervention to make them independent. So far as I know they got the same advice from all the embassies here, and the sober minded among them saw the truth of it; but the revolutionists would listen to no one. What would have happened if these societies had not been formed I do not know, but their activities have been the excuse put forward by the Turks for all the massacres and persecutions of the last twenty-five years. I shall have occasion to speak of these later on. In 1888-1889 the most serious troubles were in Armenia, where the Kurds were encouraged to harry the Armenian population without mercy. England succeeded at this time in getting one of the principal Kurdish chiefs, Moussa Bey, brought to Constantinople for trial. The atrocities which he had committed were innumerable and unspeakable; incidentally he had very nearly killed an American missionary, but his trial was a farce and changed nothing in Armenia. Here and throughout the country the hostility of the government, the imprisonment of great numbers on suspicion, and the agitation of the revolutionists excited a feeling of terror and general unrest. The number of our Armenian students was reduced more than fifty per cent.

It was not the fault of the Turks that the same state of things existed in Bulgaria, and made the position of Prince Ferdinand precarious. All the Bulgarian troubles came from Russia. As the Russian governors left in Bulgaria after the war had told them, "It was not for the beautiful eyes of the Bulgarians that Russia had sacrificed so many lives and so much treasure, but it was to build a bridge to Constantinople." Prince Alexander had been removed, but now Prince Ferdinand and Mr. Stambouloff blocked the way, supported by the great majority of the Bulgarian people. It was war to the knife against them. Murder and treason were patronized and paid for by Russia, and it was pitiful to see how some really honest and patriotic men were deceived and won over to the belief that it was necessary for Bulgaria to sacrifice everything to please the Czar. Some of them were graduates of Robert College, although in general our alumni were loyal to Bulgaria rather than to the Czar. At Constantinople Sir William White was the principal support of Bulgaria. All these foreign intrigues and the uncertainty of the future greatly delayed the development of the country and led to an excessive expenditure of money and men, in keeping up a large and efficient army. It was this generally unsatisfactory state of things which so greatly reduced the number of Bulgarian students.

The work of the College went on satisfactorily during the year, and Mr. Straus secured permission for the erection of a new building for the College and a house for the president. But when the papers finally came from the Porte there was no mention of the college building in them. Somebody in the office of the Grand Vizier had been paid by some enemy of the College to omit it. We had already commenced work on the building on plans prepared by Professor Hamlin of Columbia University, and some months of anxiety followed, although we did not stop the work. Happily the Grand Vizier was friendly. He acknowledged that the fraud had taken place in his department, although he declared that he could not find out who was responsible for it, and in the end he secured for us the necessary *iradé* from the Sultan.

In the autumn of 1888 we had the pleasure of seeing the United States flag once more on the Bosphorus. The Quinnebaug came up here again, but no American war vessel has appeared here since, although all the Great Powers of Europe have two each stationed here. It is due chiefly to the opposition of Russia and Germany that this right has been denied us. We enjoyed our acquaintance with the officers, and they challenged our students to a game of baseball, in which I am sorry to say our boys were beaten, the game having been played under stricter rules than they were familiar with. However, it did our boys good.

In the summer of 1889, as had been agreed with the trustees, I went to America to raise money for the new building. I returned in May, 1890, at the earnest request of Dr. Long, and remained here until after the Commencement, when I went back to finish my work, which occupied me until the summer of 1891. During my absence Dr. Long was acting president of the College.

The twenty-seventh year of the College opened in September, 1889, with about the same number of students as the previous year, 164 in all, of whom 104 were boarders. Forty-five were Bulgarians, 47 Armenians, 41 Greeks, 20 English and Americans, 11 others.

At the close of this year Professor Grosvenor resigned his place as professor here and returned to America, where he has ever since been a professor in Amherst College, his and my Alma Mater. First as tutor and then as professor he had been connected with the College for twenty-one years — a progressive scholar, a devoted, enthusiastic co-worker in all the activities of the College, and a successful teacher, with a charming family, he had filled a large place in the life of the College. In his well-known book on Constantinople he has associated his name with the place.

It was during this year that Professor Ormiston published an arithmetic adapted to the wants of the various nationalities in the College. It has not met with the same fate as the geography of the Turkish Empire which we published some years earlier. The geography of the empire changed so rapidly in the following years that the book became a political curiosity.

The letters which I received in America this year from the professors were not altogether optimistic, but had a good deal of criticism of the state of things in the College. Some of them thought that I ought to return at once, and others that I ought to stay in America until I had raised money enough to put the College upon a better foundation. Various schemes were proposed for improvements, which would broaden our curriculum and raise the standard of scholarship. Except as they showed some lack of harmony in the Faculty, I was neither surprised nor discouraged by these criticisms. I knew very well that we were not realizing our own ideal or meeting the demands of some of our patrons, and it was encouraging to know that the professors and teachers were not satisfied with their work. If they could not coin money, they could at least do their very best with what they had. I do not think that we had as promising material in the College at that time as in previous years, and this taken together with the serious falling off in the number of our students was discouraging, whatever might be the reason of it, whether it was due to our deficiencies or to circumstances altogether beyond our control. I am convinced that long-continued political agitation, especially when it is revolutionary in its character, is unfavorable to sound education. I believe that this is true everywhere. It is certainly true in my experience. We have a striking illustration of it to-day in Russia, and I have seen plenty of it in Turkey and the neighboring states. Boys and young men are the first to be demoralized in such movements. We have done our best always to keep the College free from such influences, but at the time of which I am writing, boys came to us whose minds were already distracted by what was going on in the political world, and it was hard to make them see that the best thing they could do for their nation was to enlighten and discipline their own minds and fit themselves by study to become intelligent and worthy citizens. In the early history of the College many of our students, especially the Bulgarians, came to us with exactly this conception of their duty; but this sort of patriotism is no longer common, although we have never relaxed our efforts to develop it.

All the nationalities were abnormally excited, the Greeks quite as much as the Armenians and Bulgarians. By way of a demonstration against the Turkish government and the Bulgarians, the Greek Patriarch had closed all the Orthodox churches and suspended religious services. It was a crisis over the question of Macedonia, where the Turks sometimes favored the Greeks and sometimes the Bulgarians — nominally a church question, but in fact purely political, as it continues to be to this day. That these warring nationalities can meet on equal terms in Robert College and live together in peace, as in general they do, is itself an important part of their education.

The graduating class in 1890 numbered 11, of whom 10 are now living. Three were Bulgarians, 3 Armenians, 4 Greeks and 1 English. Of the Bulgarians 1 is a merchant, 1 a lawyer and 1 a physician. Of the Armenians 2 are merchants, 1 a Protestant minister. Of the Greeks 1 became an editor, 1 a physician, 2 are in business.

The class of 1891 numbered 8. Four were Armenians, 3 Bulgarians, 1 Greek. Of the Armenians 1 is a teacher, 1 a dentist, 2 merchants. Of the Bulgarians 1 is an army officer, 1 a teacher, 1 in diplomatic service. The Greek is a merchant.

From this time on the Bulgarians no longer constitute the majority in our graduating classes.

I suppose that before this those who read this book have been impressed with the small number of our graduates who have become clergymen. It should be remembered that but few of our graduates are Protestants. They belong to the Oriental churches, and although serious efforts have been made to educate the clergy in these churches, this is not yet a career which is attractive to an educated young man. The higher and educated clergy are celibates, and the priests are generally uneducated. Several servants have gone from our college kitchens to be priests, but I have never been able to persuade a graduate to undertake this service in an Oriental church. It has seemed to them that it would diminish rather than increase their influence for good. Many have done good work as teachers.

CHAPTER XVIII
ANOTHER TWO YEARS IN AMERICA. 1889-1891

IN the summer of 1889 Mrs. Washburn and I went to America at the request of the trustees to raise money for new buildings and for endowment. Professor Panaretoff went with us and returned for the opening of the college year. Professor van Millingen took my classes during my absence. We were tired out when we left Constantinople, and we took our journey very leisurely, stopping to see our friends in Germany and England, and visiting Oxford and Cambridge universities. I was not at all well when I reached Boston, and one of my friends invited me to go with him to Poland Springs to recruit. A few hours before we were to start he sent a messenger to say that unexpected business would prevent his going that day, so I went out to spend Sunday with my mother in the country. That night I came down with typhoid fever, and it was two months before I left my bed. It was midwinter before I could begin my work for the College. In a few weeks I broke down again, and the doctors sent me to Florida, or, more accurately, the doctors said I must go, and Mr. Kennedy sent me with Mrs. Washburn, who was just leaving the hospital in Philadelphia.

When I entered upon my work I found the situation quite different from what it was ten years before when I made my first campaign in America, just after the Russo-Turkish War. There was much less interest in Turkish affairs and in the fate of Bulgaria. Robert College was more widely known and perhaps more fully appreciated, although by no means so generally known in America as it was in Europe. Mr. Stead, when he visited Washington in the first administration of President Cleveland, was horrified, as he told me afterward, to find that Mr. Bayard, then Secretary of State, had never heard of Robert College; and like a true newspaper man he blamed me for not blowing my trumpet so loud that all America would hear it. I protested that some things were better done with the least noise possible, but he improved the opportunity, at a dinner given to him that night by the Russian ambassador, to declare that Robert College had more influence in the East than either Russia or England, and that it would end in Americanizing Turkey, for which I did not thank him. It was a fact in America that it was chiefly in religious society that the College was known, while in

England and Russia, for example, it was best known in the ministries of foreign affairs, and known on account of the incidental influence of the College in Bulgaria rather than for its real purpose as a Christian college.

The College was not less appreciated in religious circles in America, but it was no longer unique. Its success had not only modified the policy of foreign mission boards, but had already led to the establishment of similar institutions in other parts of the world, in connection with the missions of different religious denominations. While I met with less criticism of the College than ten years before, on the part of good people who did not believe in education as a legitimate form of missionary work, the interest of the givers for such work was now divided. Other colleges in foreign lands were in need of money just as we were, and I had no desire to stand in the way of their getting it, even when they took it out from under my hands. It was the Lord's money going into the Lord's work just as much as though it came to Robert College.

I can never forget as long as I live, and I believe that I shall remember with thanksgiving in another world, all the kindness and sympathy that I met with during these two years. It seemed like a realization of Christ's promise of the hundredfold in this world. It was freely given by old friends and new, who treated me as a brother beloved when they had nothing but gratitude and love to expect in return. All that was painful in this work for the College came from a lack of confidence in my own ability to present the claims of the College in such a way as to make them understand. When I broke down in New York and was sent to Florida I felt as though my mission was a failure. We had a delightful winter, regained our health, made many friends, interested ourselves in much good work that we found going on there, and learned much of the burning questions which were agitating the country. Among other friends at St. Augustine we were specially indebted to Rev. and Mrs. Edwin K. Mitchell of the Presbyterian church, who did all they could for us and to interest others in the College. I had a letter of introduction from Mr. Kennedy to Mr. Flagler, and he was very kind. He even offered to furnish the needed funds, if I would drop Constantinople, to found a college at St. Augustine, but he had no interest in Turkey. We went as far south as Lake Worth and found kind friends there; but when I returned to Mr. Kennedy's in the spring with no money for the College, I felt as though my winter was a failure. It was not long after this that I received a note from Mr. Alanson Trask, of whom I had seen much at St. Augustine, inviting me to call on him in Brooklyn. I called and he gave me five thousand dollars. A year or two later he gave twenty-five thousand dollars more, also unsolicited.

In the spring I had to go to Washington to consult with Mr. Blaine and Senators Sherman and Edwards in regard to a treaty with Turkey which had been negotiated by Mr. Straus under the direction of Mr. Bayard, but which had not been acted upon by the Senate. In general it was a very good treaty, but it denationalized a number of persons who had long been recognized as American citizens, and on this ground I recommended that it should not be ratified, without modifications. Mr. Blaine withdrew it, with the consent of the Committee on Foreign Affairs. I had never met Mr. Blaine before, and my previous experience with American Secretaries of State had not led me to anticipate such a reception as he gave me. The charm of his manner was a revelation to me. He received me as though I had been an old friend whom he was delighted to see and asked me questions which implied that he knew all about me and Robert College, and had nothing more important to do than to enjoy an hour of social intercourse. I understood then the great secret of his popularity in the country. Senators Sherman and Edwards were very different men, but they were very cordial and asked the Senate in secret session to furnish me with all the papers relating to the treaty, that I might give them a full memorandum on the subject, which I did. Washington was not a good place to raise money, but I found many warm friends there, some of whom I had known in Constantinople.

In the autumn of 1891, by advice of the trustees, I attended the meeting of the American Board in Minneapolis. I had visited St. Paul in 1857 when it was a modern village, and the change which had taken place there seemed miraculous. I had some very dear Constantinople friends living in the Northwest Territory four hundred miles west of Winnipeg, and so I went by Montreal and the Canadian Pacific to visit them on my way to Minneapolis. When I left the train at a station fifty miles from their home, in the night, I was astonished to hear my name called by a young man, who took my valise as I stepped on to the platform in the dark, and still more astonished when I came into the light to see an old student of Robert College, who had heard accidentally that I was coming and had walked eight miles, after his day's work, to welcome me. When I returned to Winnipeg I had a very hearty welcome from the Presbyterian College and the churches there. They knew more about Robert College than the majority of similar people in the United States. I did not expect to get any money at Minneapolis, but it was a delightful and profitable experience in the renewal of many old friendships, and profitable in the opportunity it gave me to consult with others engaged in similar work, as well as to make known what Robert College was doing. I had hoped to get some money in Chicago, Detroit and Cleveland on my way back, and I was not altogether disappointed; but I found my friends too heavily burdened with good work near home to spare much for Constantinople, and that many of their gifts at home were really drafts on the future. I shall never forget two or three days that I spent at Lake Forest and the reception given me there by Dr. McClure. At Chicago I found a home with Mr. Blatchford, always a warm friend of mine and of the College.

I visited a good many colleges and universities to interest the students in our work and met with a hearty welcome, especially at Amherst, Williams, Hamilton and Princeton. I found college presidents generally ready to aid me in every way in their power, and with a keen appreciation of the value of the work we were doing in Constantinople, and I met a number of peripatetic Western college presidents on begging expeditions in the East, who could at least sympathize with me if they did not help me. One gentleman on whom I called received me almost with a groan and opened conversation with the information that I was the seventh college president who had called on him that day, and intimated that we left him no time to attend to his own business.

With the ministers I had a varied experience. Some of them evidently looked upon me as a wolf trying to enter their fold — or at least as a sneak-thief. Some wished me all possible success in churches of my own denomination, or at least in some other congregation than theirs. I did not blame them. It was easy to understand that they felt that their people were already distracted by the multiplication of the appeals made to them. On the whole I found the ministers most sympathetic and ready to do anything in their power to help me. If I had been strong enough I might have had a good congregation to speak to every Sunday, in the strongest churches; and I did a good deal of this work with profit, especially in New York, where I was received as a brother in the ministerial club, Chi Alpha, which united the leading Presbyterian, Dutch Reformed and Congregational ministers in the city. Very precious memories are connected with the members of this club. Some of the Episcopalian clergymen also were very friendly and ready to help me. So were Dr. Hale of Boston and several other Unitarian ministers. The editors of the religious newspapers were mostly old friends of mine and were always ready to lend a hand. The same thing was true of some of the daily papers. I have no doubt about the value of their support, although I have seldom known any money to come from this source alone. For that matter I never, when I spoke, appealed for a general contribution, although I know of some large gifts which have been prompted by addresses that I made. Dr. Field, Dr. Ward, Dr. Abbott and the Primes, all the professors in the Union Theological Seminary, Dr. Taylor, Dr. van Dyke, Dr. Hall, Dr. Booth, Phillips Brooks and his brother Arthur, are only a few of many devoted friends whom I might name among the ministers and editors. And I had no more enthusiastic supporters than our former tutors who were then occupying various important positions in America.

With all this sympathy and support it would seem that I ought to have found it easy to raise all the money we asked for. It was not the Lord's will. He gave us what He saw that it was best for us to have. I say this the more confidently because most of the money which has come to us since has not come from any immediate solicitation on my part, and most of what I got at that time came without my directly asking for it. As a general rule when I asked I got nothing but sympathy and often only a polite refusal without sympathy.

There were some very interesting exceptions to this which were like flowers strewed along my path. The late Cornelius Vanderbilt was one of them. I had never met him when I went to his office at the Central Station to ask him for money; but he knew something of the College, and he listened to what I had to say and questioned me as though it were a part of his business, which it was necessary for him to understand. He gave me a thousand dollars then and another donation later on. Another exception was Mr. Elbert W. Munroe. In answer to a letter he invited me to come to his house in the country, where he and Mrs. Munroe received me most cordially and carefully questioned me as to everything connected with the College. Later on they sent for me again and gave me five thousand dollars. It was not simply the cordiality with which I was received, it was not simply the money given, which impressed me so happily; it was the fact that the money was given after a careful and conscientious consideration of the real worth of the College in the Kingdom of God.

I went to America to ask for fifty thousand dollars for buildings and at least one hundred thousand dollars for increased endowment. Mr. J. S. Kennedy gave the money for the president's house, which we call Kennedy Lodge, and I found the money for the building now known as Albert Long Hall. Through Professor Newton of Yale University, the children of Mrs. Lois Newton of Sherburne, N.Y., gave the property left by their mother, about fifteen thousand dollars, for the establishment of one-hundred-dollar scholarships for the sons of Protestant clergymen in Turkey or Bulgaria, or for other Christian young men — a very timely gift. But aside from this very little was added to the endowment.

In May, 1891, I returned to Constantinople, somewhat disappointed, but thankful for what had been accomplished and with precious memories of my two years in America.

CHAPTER XIX
IMPROVEMENTS IN THE COLLEGE. 1890-1892

FOR the greater part of the twenty-eighth year I was in America, but returned before its close.

The number of students registered was 159, and for the third successive year the number of boarders was 104. Of the whole number 59 were Armenians, 41 Bulgarians, 39 Greeks, 13 English and Americans, 7 others.

The twenty-ninth year the number registered was 194, of whom 130 were boarders. Seventy were Armenians, 52 Bulgarians, 47 Greeks, 13 English and Americans, 12 others.

The increase in the number of students which commenced this year was undoubtedly due in some measure to the new signs of life in the College, in the erection of new buildings. No such outward signs had appeared for many years. We had not even built a wall around the college grounds. This also was done in 1891, and it added wonderfully to the general impression of the prosperity and dignity of the College. We continued our efforts to obtain permission to build a sewer to the Bosphorus, but it was still years later that we obtained it. No permission could be had to build it along the road through the Turkish Cemetery, as it was said that there might be graves of some of the faithful under the roadway which would be desecrated by a sewer. It was finally built by a circuitous route through the old castle.

On our return from America we went to live in Kennedy Lodge, although it was not quite finished, Professor Anderson continuing to live in Hamlin Hall. There is no more beautiful site for a house in any part of the world that I have seen than that of Kennedy Lodge, which we occupied until 1904.

The political situation during these two years was essentially unchanged — the Russian government was still plotting against the existing régime in Bulgaria in a way which tended to demoralize the people. It was about this time that Dr. Vulcovitch, the Bulgarian diplomatic agent at Constantinople, was assassinated in front of his own house by persons protected by the Russian Embassy. The conflict between the Greeks and Bulgarians over the ecclesiastical affairs in Macedonia went on as before. The Turkish government was not unfriendly to Bulgaria so long as Russia was hostile to it, but it was suspicious of Bulgarians coming to Constantinople; and in September, 1890, one of our students was arrested and thrown into prison on his return after a vacation because a copy of Freeman's "Sketch of European History" was found in his trunk. We secured his release after a few days, but the incident was typical of what our students often suffered on account of their books. I once went myself to the Ministry of Public Instruction to protest against the seizure of some French text-books which were issued by the French government. The official whom I found in charge was a native of India who spoke English very freely. He refused to give up the books, although he acknowledged that they contained nothing to object to except a notice of Voltaire's drama of Mohammed, which in fact was very complimentary to the Prophet. I asked on what principle they condemned books. He replied that they would admit nothing which mentioned the Turkish government or the Mohammedan religion favorably or unfavorably. I objected that this would exclude history, cyclopedias, dictionaries, and a great amount of literature, Shakespeare for example. "Well," he said, "what the devil do you come here for, anyway? Why can't you let us go to hell in our own way?" And then he very politely bade me good-morning. I never got the books.

There was no change for the better in the affairs of the Armenians. The agitators were not numerous, but they were active in stirring up discontent in the country and in appealing to public opinion in Europe. The Turkish government did nothing in the way of reform and was increasingly active in measures of repression. The old friendly feeling between the Turks and Armenians, who had always been regarded with more favor than the other Christian nationalities and who seemed to understand each other better, had given place to distrust and fear. It seemed as though the government was doing what it could to develop this mutual distrust, and desired to bring about a conflict, and was thus playing into the hands of the revolutionists who believed that such a conflict would bring about a European intervention. The sober-minded Armenians had no sympathy with the revolutionists, and saw plainly that the hope of their people scattered all over the country was not in rebellion, but in the peaceful progress of enlightenment. It was this feeling which had led so many to send their sons to Robert College. The event proved that the Sultan had a much more accurate knowledge of European politics than the revolutionists and their friends in Europe. We saw many European statesmen in Constantinople in those days who came here as to a storm centre to see more clearly what was to be expected. The most interesting among those whom I saw was Mr. Chamberlain, who at that time appeared to have sacrificed his own career to his loyalty to the unity of Great Britain and Ireland. I had seen him in the House of Commons, where I saw no other who was his equal in debate, and I found him one of the most intelligent and interesting investigators of the Eastern question. England suffered a great loss at this time in the sudden death of Sir William White in Berlin, where he had gone to spend Christmas. If the time ever comes when the government allows the publication of his private papers, which it took possession of after his death, it will be the most interesting of books. They sent Sir Philip Curry here as ambassador in his place, another acquaintance that I had made through Lord Salisbury at the same time that I first met Sir William White. He had never had any experience in the diplomatic service, but had been private secretary of Lord Salisbury and later Under Secretary for Foreign Affairs. He was always a good friend of mine and of the College. My relations with him were as pleasant as they had been with Sir William White, and in general I was in sympathy with the English policy here. It was neither anti-Turkish nor anti-Russian, a policy of peace and not of war, but not peace at any price. England would have resisted the conquest of southeastern Europe by Russia, and she favored the natural solution of the Eastern question in the development of the smaller states, Greece, Bulgaria, Roumania and Servia. So in regard to the Asiatic provinces of Turkey, what she aimed at was not the destruction or the weakening of the Turkish power, but the strengthening of it by good government and the fair, just and equal treatment of all the Christian subjects of the Sultan, especially of the Armenians. In securing this she did not wish to act alone but in concert with the other Powers. Whether a more active policy two years later would have prevented the calamities which followed is not a question to be discussed here.

Another old friend of the College died soon after Sir William White — Mr. Heap, who had been for some years consul-general of the United States at Constantinople. He was born in the consular service at Tunis, where his father was consul.

We lost our leading French teacher in 1892, not by death, but by the will of the Sultan, who took him to teach his sons; and he is still in service at the palace, although the last time I met him, he told me that he had not given a lesson for eighteen months. This was the second time that the Sultan had taken one of our teachers, the first being a German.

In the winter of 1891-92, following a visit from Mr. Wishard, the secretary of the Collegiate Y. M. C. A., a branch of this organization was founded by our students which was adapted to the peculiar wants of this polyglot institution and was at the same time in full harmony with the general society.

It was composed of four sections: Armenian, Bulgarian, Greek and English, each using its own language and meeting three times a month, united in one General Association, meeting once a month and using only the English language. Most of the personal work in each nationality is conducted under the direction of the respective sections. The president of the General Association is always a member of the Faculty. This society is now connected with the International Association and has been represented at various general meetings in Europe.

It was during the twenty-ninth year that I began to take some part in the preparation for the proposed Parliament of Religions, to be held in Chicago in 1893, and I had some very interesting interviews with the heads of different religious communities and others whom I invited to be present in person or by deputy. I sympathized heartily with Dr. Barrows' plans and did what I could to help him, although I had not so great faith as he had in the practical results which would follow. I found all the religious communities afraid to commit themselves by sending official representatives, but, in one way or another, they were represented. Constantinople itself is a Parliament of Religions, but the discussions are not irenic, and it is very difficult for people to understand how they can be. The Sunday congregation at Robert College comes nearer to the ideal than any that I have seen.

We did our best during the twenty-ninth year to make some advance in the College internally as well as externally. We had a very harmonious Faculty, and the work done was reasonably satisfactory. Professor van Millingen became Professor of History and English Literature. Mr. Ormiston spent the year 1891-1892 at Johns Hopkins University in Baltimore, and on his return was appointed Professor of Chemistry and Mineralogy. Professor Eliou had been made professor and the head of the Greek Department, which he had already raised to a level with the Armenian and Bulgarian. We suffered, as we always have, from the excessive amount of linguistic work which is demanded in this country. Some wag proposed, when the College was founded, that it be named Babel College, and it was not altogether a joke. We met the difficulty in part by making the College course five years in place of four, but we have not escaped giving additional time to the vernacular of each nationality, to meet the increasing demands of the Bulgarian and Greek governments and the popular sentiment of the Armenians. The Turkish government will no doubt make equal demands in the course of time. It is reasonable, and we have no desire to denationalize our students and unfit them to be leaders of their own people.

The question of elective courses had already forced itself upon us, and we yielded something in this direction. I suppose that it is heresy to confess this now, but I did not believe in elective courses in colleges and never favored them. I do not believe in them now. They belong to the university, and, as Professor Münsterberg once said, the American college of to-day seems to me to be a cross between a university and a kindergarten. The old college was a place of severe discipline, mental and moral. It has dropped out in America, and nothing has taken its place. It may be true that in this age of specialization the "all-round man" of the old time is an impossibility. Certainly it is hard to find one; but it seems to me all the more necessary for the specialist to have four years of general discipline and culture, with no option as to what he will study, before he begins to specialize; and I say this without any reference to the many obvious abuses of the elective system, which are not an essential part of it. We have yielded something in the way of electives without giving up our idea of what a college ought to be, and we are forced to have a preparatory department to meet the peculiar wants of the country. The majority of our students have never graduated or intended to graduate when they entered. We do our best for them and have reason to be proud of some of them, but we wish that all who are capable of it might have the full course of discipline and culture necessary for graduation, for their own sake and for the good of their people.

The new college building, which was then called Science Hall, but which since Dr. Long's death has been named for him, was completed in the spring of 1892. It was furnished by Mrs. Davies of New Haven, the sister of Mrs. Professor van Millingen. The Chemical Department was in the basement, the museum, library and Department of Physics on the first floor. The whole of the upper story was occupied by a hall, which was divided by a movable partition into a chapel and lecture room. It was designed by Professor Hamlin of Columbia University and built by Mr. Burness, a Scotch builder, who is one of the most respected and reliable men in Constantinople and has put up most of our buildings. The college buildings and Kennedy Lodge are all built of blue limestone quarried on the campus.

It was in the great hall of the new building that we celebrated the Commencement exercises June 26, 1892, with an audience of nearly a thousand, including the British ambassador, diplomatic representatives of Austria, Holland, Greece and Bulgaria, and many other official and distinguished guests of various nationalities. This was the formal inauguration of the building. I was not present on this happy occasion, having started for America at the end of May to recruit my health and return in September.

It was the beginning of better days, but the class which graduated was the smallest since 1874, only five in number, and smaller than any class since. Four were Armenians and 1 a Bulgarian. The Bulgarian is now a merchant in Russia. Of the Armenians 2 are merchants, 1 a dentist and 1 a physician.

The class of 1891 numbered 8, 4 Armenians, 3 Bulgarians and 1 Greek. Of the Armenians 1 is a teacher, 1 a dentist, 1 a merchant, 1 unknown. Of the Bulgarians 1 is in the diplomatic service, 1 an army officer and 1 a teacher. The Greek is a merchant.

CHAPTER XX
TRYING TIMES IN TURKEY. 1892-1894

THE number of students registered the thirtieth year was 203, of whom 143 were boarders. Seventy-three were Armenians, 60 Bulgarians, 46 Greeks, 15 English and Americans, others 9. The thirty-first year the number registered was 200, of whom 123 were boarders. Sixty-eight were Armenians, 65 Greeks, 44 Bulgarians, 14 English and Americans, others 9.

These two years were the beginning of more trying times in the country and in the College, mingled with many experiences for which we were very grateful. In Constantinople itself the thirtieth year was comparatively uneventful; but the Armenian troubles in the interior were increasing, and special complaints were made against the American schools. Hon. A. W. Terrell, an ex-Confederate officer from Texas, had been sent here by President Cleveland to represent the United States, and we were under his protection for four years. He was without diplomatic experience and in many ways a typical Texan of the old school; but he was a brave, warm-hearted, reconstructed American of great natural ability, who did his best to defend American citizens and American interests. We were under constant and great obligations to him. He had a talk with the Grand Vizier one day in 1893 which is worth noting here. The Grand Vizier said they had no reason to complain of the Jesuits, because they always spoke well of the Turks, but "where did you ever see anything good said of the Turks by an American missionary?" Mr. Terrell replied, "Why, I was at the Commencement exercises of Robert College, and I heard the president charge those young men to be loyal to the sovereign, and then I heard him pray for the Sultan." "Oh, yes!" said the Grand Vizier, "that was Robert College. That is altogether different. Did any one ever hear of the government having any fault to find with Robert College? Robert College is all right, but those people at — — are quite different."

It is easy to say good things about the Turks. We live in the most friendly relations with them and always find good things to say about them. What the Grand Vizier meant was, good things about the Turkish government. There are some good things to be said about this also. Robert College has reason to be grateful that for the last forty years it has never interfered with our work in any way, or refused any of the requests that we have made for new buildings or for the protection of our students, and that it has freed us from taxation. In return for this it has always been our purpose to respect its laws and its wishes. We have taught our students to do the same thing, and have never tolerated any seditious movements among them.

Personally, outside the College, I have expressed my own opinions as to the policy of the government and used what influence I had in favor of what seemed to me the true interests of all the people of Turkey. I love these people, and I could not do otherwise. I only regret that I have not been able to do more for them.

The saddest event of the year for the College was the sudden death of Mrs. van Millingen on a French steamer from Marseilles. She went to America with me in the spring and was returning with Professor Panaretoff. The news of her death came to us by telegraph from Athens, while we were having a general Thanksgiving Day dinner at Kennedy Lodge, as a shock never to be forgotten. No one in the College filled a larger place in our hearts and lives than she did, and her memory will be cherished as long as any of those who knew her continue to live.

The records of the Faculty show that much time was given during the year to the perfecting of the course of study. Among other things importance was given to the development of vocal and instrumental music, which had never been altogether neglected, but which had been kept in the background by our poverty, although its importance for our students had been recognized. Our students were able in June to give a concert, with the aid of their teacher, which attracted a large audience from all parts of the city and brought in about a hundred dollars for the charity fund of the Y. M. C. A. Something was also done to provide commercial instruction for those who desired it. I had taught bookkeeping in the College myself for many years, so far as I considered it an essential part of every educated man's preparation for life. I believed that incidentally it had also an ethical value.

The French Department was organized and put on a solid foundation by the appointment of a permanent instructor to direct it. It had never been satisfactory to us or to our students up to this time, as our teachers were constantly changing and often inexperienced.

The Scientific Department also made very satisfactory progress, with the advantage of the new Science Hall and the division of work between Dr. Long and Professor Ormiston. Through the kindness of a friend in Pittsburg, Pa., large additions were made to our apparatus, and our museum was enriched by a complete and beautiful collection of the fish and the algæ of the Bosphorus, besides a number of prepared skeletons of birds and animals.

The marriage of Professor Ormiston and Miss Farley left the College without a matron, and we had the good fortune to find a lady to take her place who was an experienced trained nurse, Miss Meredith Hart, who has ever since filled a large place in our college life, and to whom teachers, their families, and students who have been sick owe a debt of gratitude which cannot be expressed in words, but which is never forgotten.

In the summer of 1893 I went to America to attend the Parliament of Religions at the Columbian Fair. At Chicago Mrs. Washburn and I were the guests of our dear friends Mr. and Mrs. Blatchford. I spoke on Mohammedanism and Christianity, and was so far successful in presenting a fair statement of the former that no complaint was made of it at Constantinople, although Orthodox Mohammedans naturally could not accept the address as a whole, while some of my Turkish friends here received it with favor. I also delivered an address on the Aim of Foreign Missions. The Parliament of Religions was much discussed at the time and in the following years, bitterly attacked by some and greatly exalted by others. It is certain now that neither the fears of the one party nor the hopes of the other have been realized. My own deliberate opinion is that it did no permanent harm and much real good. It fell to Dr. Barrows to bring out, define and express to the world a thought which was already working in men's minds, and which is now the source of much of the religious controversy going on in the world. It was well that it should be brought out by a man who had unshaken faith in the Divine origin of Christianity, and there is no reason to fear that it will not in the end lead to a clearer conception of what Christianity means.

While in America and after my return I was drawn into a public and private discussion in regard to the secret society known as the Mystic Shrine of Mecca, which professes to be affiliated with the Mohammedan order of Bektashi dervishes, some of whom in Constantinople are near neighbors and special friends of mine. It is true that Orthodox Mohammedans look upon the Bektashis as a heretical sect, but they are Mohammedans. If this American society is what it professes to be, its members are Mohammedans who do not live up to their faith, for the first duty of a Mohammedan is to confess his faith and defend it. If it is a fraud and a parody on Mohammedanism, it is an insult to a great religion which is a shame to America. The Bektashis here are still in doubt as to which it is, and so am I.

When the thirty-first college year opened in September, 1893, Constantinople was surrounded by quarantine stations which made all travel very difficult, and about the same time cholera broke out in the city and continued with more or less severity until April, with sanitary regulations which caused even more excitement and alarm than the disease itself. The number of students coming from Bulgaria and other places fell off seriously. I managed to get back by way of Trieste with only one day of quarantine, but the land quarantines were more dangerous to health than the cholera, and it was a wonder to us that so many students came.

As we had deliberately increased our expenses considerably by the appointment of new teachers, and in reasonable expectation of an increased revenue from students, we found ourselves under the necessity of cutting down the salaries of all our professors until we were relieved from our financial difficulties by a special contribution from seven of our tried friends in America who came to the rescue. This is the only time in the history of the College that we have made such an appeal to our friends.

In July, 1894, just after our Commencement, came the great earthquake which caused the death of some fifteen hundred people, destroyed or seriously injured many thousand houses and public buildings, and caused such ruin in the bazaars that the seven thousand shops there had to be abandoned. The shocks lasted about a month, and great numbers of the people camped out in the fields, cemeteries and open places for much of this time. The College buildings were vigorously shaken but not seriously injured; and, so far as is known, none of the many earthquakes here have ever done serious injury on this part of the Bosphorus. The centre of disturbance is the line where the Silurian formation of the Bosphorus meets the Miocene strata in old Stamboul. At the time of the first shock Professor van Millingen and Professor Ormiston were engaged in archæological work in the dungeons of the old prison of Anema, under the old walls of the city. Their escape from being buried alive there was almost a miracle.

It was during this year that the Armenian troubles took an acute form in the massacres in the Sassoun district in Armenia and were followed by a European intervention. The Christians in that part of the empire had long been a prey to the Kurdish tribes, unprotected by the Turkish government; but in this case the Turkish troops, under orders from Constantinople, took part in the massacre and plunder of the Armenians, and the work of their extermination was officially commenced. England called upon the Powers which had signed the treaty of Berlin and guaranteed the good treatment of the people of Armenia to intervene. England, France and Russia took the lead in demanding redress for what had been done and such changes and reforms as would secure the lives, property and rights of the Armenians in those provinces where they constituted an important part of the population. The Turks soon discovered that England was the only Power to be feared in this question and that the "Concert of Europe" would not tolerate any independent action on her part.

Schemes of reform were devised by the ambassadors and discussed with the Turks, who refused to accept any kind of foreign control of the reforms demanded, but professed all manner of good intentions. So the negotiations went on month after month, while the political excitement in the country steadily increased and the condition of the Christians grew worse, until the climax was reached in the great massacre of 1895-1896. These were trying times for the College, where it required all our energy and skill to keep the minds of our students on their work; and as a result of the earthquake and the cholera there was great distress in the city, and many well-to-do families were reduced to poverty. In August the destruction of a town in Bulgaria by fire ruined several families whose sons were in the College.

I was not present at the Commencement exercises in 1894. I was in bed, attended by several doctors who could not agree as to the cause and nature of the sudden attack which seemed to threaten my life; but happily they did agree as to what should be done for me, and I survived. I was well in the morning, though tired out, as I generally was at the end of the year; but a stormy interview of two hours with a half crazy student, who threatened all kinds of vengeance on me and the College and had to be quieted down before the public exercises, very nearly finished my work in the College. I recovered in season to leave Constantinople for Switzerland the evening before the great earthquake, and thus escaped the great nervous strain of a month of earthquake shocks which caused the death of hundreds of people.

The number of graduates in 1893 was 13. Of these, all of whom are living, 6 are Bulgarians, 3 are Armenians, 3 are Greeks and 1 is English. Of the Bulgarians 1 is a merchant in West Africa, 2 are lawyers and 3 physicians. Of the Armenians 1 is a merchant, 2 are or have been teachers. Of the Greeks 1 is an instructor in Robert College, 2 are in business.

The number of graduates in 1894 was 21, all but one of whom are living. Of these 8 were Armenians, 6 Bulgarians, 4 Greeks, 2 English, 1 American. Of the Armenians 4 are merchants, 2 teachers, 1 a dentist, 1 unknown. Of the Bulgarians 3 are in the civil service in Bulgaria, 2 lawyers, 1 a teacher. Of the Greeks 3 are merchants, 1 a teacher. The English are merchants. The American is a civil engineer in America.

CHAPTER XXI
REORGANIZATION OF THE BOARD OF TRUSTEES.
1894-1896

GREAT and important changes took place during this period in the constitution of the Board of Trustees. Mr. Booth, who had been president of the Board from the beginning, died in December, 1895; and Dr. Coe, who had been secretary from the first, had to resign on account of illness and died in February, 1895. Mr. Hatch and Mr. Vermilye, the treasurer, had also died. Mr. Kingsley resigned. Dr. Coe's son, Rev. Edward B. Coe, D. D., LL. D., took his father's place. Mr. William C. Sturges, president of the Seaman's Savings Bank, became treasurer in place of Mr. Vermilye, Mr. Cleveland H. Dodge and Mr. W. T. Booth, the son of the former President, joined the Board, and finally Mr. John S. Kennedy consented to become the President.

Whatever progress the College has made since that time is due to the generous support, the wise counsels and the active efforts of this new Board of Trustees. The College opened in 1894 with 205 registered students, of whom 116 were boarders. There were 80 Greeks, 63 Armenians, 36 Bulgarians, 13 English and Americans, 13 others.

The thirty-third year there were 221 registered, of whom 132 were boarders. There were 92 Greeks, 69 Armenians, 37 Bulgarians, 8 English and Americans, 4 Turks, 11 others.

For the first time in the history of the College the Greeks outnumbered the Armenians and the Bulgarians. The Bulgarians had fallen off, owing to the establishment of government gymnasia, where students were educated at very small cost to their parents, and on account of the many difficulties put in the way of Bulgarians coming to Constantinople by the Turkish government. Constantinople was no longer a political or a business centre for Bulgaria. The Armenians were suffering from the political troubles here and in the interior. The Greeks, on the other hand, had come to realize at last that this was not a Bulgarian college, that it was no part of its object to attack or weaken the Orthodox Church, and that our Greek Department offered to them everything that they could ask in the way of mental and moral discipline. They had come to appreciate the real value and importance of our religious instruction and our efforts to build up the character of our students.

Professor van Millingen was absent on leave during the year 1894-1895. Otherwise the Faculty was unchanged. The following year the College was saddened by the death of Mr. Charles H. Durfee, a tutor who had just come to the College, but had already won the hearts of teachers and students. He had an attack of typhoid fever, and I took him to Kennedy Lodge. It seemed a mild attack, but the second week he suddenly died, when Miss Hart and Mrs. Washburn were both with him.

Mr. Hagopian had gone to America for his health at the end of the thirty-second year and on account of the Armenian troubles did not return for four years. He spent most of the time studying in the University of Edinburgh, where he made hosts of friends. He had never had anything to do with revolutionists, but the Turkish government was indiscriminate in its arrest and imprisonment of all Armenians coming from Europe or America, and it was thought better that he should delay his return. His stay in Scotland fitted him for the position of adjunct Professor of Philosophy, which he now occupies in the College.

In reading the correspondence of these years and the following one I am surprised to find that through all these trying times, when it now seems to me a wonder that the College continued to exist, we kept up our courage and were optimistic in our hopes for the future. We suffered, and suffered keenly; sometimes it seemed more than we could endure, but it was not for ourselves. Our friends in America were alarmed and anxious about us, and Mr. Kennedy offered to send us a steam yacht upon which we might take refuge in case of need. We were very grateful, but felt that the appearance of such a steamer anchored near the College might of itself create a panic which would endanger those about us. It was a serious question at one time whether we ought not to suspend the College, as Mr. Robert had advised at the time of the Bulgarian massacres, but so long as the Turkish government manifested no inclination to molest any one within our walls we felt that there was every reason why we should keep our doors open.

This is not the place to enter into any details of the events of these two years, and I have not the satisfaction of feeling that any influence of mine modified the action of the Turkish government or did the Armenians any good. I can only claim that it never did them any harm. I had influence in London and here and used it in efforts to put a stop to the extermination of the Armenians, but the real defender of Turkey through all these horrors was Russia. No doubt the Russian government looked upon the massacre of Armenians in Turkey as it has since looked upon the massacre of the Jews at home, as a matter of little consequence, with which the outside world had no concern. She made it a question of the peace of Europe that there should be no armed intervention here; and while she joined England and France in demanding reforms, it was apparently with the purpose of playing into the hands of the Turks.

After the Sassoon massacres and the official investigation of them, which had no practical result except to turn a stream of charity into the country from England and America, the negotiations here went on while the sufferings of the Armenians steadily increased. In the autumn of 1895 the embassies encouraged the Armenians here to break the deadlock in their negotiations by presenting a petition to the Grand Vizier. They asked permission and received it, but it was revoked at the last minute, when troops were sent to prevent the presentation. A collision resulted between troops and petitioners, which was followed by a cold-blooded massacre of some eight hundred Armenians in the streets, most of whom had nothing to do with the petition.

As such things never happen in Constantinople without the knowledge and approval of the government, it is generally believed that this first massacre of Armenians here was a bold and carefully devised plan to test the spirit of the European Powers, before entering upon a general slaughter throughout the empire. If it proved that such things could be done with impunity, in face of Europe, under the very eyes of the ambassadors, it would be safe to go on without fear of intervention. In England the Liberal government, which had been honestly and earnestly devoted to securing the rights of the Armenians, had fallen, and Lord Salisbury had come into power. The Turks felt that it was time to test his policy. I was in London in July, on my way to America, and was asked to see Lord Salisbury. My old friends in the Liberal government could not have expressed their determination to put an end to the existing state of things in Turkey in stronger language than he did. When I reached England on my return five days had passed since the massacre, and I went to the Foreign Office to see Lord Salisbury and get the latest news. I found that Lord Salisbury was in France, the Under Secretary, Mr. Curzon, in the north of England, and the

Permanent Secretary in Scotland. The whole Foreign Office was taking a vacation. I went to see Mr. Chamberlain, the only other minister whom I knew, and he was in Spain. It was a week later that Lord Salisbury returned. I had come on to Constantinople and did not see him, but I know that he finally realized the gravity of this crisis and was ready to send a fleet to Constantinople. He thought that it was too late to act summarily and alone, and he entered into communication with the other Powers. For a time it seemed as though something might be done, but Russia finally put her veto on it, and the "Concert of Europe" contented itself with demanding the immediate acceptance of the meagre scheme of reform which it had agreed to, which in fact amounted to nothing, and which did not delay the general slaughter which commenced in a few weeks and went on for a year. It was in vain that the terrible details of these massacres were published to the world, and that in England and America, and to some extent in France and Italy, public opinion was roused to demand some form of intervention. These publications simply exasperated the Turks and failed to interest the "Concert of Europe." Whatever plans the Sultan had he carried them out to the bitter end without fear, only tolerating the distribution of great sums of money which were contributed in Europe and America to relieve the suffering of those who survived the massacres.

During the college year of 1895-1896 we realized, as no one out of the country could realize, the significance of what was going on in the interior, and the burden of the people's suffering was hard to bear; but we had no fear of any massacre in Constantinople or any serious danger for the College. Once only we were made to feel the dangers about us.

One of our Greek students, who had friends in Pera, left the College secretly one afternoon, after having been refused permission to go, and went with his friends to the theatre. They were insulted by a Turk who sat near them, and our student complained of it to the manager. The Turk waylaid him as he came out of the theatre and murdered him. I went to his funeral in the Greek church in Pera and was startled to find hundreds of armed Cephalonians (he was from Cephalonia) ready to escort the procession through the principal streets of the city. Thanks to the precautions taken by the police, no one interfered with this demonstration. It was not the policy of the government to stir up trouble with the Greeks at this time.

KING FERDINAND OF BULGARIA

We had an alarm of cholera in the city in 1895 and the usual quarantine, which deprived us of a visit from our dear friends Mr. and Mrs. William E. Dodge, who were on their way to Constantinople, but turned back from Athens to escape the quarantine.

Later we had a very interesting visit from Bishop Potter of New York, who made an admirable address to the students.

Our most distinguished visitor was Prince Ferdinand of Bulgaria. He had at last been officially recognized by all the Powers and had come to visit the Sultan. He came to the College, attended by a brilliant retinue of Turkish and Bulgarian officials and guards, made himself very agreeable to the Bulgarian students, and took afternoon tea at Kennedy Lodge, where he was kind enough to say that Robert College had been a nursery for Bulgarian statesmen and he hoped that it would continue to be so. He did not know it, but he drank his tea out of a cup that once belonged to his grandfather, then Louis Philippe, King of France.

The question of beneficiaries became more pressing and more difficult during these years of political troubles and financial distress. From the foundation of the College this question had been discussed more than any other. Mr. Robert never favored our aiding as many students as we did, and was always cautioning us about it, while here the most trying experience that we had was the constant refusal of applications for aid of this kind. We were agreed upon certain principles: no free students; no promise of aid for more than one year; no beneficiary to be continued whose scholarship and conduct were not of the best; no aid to any but those whose parents were really unable to pay more than one half. We were also agreed that the College ought to do something for the poor as well as the rich, and we rejoiced when Mr. Walter Wood of Philadelphia and the children of Mrs. Newton and occasionally others furnished funds for this purpose; but in general we had to face the fact that the greater part of the aid which we gave had to come out of the general funds of the College, which at best were not sufficient to meet our expenses. Almost every year we have voted to reduce the number received, but we have seldom had less than fifty students (the majority day scholars) who paid only one half the regular charges. It is much easier to lay down general principles than to apply them to all special cases. So long as we had room for such additional students and they did not necessitate additional teachers and they fulfilled our requirements, there were always special and exceptional reasons why this or that one should be received, so that we generally had a few more than we intended to receive. I think that this liberality on our part has been appreciated by the different nationalities in the East and is one of the reasons why they support the College, and it has always seemed to me that while it is unwise to receive free students, who are not likely to appreciate what costs them nothing, in aiding a certain number we are simply carrying out the purpose for which the College was founded. Some of our most distinguished graduates were half-pay students. Some have disappointed us, but on the whole I see no reason to regret that, out of our poverty, we have aided so many to secure the advantages of an education in Robert College.

The Commencement exercises in 1895 and 1896 brought together great crowds as usual, with many distinguished guests who were afterward entertained at Kennedy Lodge. The government had prohibited all such gatherings in the city, but they treated our case as exceptional and made no objection to it, probably because the American minister presided on these occasions and the English ambassador and other ministers always attended. Still we felt it necessary to take every precaution against any appearance of anything like a political demonstration. We had no address by any of the guests, and the orations were all in English or French. The only really trying moment on these occasions was when the band opened the exercises with the Hamidie March, the Turkish national air, and the audience was expected to rise. If they had kept their seats this would have been a political demonstration beyond our control, which would have made trouble. Happily they did not.

The number of graduates in 1895 was 15. Six were Bulgarians, 5 Armenians, 3 Greeks, 1 was English. Of the Bulgarians 3 are teachers, 1 a judge, 1 in diplomatic service, 1 in business. Of the Armenians 3 are merchants, 1 a civil engineer, 1 pastor of a Protestant church in Constantinople. The 3 Greeks are in business, and the Englishman is the agent of the Cunard Steamship Company in Constantinople.

The number of graduates in 1896 was 6, of whom 5 are living. Three were Bulgarians, 2 Armenians, 1 a Greek. Of the Bulgarians 2 were lawyers, 1 a teacher. Of the Armenians 1 is in business, 1 a Protestant minister. The Greek is a musician.

CHAPTER XXII
THE GREAT CONSTANTINOPLE MASSACRE. 1896-1897

IN the summer of 1896 everything in Constantinople seemed to be quiet, and most of the gentlemen connected with the College went away for the vacation. Professor Panaretoff and I went to Austria to the Saltzkammergut. We found nothing but rain and floods there and started for the Carpathians; but in Vienna Professor Panaretoff was ordered by his doctor to go to Carlsbad. As I was left alone I went to the Millennial Exhibition in Budapest for a few days and returned to Constantinople on Saturday, August 22. The following Wednesday I went up the Bosphorus to call at the English Embassy and to lunch with Mr. Dimitroff at Buyukdere. I returned about 4 o'clock, and, soon after, some one came in great excitement to say that the Turkish army had revolted, plundered the Ottoman Bank and were slaughtering people in the streets. I at once took all possible precautions for the protection of the College and the families. It turned out that the news which I had received was incorrect, but that something equally terrible was going on in town. It had been a beautiful day, and several of our lady friends had been in town and found it very difficult to get back through streets which were already running with blood.

What had happened was this. About noon a band of Armenians, most of them from Russia, entered the Ottoman Bank, with arms and dynamite, took the employees prisoners and barricaded themselves in the building, with the threat that, unless the ambassadors at once secured a pledge from the Sultan of certain reforms, they would blow up the bank with dynamite. To finish with this part of the story, soldiers soon surrounded the bank, and negotiations began with the captors which in the evening resulted in their being permitted to leave the bank, go on board the yacht of the chief manager and leave the country unmolested.

Who originated this plot I do not know, but it is certain that the Turkish government knew all about it many days before, even to the exact time when the bank was to be entered; and the Minister of Police had made elaborate arrangements, not to arrest these men or prevent the attack on the bank, but to facilitate it and make it the occasion of a massacre of the Armenian population of the city. This was to be the crown of all the massacres of the year, one worthy of the capitol and the seat of the Sultan, a final defiance to the Christian world. Not many minutes after the attack on the bank the bands of Turks, who had been organized by the Minister of Police in Stamboul and Galata, commenced the work of killing every Armenian they could find, protected by large bodies of troops, who in some cases took part in the slaughter. Through Wednesday, Wednesday night, Thursday and Thursday night the massacre went on unchecked. An open telegram was sent by the ambassadors to the Sultan Thursday night, which perhaps influenced him to give orders to stop the massacre, and not many were murdered on Friday. I do not care to enter at all into the horrible details of this massacre of some ten thousand Armenians. Very few of them were able to make any serious resistance. Very few women or children were killed, and these only in certain quarters where the houses were attacked and looted. Many Turks looked upon the whole thing with horror and protected the Armenians in their own houses. An American negro sailor, stranded here, whom the Turks took to be a Mohammedan, saved one house full of refugees. We had a number of Armenian servants in the College, and a few others took refuge there. Thursday night there was a massacre of Armenians just below us at Bebec and another opposite us at Candilli. The British gunboat came and took off the British residents and offered to take us, which we declined. Ruffians gathered at Hissar to massacre and plunder the Armenians here, but the leading Turks drove them off in the early evening. We had five Montenegrans at the College, and about midnight I left them to patrol and guard the grounds, with orders to wake me if any attack was made on us. We had already buried what we could of our valuables.

Not long after we retired, the gate-keeper came to say that a company of Turkish soldiers was at the gate and demanded admission, saying that they were sent by order of the Sultan to protect us. It seemed wise to assume that this was true and admit them to the grounds, while the Montenegrans still guarded Hamlin Hall, where all our Armenians had taken refuge. The colonel who came with them went away, and the captain left in command told the gate-keeper that they had come because they knew the College was full of Armenian revolutionists whom they expected to capture. Which of these statements was true I do not know, but it was a very anxious morning for us, as we and our Armenian servants were at the mercy of these soldiers, of whose real mission we were in doubt. The next day these men were replaced by twenty other soldiers under the charge of a captain whose family lived in Hissar. The government claimed that they were necessary for the protection of the College, and I furnished them with quarters in the back part of the study hall building. We were not expected to do anything else for them. They were of the regular army, genuine Turkish peasants from Asia Minor, quiet and good natured; and the four months they remained there was a continuous holiday for them, as the captain did not trouble himself to drill them. They never made any disturbance or gave us any trouble of any account; but after the College opened in September they were a source of constant anxiety, and we had to watch our students with untiring vigilance to see that they did not get into conflict with the soldiers, especially as we had a number of new Turkish students along with some sixty Armenians.

The massacre of the Armenians came to an end on Friday, the day after the soldiers came to the College; but the persecution of them which went on for months was worse than the massacre. Their business was destroyed, they were plundered and blackmailed without mercy, they were hunted like wild beasts, they were imprisoned, tortured, killed, deported, fled the country, until the Armenian population of the city was reduced by some seventy-five thousand, mostly men, including those massacred. They were replaced by Kurds and men of other wild tribes. Since that time it is very difficult for an Armenian to get permission to come to Constantinople from the interior. The poverty and distress of those left alive in Constantinople was often heartrending, and many women and children died of slow starvation. That this persecution still continues in a milder form is undoubtedly due to the criminal agitation kept up by a few revolutionists in Europe and the United States, whose chief business is the blackmailing and murder of their own people.

Sir Michael Herbert, the British *chargé d'affaires,* and some of the ambassadors did what they could to stop the massacre of the Armenians, and some of the consuls aided the Armenians to escape from the country after the massacres; but the "Concert of Europe" did nothing. It accepted the situation. The Emperor of Germany went farther. He sent a special embassy to present to the Sultan a portrait of his family as a token of his esteem.

Under all these circumstances, and in doubt as to what worse calamities might be in store for us, it was with much hesitation that we opened the College as usual on the 15th of September, only eighteen days after the massacre. Most of the Faculty was absent, and the decision had to be made by the president. It was a terrible responsibility to assume, but it seemed to me that we must go on and trust in God to protect us, as we had done at the time of the Bulgarian troubles. We were surprised at the number of students who appeared and at their assurance that the College was a safe place. The whole number registered was 200, of whom 130 were boarders. There were 77 Greeks, 61 Armenians, 38 Bulgarians, 8 English and Americans, 9 Turks, 7 others, about the same number of boarders that we had the previous year. The head of our French Department was prevented from returning by the fears of his wife's family, but the newly engaged French tutor, Mr. Reymond, came and has ever since been at the head of the department. Mr. Pollock, a new American tutor, broke down in health in the middle of the year and returned to America. The rest of us survived the terrible strain of months of painful anxiety and sympathy with suffering which we were powerless to prevent and could do little to alleviate, but at the end of November my health broke down so completely that I was forced to spend three months in Egypt to recruit. As at other times, Dr. Long took up the burden, and I was not missed. On our return from Egypt Mrs. Washburn and I improved the opportunity to stop at Beirut, with our dear old friends of the Syrian Protestant College, and rejoice with them in their prosperity. We greatly enjoyed this visit and our stay in the new Egypt of Lord Cromer, the renewal of our acquaintance with the American missionaries there, and our study of ancient Egypt. We felt sometimes that we never wished to see the blood-stained streets of Constantinople again.

We came back to new and unexpected troubles and greater anxieties than ever. War broke out with Greece, followed by an order for the expulsion of all Greek subjects from the empire, and the fanaticism of the Turks was roused to a higher pitch than at the time of the massacres. Constantinople was like a powder magazine which might be exploded by a chance spark. Our students were intensely excited, all of them, and we felt that the dreaded spark might be kindled in the College at any moment. That it was not was due chiefly to the untiring efforts of the professors and tutors of the different nationalities to quiet and restrain the students. Five of the Greeks ran away to enlist in the Greek army, but the Turkish government was considerate enough not to molest our Greek students or servants.

This war was an act of supreme folly on the part of the Greeks. The government was driven into it by popular clamor against its own judgment. It was hardly less a folly for the Turks. It is generally believed that the final decision to declare war was due to German influence, exercised chiefly through the distinguished German officers who had reorganized the Turkish army, and that the popular demonstrations here were not spontaneous. The Greeks had no army to meet the Turks, who would have been in Athens in a few days if the Powers had not intervened. The Turks had no fleet which they dared to send outside the Dardanelles, and in the end they lost Crete. The Greeks might have had an alliance with Bulgaria and been supported by an insurrection in Macedonia, but here also it was the mob which decided the government to reject this alliance. It was well for Bulgaria that they did. There was no reason why they should go to war with Turkey at that time.

Our interest in the Greeks naturally led us to sympathize with them, but we could not sympathize with the spurious patriotism which had forced the government into war, and which has so often brought them into trouble. The Christian world owes so much to ancient Greece that it naturally interests itself in modern Greece and in every effort of the kingdom of Greece to improve its position. It welcomes every advance in the prosperity and enlightenment of the nation; but sometimes its enthusiasm is cooled by evidence that the same spirit of revolt against reason which ruined ancient Athens is still prevalent. The seventy-two Greeks in the College who did not run away and go to the war were not less patriotic and were much wiser than those who went.

When the end of the year came and found us all alive, in relative peace and quiet, after the long months of terror, war, massacre, and the rage of the wildest passions about us, we felt like making our Commencement a day of thanksgiving; but the city was still full of misery and distress, and the political horizon still dark, so that we felt the need of unusual caution in arranging our programme. We gave special importance to the music and had one of the principal musicians of the palace to take a prominent part. Mr. Riddle, the American *chargé d'affaires*, presided, the audience was as large as ever and everything passed off happily.

The number of graduates was 14, of whom 13 are living. Five were Bulgarians, 4 Armenians, 4 Greeks, 1 a German from Russia. Of the Bulgarians 1 was a teacher, 1 a judge, 2 in civil service, 1 died while studying medicine. Of the Armenians 2 are merchants, 1 an architect in New York, 1 a teacher in Robert College. Of the Greeks 2 are merchants, 1 a lawyer in Roumania, 1 a physician. The German is in Russia.

CHAPTER XXIII
FURTHER DEVELOPMENT OF THE COLLEGE. 1897-1899

THE reorganized Board of Trustees did not disappoint us. When the reorganization took place it seemed almost too much to hope that a new day had really dawned upon us, that we were no longer to bear alone the burden which we had carried for so many years. The old Board was sympathetic, gave us its blessing and looked after our funds carefully, but it was so constituted that it could do little more. I remember Dr. David B. Coe, Mr. W. A. Booth and Mr. William C. Sturges with gratitude and affection. They were real friends of the College, and when I was in America they were always ready to listen to me and do what they could. The fact that they were so well known and universally respected was a guarantee of the standing of the College which I fully appreciated; but the new Board assumed a responsibility for the College which was an unspeakable relief to us. The Constitution was modified and the Board enlarged. At this time it consisted of Mr. John S. Kennedy, President, Rev. Dr. E. B. Coe, Secretary, Mr. Frederick A. Booth, Treasurer, Mr. John Sloane, Mr. Robert W. De Forest and Mr. William C. Osborn. The Board not only listened to our wants and appreciated our needs, but undertook to supply them as far and as soon as possible. This could not be done in a day, but the work of enlarging and strengthening the College began in this period, and it has been going on ever since. They were undoubtedly encouraged by a happy event which occurred in the summer of 1898. We had long felt the pressing need of a new building for our Preparatory Department, which we could not dispense with, but which could not be managed satisfactorily while it was under the same roof with the College. I went to America that summer with the special purpose of trying to interest Miss Stokes of New York in this need. I hardly know why I had thought particularly of her, although she had visited Constantinople and interested herself in the education of two Bulgarian students here, but I was very hopeful. When I reached America, to my great disappointment I found that she was not in the country, and I came back with a heavy heart. When I reached Kennedy Lodge and met Mrs. Washburn her first words were that she had a letter for me that would interest me. It proved to be a letter from Miss Stokes in which she said that she had been thinking of the wants of the College and would be very glad to put up a building for the Preparatory Department. I could hardly believe my eyes. It seemed to me almost like a miracle, and when the building was finished I sympathized most heartily with Miss Stokes' request that it be called Theodorus Hall, the gift of God. The trustees were also encouraged by two legacies left to the College, — five thousand dollars by Mr. W. H. Stickney of Baltimore and ten thousand dollars by Mr. Charles F. Wilder of Boston, — and they made arrangements for the appointment of a Professor of Mathematics, which had long been a crying need of the College.

For the thirty-fifth year, 1897-1898, the number of students registered was 250, of whom 145 were boarders. There were 88 Greeks, 87 Armenians, 49 Bulgarians, 10 Turks, 7 English and Americans, 9 others.

For the thirty-sixth year, 1898-1899, the number registered was 292, of whom 173 were boarders. There were 108 Greeks, 105 Armenians, 45 Bulgarians, 10 English and Americans, 14 Turks, 10 others.

The increase of Greek and Armenian students after the massacres and the war was altogether unexpected, and we had to refuse a number of applicants in the fall of 1898. We could not accommodate more.

One of the pleasantest experiences of this period was the coming here of President Angell of Michigan University as American minister, who was not only a college president, but a scholar and a statesman. He and Mrs. Angell were the most delightful of friends. We rejoiced in them and were proud of them as representatives of our country, which he had already represented in China. We were disappointed but not surprised that he found Michigan University more attractive than the Sublime Porte and resigned his place here after a year of fruitless negotiations, which, as he had been in China, had not even the interest of novelty. In fact he found that the Sublime Porte surpassed the Yamen in the style of diplomacy common to both.

On his departure our old friend Mr. Straus returned to the post which he had occupied under President Cleveland, an appointment which was supposed to be agreeable to the Sultan.

There was also a change in the British Embassy. Nearly all the ambassadors who had been here during the massacres were recalled and among them Sir Philip Currie, who was replaced by

Sir Nicholas O'Conor, an experienced diplomatist, a kind-hearted and agreeable gentleman, who has been most friendly to the College, who has carried out his instructions to keep peace between England and the Porte, and who has given the Sultan endless good advice which has seldom been followed. Since the massacres we have lived here through an era of German influence which seems now (1907) to be waning. It was in the autumn of 1898 that the Emperor William II made his pilgrimage to the Holy Land and visited Constantinople. It is believed here that this visit cost the Sultan more than ten million dollars, and the Turks say that all he got in return was a marble bust of the Emperor and of his grandfather. He was not welcomed by the people here, either Turks or Christians, but he cemented an alliance with the Sultan which freed Turkey from all fear of the "Concert of Europe" and in return opened a wide field for German enterprise in Turkey and for the development of German influence in Asia Minor. German influence here has been as strongly anti-American as it has been anti-English.

In 1898, in the time of the Spanish War, we had all Europe, except England, against us and had to listen to much that was unpleasant here in Constantinople, where in diplomatic circles it was universally believed that we should be ignominiously defeated. Curiously enough the Turks were on our side, and rejoiced over the defeat of Spain as a divine punishment for her treatment of the Moors in the sixteenth and seventeenth centuries. It was said that prayers were offered in our behalf in some of the mosques.

I am tempted to quote here from a letter of one of the most distinguished statesmen in England, which I find among my papers, written in September, 1898, apropos of the feeling in America. "The change of sentiment in regard to foreign possessions in the U.S.A. is not more sudden than surprising to us. Whatever benefit there may be in it for Britain, it seems to me full of trouble for America. Your constitution and government were not framed for the sort of work which oceanic Powers ruling half-savage tropical dependencies have to do, but I see that good men in America believe that, because it has come in the dispensation of Providence, Congress will be endowed with the necessary wisdom for it and it will even lead to an improvement in political methods and public life. England, as you will see, views it with sympathy."

For ourselves, we regretted the war, but we rejoiced in its victories and hoped, as this gentleman says, that Congress might be endowed with wisdom to manage our new possessions. We are still hoping. But our Congress is not, thus far, made up of men whose knowledge or interests fit them to legislate for a world-power such as we have become. They are chiefly local politicians with little interest in the welfare of the country as a whole, and ignorant of foreign politics. There is no choice for any nation now but to be a world-power knowing how to defend its own interests, or to be dominated by the Great Powers of Europe and exploited in their interests. In 1896 we could not send a gunboat to Constantinople to protect the lives of American citizens because Russia and Germany did not wish it. Our trade with Turkey has been limited for years in the same way. From the standpoint of Constantinople it seems that the great need of America is more international statesmen.

To go back to the College, it was in 1897 that we had our first public field day for athletics. An athletic club had been organized the previous year by Mr. Ostrander, then a tutor in the College. We had never ignored our responsibility for the physical culture of our students. As far as our means allowed we had provided gymnastic apparatus, and had exercised our students in some system of light gymnastics; but our chief dependence had been in encouraging all sorts of out-of-door games — cricket, baseball, football, etc. The Athletic Club had rather a precarious existence for several years, but it has grown stronger every year, and its annual field days have attracted much attention in the city and developed the interest of the students in athletics. Some of our students have distinguished themselves by breaking world records and winning international prizes. For myself I rejoice that the interest in athletics has not yet reached a point where it overshadows the proper work of the College, and I hope that it never will. I believe that systematic work in the gymnasium is a far more important means of cultivating the physical powers, and that out-of-door games, if not confined to a chosen few, are equally important. Our games have never degenerated into gladiatorial shows. We have sometimes been troubled by international rivalries in athletics, but our own neutral position has generally enabled us to restore harmony, and on the whole the conduct of our students in these contests has been praiseworthy.

Our chief source of anxiety in 1898-1899 was in regard to our water supply. We talked about it every day and dreamed about it every night. At times we had not a two days' supply in sight simply for cooking and drinking. We had a well one hundred and eighty feet below the College which furnished water for other purposes, but one horse pumped this dry every morning in two hours. We had several large cisterns and had always depended upon rain-water caught on our roofs for our supply. We had been in trouble before, but this year, with a greater number of students than ever before, we had to face a drought which had continued for two or three years with an annual rainfall of only twelve to fifteen inches. The first part of the year we sent our students to the Turkish bath in Hissar, but in the early spring this burned down. Then the well threatened to give out, and we saw the bottom of our cisterns. I arranged to have water brought on horses, in barrels, from a spring two miles away. The evening before this water was to begin to come a storm came down from the Black Sea with a deluge of rain, and that was the end of the drought. But this was an experience which it was not safe to repeat, and Mr. Kennedy came to our rescue and furnished the means to put in a steam pump and connect us with the city water supply in a building which we erected for this purpose. Our supply is now unlimited, but we still depend on our cisterns for drinking and cooking purposes.

Professor Anderson's health broke down in 1898 under the strain of life in Hamlin Hall, where he had lived with his family since a similar experience had forced me to withdraw to Kennedy Lodge. Since that time no family has lived in Hamlin Hall. The family rooms are now used as the college hospital and Miss Hart's apartments. There are also twelve teachers living in the building. The president's house is only a stone's throw from Hamlin Hall. After a year's absence, Professor Anderson returned to the College.

Mr. Hagopian returned to the College in November, 1898, and like other Armenians returning to the city, although his papers were in perfect order, he spent twenty-four hours in the city prison, when by our intervention he was set at liberty. The neglect of a friend of his in London to post a letter to me prevented our meeting him on his arrival. If I had known of his coming on that day, I could have saved him this trying experience, through the intervention of the American consul.

In March, 1899, Lord Rosebery came to Constantinople, and Mrs. Washburn and I lunched with him at the British Embassy. I had never met him before, although when he was Foreign Minister I was in correspondence with him. I had a long talk with him on Eastern affairs and English policy. I found him quite as interesting a man as Lord Salisbury, though of a different type, and less inclined to express decided opinions. He related to me one or two most interesting incidents of his experience when Minister of Foreign Affairs.

The number of graduates in 1898 was 14. There were 6 Bulgarians, 4 Greeks, 2 Armenians, 1 English, 1 Italian. Of the Bulgarians 2 are in business, 1 a judge, 1 a lawyer, 1 a teacher, 1 in diplomatic service. Of the Greeks 2 are in business, 1 a lawyer, 1 an engineer. Of the Armenians 1 is a mining engineer in Mexico, 1 a physician in America. The Englishman is a merchant; the Italian, unknown.

The number of graduates in 1899 was 13. There were 5 Greeks, 4 Armenians, 3 Bulgarians, 1 Hebrew. Of the Greeks 2 are in business, 2 have studied medicine and 1 is in the treasurer's office in Robert College. Of the Armenians 3 are in business, 1 has studied law in America. Of the Bulgarians 2 have studied law, 1 is in diplomatic service. The Hebrew is an assistant in the physico-chemical laboratory of the University of Leipsic.

We had our usual crowded and distinguished audience on both the Commencement days, and an admirable address from Mr. Straus, who presided in 1899. The subjects treated by the graduates in their orations were the following: The Russian Woman, The Temptations of Poverty, The Social Problem, Life a Conflict, The East and the West, The Value of Self-reliance, La Dette de 1'Occident, La Puissance de la Volonté, Les Progrés des Sciences et la Misére Sociale.

I suppose that few foreigners have had a better opportunity to acquaint themselves with the people of Asia Minor than Sir William Ramsay, and I quote here what he says in his "Impressions of Turkey" of our graduates: "I have come in contact with men educated in Robert College, in widely separated parts of the country, men of diverse races and different forms of religion, Greek, Armenian and Protestant, and have everywhere been struck with the marvelous way in which a certain uniform type, direct, simple, honest and lofty in tone, has been impressed upon them. Some had more of it, some less; but all had it to a certain degree; and it is diametrically opposite to the type produced by growth under the ordinary conditions of Turkish life."

CHAPTER XXIV
DEATH OF DR. HAMLIN. 1899-1901

THERE was nothing in the history of the College in Constantinople the thirty-seventh year which demands special attention. Everything was quiet and peaceful in the city. The Sultan completed the twenty-fifth year of his reign and the six hundredth of the Ottoman dynasty, and all Europe united to congratulate him.

The prosperity of the College continued unabated. The number of students registered was 297, of whom 176 were boarders. One hundred and twelve were Greeks, 108 Armenians, 39 Bulgarians, 14 Turks, 13 English and Americans, 11 others.

For the thirty-eighth year the number of students registered was 311, of whom 182 were boarders. One hundred and twenty-seven were Greeks, 108 Armenians, 34 Bulgarians, 14 Turks, 12 English and American, 16 others.

The number of students for these two years represented the extreme limit to which it was possible for us to go in receiving students. We were overcrowded in the buildings which we had at that time.

In the spring of 1900 the trustees of the College requested me to go to America and consult with them as to what measures should be taken to meet the immediate needs of the College and secure its future development. This was the most important step ever taken by the trustees and was the beginning of the development which is still in progress. It was a recognition of responsibility on their part which the Faculty welcomed with enthusiasm and new hopes for the future. At their suggestion I started in season to attend the Ecumenical Missionary Conference, which was held in New York that year, where it was thought advisable to have Robert College represented. The importance of the College and its world-wide influence were fully recognized. I presided at one of the great meetings in Carnegie Hall and spoke on different occasions, and had many opportunities for consultation with those engaged in similar work in other parts of the world, most of whom realized that it was the founding and the success of Robert College which had changed the policy of American missionary societies and led to the establishment of colleges in so many missionary fields. I found these personal conferences very profitable, and greatly enjoyed meeting so many great and good men of various nationalities from all parts of the world. It was natural to compare this meeting with the Parliament of Religions at Chicago, in which I had taken a prominent part, and I did so in the brief address which I made at the last meeting. They were not antagonistic in spirit or purpose, but the more definite aim of the practical workers of the Missionary Conference was certainly more inspiring and seemed to promise more immediate results.

Soon after the Conference the trustees met informally at dinner at Mr. Kennedy's, where I had an opportunity to present to them the views of the Faculty as to the present conditions — the needs and the prospects of the College. What was generally agreed to there was afterwards adopted at a formal meeting of the Board. They resolved to carry out as far as possible the recommendations submitted by the Faculty. They resolved "to do everything that was necessary for the development of the College on the model of the best colleges in America, to make it thoroughly up to date in its material equipment and in its curriculum, personnel and spirit." Professor Lybyer had already been appointed professor of mathematics; and it was agreed to appoint, in addition, a principal of the Preparatory Department, a professor in the Scientific Department who should also be a physician, and a college treasurer who should also be a professor in the Commercial Department. It was also decided to erect a new building for study halls and recitation rooms, a gymnasium and three houses for professors, to supply new chemical and physical apparatus, and to increase the library, also to purchase adjacent land. As all this would increase the running expense of the College, it was resolved to take immediate steps to raise two hundred and fifty thousand dollars to increase the endowment. A building for the Preparatory Department had already been provided for by Miss Stokes, and Mr. Cleveland H. Dodge, at the meeting, promised to put up a gymnasium. Mr. Kennedy promised to put up the professors' houses.

It should be noted that this action of the trustees was not the result of any special appeal made by us, but was the result of their own investigations and of their own purpose to make the College worthy of the position which it occupied in the East, and the reputation which it had attained in the world. No one, outside the Faculty, can fully appreciate what this meant to us who were on the ground, who knew what the College had done and might do, who had had a part in all its trials and triumphs.

This was not the only evidence which we had of the interest which was taken in the College in educational circles in America. I received most cordial invitations to visit colleges and universities. Princeton and Michigan Universities, Amherst College, and later the University of Pennsylvania, honored Robert College by conferring on its president the degree of Doctor of Laws. I took special pleasure in my visit to President Angell of Michigan University, who had so greatly endeared himself to us when he was United States minister here, and to Williams College, whose president had long been a faithful friend of ours and had done no little work in finding tutors for us, and to Amherst, my own Alma Mater.

In August we arranged for a gathering at my son's summer home at Manchester-by-the-Sea of all who could be got together of the Hamlin family. Dr. Hamlin, then nearly ninety years old, was there in good spirits and apparently good health. He was much pleased to hear of what the trustees had done and promised to do for Robert College and rejoiced in its present prosperity. The next morning, August 8, he went with Mrs. Hamlin to Portland to assist in the celebration of "Home Week" there. That evening, on his return from a public meeting, where he had spoken, he complained of feeling ill and soon died. His funeral took place at Lexington, near Boston, which had been his home for some years. His body was carried to the grave by Armenian friends, who afterward erected a monument over it, in memory of what he had done for the Armenian people in Turkey. After our return to Constantinople and the opening of the College we had a memorial service for him in the college hall, conducted by Dr. Long, with most interesting and appreciative addresses. There was a large audience of his old friends and of the college students. It was twenty-seven years since he had been in Turkey, but his memory was fresh in the minds of those who had known him. No one who had been a student under him in the Bebec Seminary or Robert College could possibly forget him, and the tradition of him still lingers in the city among those who had not known him personally. His name, attached to Hamlin Hall, is familiar to all our students, and his portrait hangs in the college chapel. Of his work as one of the founders of the College I have written in the earlier chapters of this book. Those who would know him as a man should read his autobiography, "My Life and Times." It was an interesting fact that, though Dr. Hamlin was a

typical New Englander, he, like Mr. Robert, was of French Huguenot stock.

On our return to Constantinople we stopped for a few days
in Paris as the guests of Mr. Dimitroff, who was the Bulgarian
Commissioner at the Paris Exposition. For us who had known
Bulgaria as a Turkish province, chiefly inhabited by peasants who
were practically serfs, a country with no sign or promise of modern progress, the Bulgarian exhibit was the most wonderful thing
that we saw. It compared favorably with the exhibits of the smaller
states, even in the department of art, and showed that the progress
of the country in twenty years of freedom had been unexampled.
We could not but feel that something of this progress was due to
Robert College.

The Commencement exercises in 1900 were unusual. The
plague had broken out in Egypt, and it was believed that cases had
occurred in Constantinople. We were in daily expectation that we
should be shut in by quarantines, which would make it very difficult for our students to reach their homes. We closed the College
a week earlier than usual and excused the Seniors from delivering
orations. Professor van Millingen and Mr. Lloyd C. Griscom, the
American *chargé d'affaires*, made addresses which were highly appreciated by a crowded and distinguished audience. Mr. Griscom
represented the United States here as *chargé d'affaires* for about a
year, and won golden opinions, not only from all Americans, but
from the representatives of foreign Powers, and was specially honored by the Sultan. It was he who finally arranged for a settlement
of American claims for indemnity for losses during the massacres.
We do not wonder at the successive and rapid promotions which
have made him American ambassador at Rome. He was followed
here by Mr. John G. A. Leishman, who was raised to the rank of
ambassador in 1906 and still holds this position.

One of the curious incidents of the thirty-seventh year was the
arrest of one of our Greek students and his imprisonment for two
months in the common prison along with those charged with being incendiaries, burglars and murderers. The only charge against
him was that when he arrived by steamer in Constantinople he
had in his pocket a patriotic Greek song, with music, which could
be bought in any music store in Pera. We begged the Minister of
Police not to imprison him on such a charge, and he sent him to
the College; but some of the officials knew that his father was rich,

and after some weeks made a formal charge against him of bringing incendiary documents into the country, the penalty of which is three years' imprisonment. His father had to come and bargain with the judges to acquit him when he was tried. The trial was really a farce, but it cost the father a round sum. Mrs. Washburn and Miss Hart went to see him several times in prison and became so much interested in the pitiful condition of the prisoners that on our Thanksgiving Day, with the consent of the officials, they gave them a good Thanksgiving dinner. This was after the release of our student.

The thirty-eighth college year, 1900-1901, was one of continued prosperity in the number of our students and the work done by them. We had one addition to our Faculty, Mr. Lybyer, who came to take charge of the Mathematical Department. The one cloud that rested upon the College was the failing health of Dr. Long, and it was arranged that he should take a year's vacation in America with full salary. In the spring of 1901 we had the pleasure of a visit from the president of the Board of Trustees with Mrs. Kennedy. Nothing could have been more grateful to us or more profitable for the College, and I am sure that Mr. and Mrs. Kennedy not only enjoyed their visit and appreciated the unsurpassed beauty of the site of Kennedy Lodge, but carried away with them a stronger impression of the importance and worth of the College, as well as its needs.

The work on the new building for the Preparatory Department was begun in the autumn of 1900, although, through the rascality or enmity of some officials at the palace, the *iradé* which was issued had been lost, and the new one obtained after much delay was so ambiguous as to be worthless. None of the accredited authorities of the Porte or the city dared to take the responsibility of giving us permission to go on, but they were all friendly and had no desire to stop the work, and we went on unmolested. After the building was finished we got the proper official *iradé* to erect it. We also commenced the improvements in Hamlin Hall and bought in Paris and Vienna more than a thousand dollars' worth of physical apparatus. The most remarkable event of the year was the completion of the sewer from the college grounds to the Bosphorus, after thirty years of negotiation with the Turkish authorities, which enabled us, for the first time, to complete our sanitary arrangements on scientific principles. This also was accomplished through our friendly relations with the local officials, and the work was thoroughly done, not only to our advantage, but equally to that of our Turkish neighbors, as we built up and covered in what had been an open sewer through the old castle to the sea.

The most interesting events at the Commencement in 1901 were the gathering of the alumni and a letter received from the Greek Patriarch. For the first time we had an alumni dinner, at which more than sixty were present, a large number considering that our alumni are scattered over the world and that the obstacles put in the way of travel prevent those from abroad coming to Constantinople. Two of our most distinguished alumni had died during the year, both of the class of 1871. Mr. Slaveikoff was Minister of Public Instruction in Bulgaria at the time of his death. Mr. Stoiloff had been intimately connected with the whole history of the principality, was the most widely known of Bulgarians, had held the highest offices of state, was a patriot and an honest man.

We had no speeches at our Commencement, and the next day I received the following letter, which was also published in the official organ of the church by the Patriarch: —

TO THE MOST NOBLE AND MOST LEARNED DIRECTOR OF ROBERT COLLEGE

MOST NOBLE SIR: The following is an address which his Holiness directed me to deliver yesterday on my visit to your College, which I now have the pleasure to transmit to you.

"Having come among you, Honorable Gentlemen, by order of his Holiness, my most venerable Master, it gives me great pleasure to say that his Holiness has always followed with great interest the work of your most important and most noble institution. His Holiness duly appreciates your labors and cares that the education which you give shall make good citizens and moral men, who will act in society as worthy and honest members of it, loving their neighbors, not rendering evil for evil, but good for evil.

"But the appreciation of his Holiness surpasses this limit, for he admires and praises you for working in harmony with the teaching of the Apostle; doing good without any afterthought, which might bring forth scandals, you respect the teaching of our Lord Jesus Christ, who said, 'Woe unto him through whom scandal comes.' Your enviable mission, as is proved by facts, is the mission of making good men, not of corrupting consciences: to make good Christians, not perverts from the church. For these reasons his Holiness gave me the fatherly order to express to you his thanks and praise for your work, inasmuch as our nation on account of unhappy circumstances has not been able to found such an institution as Robert College." Transmitting to you word by word this fatherly message of his Holiness, I take the opportunity to sign myself, with great respect and brotherly love for you,

THE GRAND VICAR CHRYSOSTOME.

There were 18 graduates in 1900, of whom 8 were Armenians, 5 Greeks, 3 English, 2 Bulgarians. Of the Armenians 7 are in business, 1 a civil engineer. Of the Greeks 3 are in business, 1 an engineer, 1 a teacher in Robert College. Of the English 1 is a teacher, 2 are in business. The two Bulgarians are lawyers.

There were 11 graduates in 1901. Five were Greeks, 4 were Bulgarians, 1 was Armenian, 1 was French. The Greeks are all in business. Of the Bulgarians 2 are in business, 1 is a lawyer, 1 a librarian. The Frenchman is in business in Central Asia. The Armenian is in business.

CHAPTER XXV
NEW PROFESSORS AND NEW BUILDINGS. 1901-1902

THESE recollections of Robert College I am writing in what was, for many years, Dr. Long's study, in the college house in Roumeli Hissar, and I feel it to be a more sacred place than any other about the College. He left us with his family in June, 1901, for a year of rest in America. He had been failing in health for several months, but his physician believed that a sea voyage would revive him. We took him in a chair down to the landing stage, where the people of the quarter gathered to give him their parting blessing. The American minister had sent his steam launch to convey him to the steamship which was to take him to Liverpool. It was a sad parting on the deck of the steamer, and our worst fears were realized. He reached Liverpool only to die there in a hospital July 28, 1901, and there he is buried. He had been a professor in the College for twenty-nine years and acting president whenever I was absent, twice for two years at a time when I was in America raising money. He was born in December, 1832, graduated at Alleghany College, taught two years and came to Turkey as a missionary of the Methodist Episcopal Church to the Bulgarians. It was through his influence that the first Bulgarian students came to Robert College, and no foreigner has ever been more trusted and beloved by the Bulgarian people than he. He came to Constantinople to join Dr. Riggs in the revision of the Bulgarian Bible, and when this work was done he was persuaded to accept a professorship in Robert College. No man ever had a wiser, more loyal and loving associate than I found in him, and much of the reputation of the College as a seat of learning was due to his broad scholarship. His religious influence was that of a man filled with the spirit of Christ. Even his Mohammedan neighbors regarded him as a holy man. Robert College was never the same to me after he left it. Mrs. Long died, in December, 1901, at Enfield, N. H., a few months after her return to America, leaving two daughters who still reside in that town.

The number of students registered the thirty-ninth year was 308, of whom 181 were boarders. There were 131 Greeks, 98 Armenians, 29 Bulgarians, 15 Turks, 14 English and Americans, 21 others of 11 different races.

So far as the College was concerned, the year in Constantinople was a quiet and peaceful one, although if we had chosen to interest ourselves in political affairs we might have occupied ourselves with much that was exciting and much that was trying to the people of the country. German influence was dominant at the palace and the reign of the Camarilla unchanged. The Armenians were suffering from all sorts of oppressions and the Turks still more from the terrible system of espionage which left them no peace or sense of security day or night. The storm centre was in Macedonia, and incidentally it became a matter of interest to us and to all Americans, through the capture of Miss Stone, an American missionary, by a band of revolutionists. The treaty of Berlin, Art. 23, had provided for a reformed government in Macedonia; but nothing had been done to carry this decision into execution, and the condition of the Christian population was worse than ever. Large numbers of the young men had fled into Bulgaria, and a revolutionary organization had been formed there. A similar organization on a vast scale was formed in Macedonia, with its headquarters at Salonica. The insurrection broke out in 1901, and Miss Stone was captured in Macedonia by a band connected with this organization in the autumn of this year, when traveling on what was supposed to be a perfectly safe road and not far from a Turkish guard house. She was held for ransom. This is not the place to enter into the details of this unfortunate affair or to criticise the management of it. I believe that it is universally acknowledged that it was sadly mismanaged up to the time that Mr. Gargiulo, Mr. Peet and Mr. House went to Macedonia in December and finally secured her release in February, 1902. It was not until things had come to a deadlock in December that it was possible for me to do anything. I then went privately to Sofia, saw the Bulgarian ministers, four of whom happened to be graduates of the College, and the military officers who knew what was going on along the frontier, also graduates, and the chief of the revolutionary committee, who had never been in Robert College, but whom I found to be an educated gentleman who had studied in Paris. I saw others also and satisfied myself as to what needed to be done. I returned to Constantinople, made my report, which was telegraphed to Washington, and my recommendations were carried out. It is my belief that she might have been set at liberty within a few days after her capture and for a small sum of money if the affair had been settled quietly at the outset. But whatever mistakes may have been made here, it was the American newspapers and the public there which was chiefly responsible for the long delay and the large sum paid for her ransom. The telegraph kept the revolutionists informed every day of what was going on in America and of the sums raised for her ransom. No finer work has ever been done in Turkey than that of Mr. Gargiulo, the first dragoman of the Legation, and his associates, in securing her release, in the midst of difficulties which seemed to be insurmountable. The brigands got the money contributed in America, and it is generally believed that it went to pay for the arms which were used against the Turks the following summer.

The college year had hardly opened when we were shocked by the news of the assassination of President McKinley at Buffalo. At the request of Mr. Leishman a public service was held in the college chapel on the day of his funeral, which was attended by all the American officials, by the staff of the French Embassy and the American colony. A formal service had been held in the morning of the same day in the chapel of the British Embassy at Therapia. This was the third time since the founding of Robert College that we had been called to mourn the death of a President of the United States by assassination. What could we say to our students in view of such crimes, we who had come out here professing to represent a higher Christian civilization and the blessings of a free government — a government of the people by the people? We told them that the people repudiated and condemned these crimes, that they did not disturb the stability of the government, that they were the work of individuals such as were to be found in every country; but in our hearts we knew that the principles which we represent here had been dishonored in the minds of the people of this country and our influence in some measure diminished. These great crimes have confirmed the belief of Europeans in the picture of American society, which they get from their newspapers, which represents us as worshipers of the almighty dollar, given over to lawlessness and regardless of human life, with little real respect for God or man. They make this impression, not by inventions of their own, but by quotations from New York newspapers. Robert College is a standing protest against this conception of our country, and we defend its honor as best we can, without concealing the fact that the conflict between good and evil is as fierce there as in other parts of the world.

We sometimes have visitors at the College from America who

impress on our students the idea that America is after all a Christian state founded on the same principles which we are inculcating upon them. Such a company visited us one Sunday in March, 1902, two hundred and fifty of them, and we had three admirable addresses from Dr. Josiah Strong of New York, Dr. Barton of Chicago and Dr. Foote of Brooklyn, in place of our usual Sunday service. In general the crowds who come in excursion steamers every spring have but a day or two in Constantinople and find the bazaars more interesting than the College, although we exchange friendly salutes when they pass up the Bosphorus, and the evening of their arrival they often hear an address from Professor van Millingen, on Constantinople.

The year 1901-1902 was a very important one in the internal development of the College. The professorship of mathematics had already been filled by the appointment of Professor Lybyer. At the beginning of this year three additional professors were added to the Faculty, Professor William S. Murray as principal of the Preparatory Department, Dr. Charles W. Ottley as resident physician and Professor of Biology, Professor George S. Murray as treasurer and to take charge of the commercial studies. Before the close of the year Professor George L. Manning, Ph. D., was appointed Professor of Physics, and Rev. C. F. Gates, D. D., LL. D., was appointed Vice-President, with the understanding that he should come to the College after a year and take my place whenever I might resign, as I had informed the trustees that I should at the end of the year, after I had reached the age of seventy.

In making these appointments the trustees were simply carrying out their purpose "to make the College thoroughly up to date in its material equipment, in its curriculum, personnel and spirit," a model college, not necessarily exactly like an American college, but adapted to its environment. It is needless to add that Professor van Millingen and I, the old stagers, looked upon this as the realization of the hopes which we had cherished through long years of effort to make the most of such means as we had, to keep the lead in the educational development of this part of the world. The other members of the Faculty — American and native — welcomed the dawn of the new day with equal enthusiasm, and our alumni were encouraged to believe that they would never have reason to be ashamed of their Alma Mater.

We were equally fortunate in finding men for our Turkish and

German departments, for which we had never before been able to provide in a manner satisfactory to us or to our students. Tevfik Fikret Bey, who has since been at the head of the Turkish Department, is a man of high character and one of the most distinguished scholars in Constantinople, of whom we can be proud as an associate.

We were indebted to the Moravian Brethren at Herrnhut in Saxony for a German teacher who is in hearty sympathy with the spirit of the College, Mr. Friedrich W. Kunick, the first satisfactory German teacher that we have ever found. I once wrote to a professor in the Berlin University to find a man for us, explaining to him what sort of a man we wanted; and he replied that there was a great demand for just such men in Germany, but that the supply was very small.

Our whole staff of teachers at this time, thirty-five in all including the professors, was worthy of the high ideal which the trustees had in view for the College, many of them among the most promising graduates of the College, representing many nationalities but working together in harmony and mutual goodwill.

Theodorus Hall was ready for occupation at the close of the year, and we had also applied to the Government for permission to erect a new study hall, a gymnasium and three houses for professors. We had also completed the purchase of about seven acres of land just beyond the campus, for which Mr. Kennedy had furnished the money when he was here. Theodorus Hall was paid for, and Mr. Dodge had promised to build the gymnasium, but where the money was to come from for our greatly increased current expenses and the proposed buildings we did not know; but the responsibility for the steps taken in advance had been assumed by the trustees, and it cost me no more anxious days and wakeful nights such as I had known in former years.

Much time was given during the year to a careful revision of the course of study in both the Collegiate and the Preparatory departments. One year was added to the preparatory course, and in the Collegiate Department we arranged for a division of the course from the beginning of the Sophomore year — one division leading up to the degree of A.B. and the other to that of S.B., with a certain number of electives in each. Except in the matter of commercial studies, which may be chosen, there was no departure from the general principles which had guided us in former years, but we were able to give new importance to physical culture and to such studies as physics and biology. We introduced no university methods, but we did what we could to adopt modern methods of study in the sciences. The buildings which have been erected since have enabled us to make still further progress in this direction. We did not in any way relax our efforts to make this a Christian college and to develop the Christian character of our students. We believe that the primary object of college education is disciplinary — the forming of character, the education of the moral powers, the heart and will, and this in the spirit of the Lord Jesus Christ and in accordance with His teaching, the development of true manhood. We put this first, while we would neglect nothing in the way of essential physical and intellectual culture to make not only good men, but strong men.

The class which graduated in 1902 numbered 13, of whom 6 were Armenians, 4 Greeks, 2 Bulgarians and 1 Austrian. Of the Armenians 4 are in business, 1 a teacher, 1 in journalism. Of the Greeks 3 are in business and 1 a teacher. The Austrian is in business. The Bulgarians both continued their studies.

CHAPTER XXVI
MY RESIGNATION OF THE PRESIDENCY. 1902-1903

I SPENT the summer vacation of 1902 in America, and, at his request, I went to Washington to see President Roosevelt. I had met him many years before, at a club in Boston, when he was interested in the reform of the government of New York City, and consequently had formed some idea of him as a young man. I went to see my old friend Secretary Hay first, to talk over Turkish affairs with him, and he arranged my interview with the President. When I reached the White House I found about fifty people in the reception room waiting to see him — Senators, Representatives and petitioners for all sorts of favors — together with some who seemed to have come as they would have to a zoölogical garden to see the elephant. The scene was not new to me, but I was more than ever impressed with the absurdity of it. It seemed to be a relic of the old idea that the Caliph should sit in the door of his house or tent every day and personally deal with every case that any one chose to present to him. Even the Sultan has given up this, although the shadow of it remains in the Friday Salaamlik. In America it is a traditional symbol of a republican form of government; but it is not an evidence of republican good sense to make such demands upon the time and strength of the President. On this occasion President Roosevelt appeared suddenly in the room and disposed of the whole crowd in less than half an hour, listening and speaking to each one in a voice loud enough to be heard by all. After this I had a long talk with him in his private office on our relations with the Turkish government. He talked with a freedom which astonished me at first, but it was soon clear enough that I was expected to distinguish between what he said as Theodore Roosevelt and what he said as President of the United States, and that he took it for granted that what he said would not be made public by me. It was four years later when I saw him again and afterward lunched with him at the White House, with much the same experience. Theodore Roosevelt is certainly one of the most interesting men whom I have ever met; and President Roosevelt, from my point of view, which is European, is one of the greatest statesmen in the world. I know of no statesman in Europe who ranks above him.

The college year opened in September, and the number of students registered was 318, of whom 190 were boarders. There were 145 Greeks, 101 Armenians, 28 Bulgarians, 9 English and Americans, 17 Turks, 18 others.

The relations of our government with Turkey were strained at this time on account of concessions made to the French government as a result of its naval demonstration and occupation of the island of Mytilene. These concessions granted certain privileges to schools, hospitals and other institutions under Turkish protection which were denied to Americans, although, after having been granted to the French, they had been extended to English, German and Russian institutions, by special *iradés*. It was our right to enjoy the same privileges. The Turkish government did not deny this, but would not issue the *iradé* necessary to enable us to profit by the right as they had done for the other Powers. Mr. Leishman pressed this question as vigorously as he could, but it was not finally settled until 1907. Robert College was not directly interested in it, as our position was established by our original charter given by Sultan Abd-ul-Aziz; but the prestige of the United States in Turkey was at stake, and most of the American institutions, including the Beirut College, were directly interested in securing these rights. It was not a question to go to war about, and there were occult influences at the palace, probably of foreign origin, which led the Sultan to resist all Mr. Leishman's demands, until the tables were turned and he had something to ask of the United States. Great credit is due to Mr. Leishman for the skill with which he took advantage of this opportunity, not only to settle this question, but to establish our position here as entitled to the same rights as the European Powers. The year 1903 was marked by the outbreak of the revolution planned by the Macedonian committee, not only in Macedonia, but in the province of Adrianople. The insurgents were Macedonian Bulgarians, but were not supported by the government of free Bulgaria, or by any European Power, and they failed, although they demanded nothing more than the execution of the treaty of Berlin. Russia and Austria intervened, but neither of the Powers wished to have the Macedonian question settled until they could settle it in their own interest. They intervened to maintain the *status quo*. This is not the place to tell the story of the horrors of that year or those that have followed, or to discuss the Macedonian question. It need only be said here that one result of the troubles there has been to stir up a bitter enmity between the Greeks and Bulgarians, not only in Macedonia, where their bands have rivaled the Turks in barbarity, but wherever they meet, even in Robert College. This conflict between them is as foolish as it is unchristian. It has been playing into the hands of their worst enemies, Austria and Russia. It has been a source of constant anxiety to us in the College; but happily, and to the credit of our students, it has not led to any serious disturbance up to the present time (1907). The College is a perpetual peace conference between all the nationalities and religions of this part of the world.

While I am writing (1907) I learn that the two representatives of Bulgaria at the Hague Conference are General Vinaroff and Judge Karandjuloff, both graduates of Robert College, of the classes of 1876 and 1879.

Theodorus Hall was opened for students in September, 1902, and proved to be admirably adapted to its purpose, and up to date in all its equipment. It accomplished what we had long felt to be essential — the entire separation of the younger boys in the Preparatory Department from the college students. Professor William Murray went to live in the building with the boys, and he and Mrs. Murray were tireless in their devotion to them. Mr. Hagopian had been appointed adjunct professor and assistant principal; and he assisted in the opening of the school, but was so unfortunate as to break his leg on New Year's Day, and after seven months in the hospital came back too feeble to do much work for a year. Two American tutors and several other teachers lived in the building and assisted in the care of the boys.

We commenced work on the gymnasium in the summer of 1903, although no progress had been made in securing an *iradé*. The government never interfered with the work, and it was completed and occupied the following year. Like our other buildings, it is of blue limestone. It has been a great boon to the College, and there is nothing of the kind in Constantinople to compare with it. We call it the Dodge Gymnasium, as it was the gift of Mr. William E. Dodge and his son, Cleveland H. Dodge, one of our trustees.

In May, 1903, we welcomed Dr. Coe here as a representative of the trustees, and he brought Dr. Gates with him from Switzerland, where he was spending a year before taking up his work in the College. The visit was prompted by some criticisms which some of the new professors had made upon the administration of the College, and was a new proof of the desire of the trustees to meet their responsibilities here with a full understanding of the condition and the needs of the College. Dr. Coe and Dr. Gates spent three weeks in Kennedy Lodge, had meetings with the Faculty and private conferences with the professors, teachers and others interested in the College. For all of us it was not only a great pleasure to have them with us, but most profitable to us as individuals and as a Faculty, in the opportunity which it gave us to hear their views on many important questions and to discuss them with the secretary of the Board of Trustees. So far as I know there was no exception to the general satisfaction of all concerned, in the results of this visit. It was a happy introduction of Dr. Gates to the position which he was about to assume as president of the College.

We received some gifts about this time which are worth recording — the first from a Greek gentleman, Nicolaki Bey, a judge of the Court of Appeals in Constantinople. He gave us his house in Pera, which we have since sold, and the income of the fund goes to the aid of beneficiaries. Mr. S. M. Minassian also gave us a house in Pera, but we have not yet been able to obtain possession of it. Both these gentlemen had been students of Dr. Hamlin in the old Bebec Seminary.

We were also indebted to Mrs. Frederick F. Thomson of New York for a fine pipe organ for our college chapel, which has added new interest to our public services, and to the British government, the British Museum and the Clarendon Press for very valuable additions to our library, secured through the influence of Professor van Millingen.

The Commencement exercises were held two weeks before the close of the college year — an experiment which proved so satisfactory that this arrangement has been continued ever since. Mr. Leishman, the American minister, presided, and we had the usual crowd with the usual distinguished guests. The most interesting event of the day was the Turkish oration, delivered by our first Turkish graduate, Houloussi Hussein Effendi. In form, substance and delivery it was the best oration of the day. We have had many Turkish students during these forty years, but only this one has gone farther than the Sophomore class.

The whole number of graduates was 19. There were 7 Bulgarians, 6 Armenians, 5 Greeks, 1 Turk. Of the Bulgarians 2 went to Germany to study, 2 are in business, 1 is in the American consulate at Batoum, Russia, 1 in the diplomatic service. Of the Armenians all are in business. Of the Greeks 4 are in business and 1 in the service of the British government in Macedonia. The Turk is a teacher in Robert College.

March 1, 1903, I completed my seventieth year, and I had long before determined that it would be my duty at that time to resign my place as president to a younger and better man. I had informed the trustees of my intention, and happily they had found the right man in Dr. Gates. It was at my earnest solicitation that he consented to allow me to suggest his name to the trustees. I knew of no other man who could fill the place so well, and after full consideration the trustees came to the same conclusion. At the request of Dr. Gates and the trustees I retained my position in the College as professor and continued my work until the close of the following year, when I bade farewell to Constantinople, as I believed for the last time, and spent the next two years in work for the College in the United States. In 1906, at the earnest request of the Faculty, I returned to the College, and have since been teaching my old classes here, feeling much more at home than I did in America. The generous contributions made by Mr. Kennedy and Mrs. William E. Dodge while I was in America have given new life to the College, transformed the appearance of the grounds, renovated Hamlin Hall, and given us the beautiful building known, at Mrs. Dodge's request, as Washburn Hall, with two new houses for professors; and the number of students has risen to more than four hundred.

But these recollections properly end with the close of the fortieth year, when I resigned; and what my feelings were at that time will best appear from an extract from my last report to the trustees in 1903.

"I look back upon these thirty-four years in Robert College with the deepest gratitude to the trustees in New York and to my associates in Constantinople. The trustees have given me their unvaried and absolute confidence and support, and no man ever had associates more loyal and true. We have all been of one heart and mind as to what the College ought to be, what the chief end which we had in view in our work, and each one has been wholly consecrated to it. This has been true, not only of the professors, but also of most of the instructors and tutors, many of whom have done as good work as any done in the College. This has been the secret of our success. Of my personal affection for these men, here and in America, the living and the dead, it is impossible for me to write.

We have worked together, with all our hearts, for what we believed to be the good of the people of this part of the world, have helped them in every way in our power and have sought to inspire them with the true Christian ideal. We have made no secret of our own opinions, but we treated theirs with respect and have done our best to enter into sympathy with their life and their habits of thought. In return our students and the various communities which they represent have trusted us, believed in us and given us their sympathy and affection. I count this the most precious reward that they could give us for all the work that we have done. To all these dear friends in the East and to those in America, England and elsewhere who have given us their sympathy and support I owe a debt of gratitude which I can never repay.

"I hope that my wife will pardon me for mentioning her in this report, but every one who has known the inner life of the College for the past thirty-four years knows that no small part of my success and the success of the College has been due to her untiring devotion to all its interests, her intimate knowledge of the people of different races, her power of winning the hearts of our students and all our neighbors, and, not least, her deep sympathy with the spiritual aims of the College."

CHAPTER XXVII
THE WORK OF FORTY YEARS. 1863-1903

I CANNOT say that I or my associates were ever satisfied with the work that we were doing in Robert College, or that at any time we ever realized our ideal of what it ought to be. But I feel no inclination now to complain of our poverty or of other circumstances beyond our control which hindered our progress, for circumstances equally beyond our control have given the College an influence in the world far beyond anything that its founders could have hoped for. Those who have read the preceding chapters of this book will understand something both of the adverse and the favorable conditions under which we have worked.

At the end of forty years we had done something for the education of more than 2500 young men of many nationalities. The average length of time spent in the College by these students was about three years; 435 of them had graduated with honor, after from four to seven years in the College. Of these 144 were Armenians, 195 Bulgarians, 76 Greeks, 14 English and Americans, 3 Germans, 2 Hebrews, 1 Turk.1

In the early history of the College these boys came to us as very raw material so far as school training was concerned, and even at the present time this is of a very miscellaneous character, generally not including any knowledge of the English language. We were forced to have a Preparatory Department, even for those who were otherwise advanced enough for college studies. So far as home training was concerned they generally came with habits of obedience and respect for their elders which fitted them to submit readily to school discipline. On the whole I think that our students have been less difficult to control, less unruly than American boys, and no hazing traditions such as disgrace our American colleges have been established here, although we have had occasional examples of similar brutality.

I have been more and more impressed every year with the feeling that boys are by nature very much the same everywhere

---

1 In the Appendix will be found tables giving the details for every year of the number of students, the amount received from them and the amount of the current expenses of the College.

— that while different environments and varied conventionalities modify them externally, boys of different races are at the bottom essentially the same. I am often asked which of the nationalities in the College is the most intelligent and how they compare with Americans. As to the different nationalities it is a question to which there is no answer. None could be given from reference to our records for forty years. Our best scholars have sometimes been of one nationality, sometimes of another. In comparison with American students, most of our students come to us with less of that unconscious education which every American boy has acquired outside the school, but when it comes to his work in the College the student here is equal to any American.

The question what Robert College has done for these students can best be answered by the extraordinary reputation which the College has gained in this part of the world. We are known by the character of our students and especially of our alumni. We have been sadly disappointed in a few of them, but the great majority have done honor to the College, wherever they have gone, in the universities of Europe as scholars and in active life as men.

Our theory of college education is not new. In substance it is as old as Plato and Aristotle. Its chief end is the highest possible development of character. The principal work of the College is disciplinary. It also does something in the way of storing up in the mind of the scholar a certain amount of useful knowledge, but much of this is soon forgotten and the greater part of the knowledge which we use in practical life is not learned in college, not from the teachers at any rate. The greatest scholars are often the most unpractical and helpless of men.

The most important work of the College is to train and develop the physical, intellectual and moral powers of the student. These powers exist in him. They are the gift of God.

The work of the teacher is to draw them out, to cultivate them, to bring them into harmony, to develop them symmetrically so that the lower shall be under the higher, so that the will shall habitually choose the higher rather than the lower motive. It is a well-known fact that most of our actions are determined by instinct or by habit. Youth is the time when instincts may be modified or brought under control and when habits are formed which generally go with us through life. When we say, then, that education is disciplinary and designed to develop and mould the character, we

PANORAMA OF ROBERT COLLEGE

have in view the formation of those habits which will determine the actions of after life. This discipline may be directed specially to the physical powers, as where athletics stand first in the eyes of the student. It may be and often is confined to the intellectual faculties, to forming habits of study, of investigation, of reasoning, which will develop mental powers. Neither of these things should be neglected. Habits which will secure good health, with strong minds, capable of comprehending and mastering the problems of life, are precious acquirements. But when we speak of character we mean something more than these things and something far more important. We are thinking of the affections and the will. These dominate the life, constitute the character and fix the destiny of the man. The discipline of these powers, the training of the will, the formation of habits which will bring the life into harmony with the will of God, this is the highest and best work of the College. Such is our theory, and we have done our best to live up to it. We have been so far successful that our students are recognized everywhere as representing a different type of manhood from that commonly seen in the East, and some of our alumni are striking and illustrious examples of this type. This is the real work of the College, and by this we are to be judged; but unconsciously and incidentally the College has exerted an influence in this part of the world and in other lands which is worthy of notice.

It has revolutionized the policy of missionary societies in America in regard to education and led to the establishment of scores of similar institutions in different parts of the world. In Turkey alone there are now six American colleges and many more high schools. It has led to the founding of a large number of government and national schools in Turkey. This development of education was the direct result of what it was believed that Robert College had done for Bulgaria, and the progress made has been marvelous. These government schools are not what we might wish them to be, for the moral training is wanting, and the mental discipline is unsatisfactory; but they have their value in the enlightenment of the people. The schools of the Christian nationalities have felt the influence of the moral and religious training in Robert College and have greatly improved in this respect. This view of education has been much discussed in the kingdom of Greece during the past few years, its importance recognized and Robert College held up as a model. The Greek newspapers have been full of eulogies on our principles and our work. In Austrian Croatia and even in Russia there have been evidences of our influence. The fact that the heads of the Oriental churches in Turkey have long been warm friends of Robert College is an evidence that we have had an influence with them in removing their prejudices and leading them to realize the importance of a spiritual training for their young men.

We have also had some influence, not so much as I could wish, in bringing about a less hostile state of feeling between the different races in the East. At least they meet together on equal terms in the College and develop a certain amount of mutual respect, in some cases of warm personal friendship. They learn that it is possible to work together for a common end, and they find a common bond of sympathy in their relations to us. We have had some remarkable illustrations of sacrifices made by students of one race to help those of another.

We have certainly had great success in winning the confidence of our Mohammedan neighbors, removing their prejudices, securing their respect and friendship and giving them new conceptions of Christianity, as well as of America.

The Germans think that this and the other American colleges in Turkey have a great influence in directing the commerce of the country to America and England. There is no doubt some truth in this. The trade of Turkey with America has greatly increased of late years, and the spread of the English language is an advantage both to England and America, but we have never presented this as one of our claims to support.

The College is best known in Europe for the influence that it had in building up a free state in the Balkan Peninsula. Fifty years ago, except to a few students of history, the Bulgarians were a forgotten race in America and western Europe. We did not exactly discover them, but we played an important part in making them known to the Western world at a time when they most needed help. Years before this they had discovered us, and through the young men who studied in the College they had come to have faith in our wisdom and goodwill. The most important thing that we ever did for them was the educating of their young men to become leaders of their people at a time when there were very few Bulgarians who knew anything of civil government in a free state.

This was our legitimate work and naturally and inevitably led to our doing what we could for them after they left the College, to give them the advice which they sought in their new work, and to defend their interests where we had influence in Europe. That, in this way, we had an important part in the building up of this new state is a fact known to all the world and best of all by the Bulgarians themselves, who have never failed to recognize their obligation to the College and to manifest their affection for us as individuals.

We have done what we could for the other nationalities of the College, and they understand that we take a deep interest in everything which concerns their prosperity and progress. They have not had the opportunity to distinguish themselves in statecraft, but they have won honor and success in other fields of labor, both in the East and in other parts of the world. We have had relatively few Turkish students, only one who has graduated, as it has been the policy of the Sultan to forbid Turkish students attending any but government schools. Notwithstanding this prohibition, we now have (1907) more than twenty Turks in the College, and its reputation among enlightened Turks is quite as high as with other nationalities.

The burden of the work during these forty years was to make the College worthy of its reputation and to meet the ever increasing demand for a higher education. As I have explained in the earlier chapters of this book, the College, at the outset, was a very primitive institution, better than any other in the Turkish Empire, but lacking in most of the appliances which a college is supposed to possess. It was a long step in advance when we moved into Hamlin Hall in 1871, but many years passed after that before we were able to improve our material conditions to any extent. We devoted these years to what is really more important than buildings or apparatus, to the inner development of the College, to the development of our Faculty and staff of teachers, and the adaptation of our course of instruction to our environment. Such men as Dr. Long and Professor van Millingen were worth more than new buildings. But the time came when these also were essential to our work and to our reputation. We had already been forced after Mr. Robert's death to seek for new friends in America to enable us to meet our current expenses. In the two years which I spent in America on this errand, in 1880-1882, such friends were found; and in 1889-1891 we had to appeal to them again, or to find others who would lend a hand to save the College. It was twenty years after the erection of Hamlin Hall before we were able to put up the Albert Long Hall, at the

GRADUATES AND THEIR WIVES, SOFIA, 1904

same time that Mr. Kennedy erected Kennedy Lodge for the president's house. We made other improvements at this time which made our grounds and buildings attractive. It was a turning point in our history so far as our influence here was concerned. A still more important event came five years later in the reorganization of the Board of Trustees in New York, which may be regarded as the beginning of a new era. After Mr. Robert's death the responsibility for the management, the support, the life of the College, rested upon the Faculty here. It was a burden too heavy for us to bear and not a desirable arrangement for the College; but we put our whole lives into the work and have no reason to be ashamed of the result. I am proud of my associates here, both Americans, natives and Europeans, whenever I think of it — of their self-sacrifice, their tireless devotion to all the interests of the students and the general interests of the College, their wisdom and their faith. To work with such men in such a cause was a life worth living.

The reorganization of the Board of Trustees has given new life to the College and been followed by the erection of Theodorus Hall for the Preparatory Department, the Dodge Gymnasium, Washburn Hall, the renovation of Hamlin Hall, the erection of five professors' houses, and many other important improvements. Equally important has been the inner development of the College, made possible by the appointment of five new professors, additional instructors, with new appliances and a revision of the course of study. All this work was not completed in 1903, the close of the period of forty years, but it was all initiated in that period and has been most happily carried to completion under the wise administration of my successor, Dr. Gates, and the Board of Trustees organized in 1895.

The demand for progress and development will be as inevitable in the future as in the past, and this will mean more money and more strong, consecrated men to devote their lives to the work. No doubt there will be new trials and difficulties to encounter as well. But Robert College has been a work of faith from the beginning. It is now and it will be in the future. The motto on our college seal is

PER DEUM OMNIA

APPENDIX

A. NUMBER AND NATIONALITY OF STUDENTS AND GRADUATES EACH YEAR

	REGISTERED STUDENTS						GRADUATES				
Year	Registered	Boarders	Armenians	Bulgarians	Greeks	Others	Graduates	Armenians	Bulgarians	Greeks	Others
1	20	16	0	0	2	18	0				
2	28	25	1	1	4	22	0				
3	51	44	20	9	6	16	0				
4	96	76	19	13	18	39	0				
5	102	79	14	16	33	34	2	1	1	0	0
6	95	73	11	41	17	23	6	0	5	0	1
7	96	66	35	38	22	25	1	1	0	0	0
8	143	98	35	41	33	34	5	0	5	0	0
9	218	164	80	40	34	64	8	0	6	1	1
10	257	189	98	38	48	73	1	0	1	0	0
11	237	172	87	43	43	64	5	0	5	0	0
12	208	163	55	45	48	60	11	3	7	1	0
13	191	152	54	33	39	65	15	7	7	1	0
14	135	98	43	42	14	38	14	6	5	2	1
15	128	93	35	50	11	32	8	3	3	1	1
16	162	111	50	54	32	26	11	5	6	0	0
17	200	149	74	77	27	31	7	3	4	0	0
18	232	158	85	89	28	23	12	2	9	1	0
19	259	173	94	105	24	37	9	4	5	0	0
20	243	165	83	110	26	24	10	4	5	1	0
21	215	142	82	91	29	13	22	7	14	1	0
22	173	115	63	71	28	11	15	4	9	1	1
23	182	120	64	71	37	10	20	8	12	0	0
24	182	130	53	70	36	23	26	10	13	3	0

APPENDIX
NUMBER AND NATIONALITY OF STUDENTS AND GRADUATES—
Continued

	REGISTERED STUDENTS						GRADUATES				
Year	Registered	Boarders	Armenians	Bulgarians	Greeks	Others	Graduates	Armenians	Bulgarians	Greeks	Others
25	170	113	55	60	33	22	28	12	15	1	0
26	158	104	43	52	33	30	11	3	3	4	1
27	162	104	47	45	41	31	8	4	3	1	0
28	159	104	59	41	39	20	5	4	1	0	0
29	194	130	70	52	47	25	8	4	3	1	0
30	203	143	73	60	46	24	13	3	6	3	1
31	200	123	68	44	65	23	21	8	6	4	3
32	205	116	63	36	80	26	15	5	6	3	1
33	221	132	69	37	92	23	6	2	3	1	0
34	200	130	61	38	77	24	14	4	5	4	1
35	250	145	87	49	88	26	14	2	6	4	2
36	292	173	105	45	108	34	13	4	3	5	1
37	297	176	108	39	112	38	18	8	2	5	3
38	311	98	108	34	127	42	11	1	4	5	1
39	308	181	98	29	131	61	13	6	2	4	1
40	318	190	101	28	145	45	19	6	7	5	1
41	320	188	94	23	168	35	17	6	1	9	1
42	342	222	97	34	171	40	10	5	1	4	0
43	373	257	88	37	195	53	12	6	0	6	0

APPENDIX

B.   RECIPTS FROM STUDENTS, AND EXPENSES AT CONSTANTINOPLE, EACH YEAR

YEAR	RECEIVED FROM STUDENTS	EXPENSES AT CONSTANTINOPLE *Not* including Building, Improvements, or Apparatus
1	$2,578	$5,181
2	3,845	5,630
3	5,808	6,107
4	7,858	9,111
[1]5		
[1]6		
7	10,300	11,052
8	14,869	13,939
9	26,906	22,308
10	31,548	27,874
11	26,364	28,380
12	24,697	26,778
13	20,014	24,648
14	14,780	20,490
15	14,511	18,981
16	16,746	21,890
17	23,720	25,647
18	25,280	28,350
19	29,493	32,371
20	29,020	34,185
21	24,535	32,792
22	19,144	26,131
23	17,384	25,694
24	20,552	28,164
25	18,889	29,488
26	16,227	28,987
27	15,891	26,004
28	16,033	26,998
29	20,227	30,088
30	22,426	30,728

[1] The accounts of these two years cannot be found in Constantinople.

APPENDIX

RECIPTS AND EXPENSES — *Continued*

YEAR	RECEIVED FROM STUDENTS	EXPENSES AT CONSTANTINOPLE *Not* including Building, Improvements, or Apparatus
31	$19,919	$36,169
32	20,845	31,442
33	24,987	36,753
34	24,070	35,640
35	28,300	36,682
36	33,117	40,731
37	32,577	42,539
38	34,636	43,670
39	34,295	48,302
40	37,028	59,006
41	37,434	59,457
42	45,320	60,031
43	50,782	68,189

C.   THE FACULTY OF THE COLLEGE, FORTY-FIFTY YEAR, 1907-1908

President, Caleb Frank Gates, D. D., LL. D.,	appointed 1903.
George Washburn, D. D., LL. D.,	appointed 1869.
Hagopos H. Djedjizian, A. M.,	appointed 1872.
Stephan Panaretoff, A. M.,	appointed 1877.
Alexander van Millingen, D. D.,	appointed 1878.
Charles Anderson, D. D.,	appointed 1888.
Louisos Eliou, Ph. D.,	appointed 1890.
William T. Ormiston, A. M.,	appointed 1892.
Ion E. Dwyer, A. M.,	appointed 1904.
Bertram V. Post, M. D.,	appointed 1904.
George L. Manning, Ph. D.,	appointed 1905.
Abraham D. Hagopian, A. M.,	appointed 1905.
George H. Huntington, A. M.,	appointed 1907.
(One vacancy.)	

APPENDIX

PERMANENT INSTRUCTORS

Peter Voicoff, A. M.,	appointed 1883.
Constas Constantinou, Ph. D.,	appointed 1895.
Henri Auguste Reymond,	appointed 1896.
Tevfik Fikret Bey,	appointed 1900.
Stavros S. Emmanuel, A. M.,	appointed 1893.
Caspar H. Tuysizian, A. B.,	appointed 1897.
Friedrich W. Kunick,	appointed 1902.
(14 other teachers.)	

D.   FORMER MEMBERS OF THE FACULTY

*Cyrus Hamlin, D. D., LL. D., *President*.	1863-1877.
*George A. Perkins, A. M.,	1863-1865.
*Henry A. Schauffler, D. D.,	1863-1865.
John A. Paine, Ph. D.,	1867-1869.
*Albert L. Long, D. D.,	1872-1901.
Edwin A. Grosvenor, LL. D.,	1872-1890.
George S. Murray, A. M.,	1901-1904.
*Charles W. Ottley, M. D.,	1901-1904.
A. H. Lybyer, A. M., Ph. D.,	1900-1907.
William S. Murray, M. S.,	1901-1907.

E.   FORMER AMERICAN TUTORS

Harry H. Barnum,	University of Chicago.
Ward M. Beckwith, M. D.,	Westmoreland, N. Y.
Philip M. Brown,	U. S. Embassy, Constantinople.
Alvey M. Carter,	Art Museum, Boston, Mass.
Rev. W. V. W. Davis, D. D.,	Pittsfield, Mass.
Prof. Frank L. Duley,	Mount Hermon, Mass.
Charles H. Durfee,	Deceased.
Handford W. Edson,	Indianapolis, Ind.
Judge W. T. Forbes,	Worcester, Mass.
Francis E. Garlough,	Boston, Mass

Deceased.

APPENDIX

Miles T. Hand,	Honesdale, Penn.
John H. Haynes,	North Adams, Mass.
Frederick M. Herrick, Esq.,	New York, N. Y.
Winthrop H. Hopkins,	Auburn, N. Y.
Prof. Arthur S. Hoyt, D. D.,	Auburn Theological Seminary, New York.
Rev. Charles S. Hoyt, D. D.,	Deceased.
Rev. George E. Ladd,	Red Oaks, Iowa.
Rev. Clement C. Martin,	Fostoria, Ohio.
Rev. Eneas McLean,	Deceased.
Rev. D. S. Muzzy,	Yonkers, N. Y.
Prof. Charles Nash, D. D.,	Oakland, Cal.
Rev. Luther A. Ostrander, D. D.,	Lyons, N. Y.
Rev. Leroy F. Ostrander,	Samokov, Bulgaria.
Prof. George E. Pollock,	Deceased.
Lansing L. Porter,	Evanston, Ill.
Rev. Lewis T. Reed,	Brooklyn, N. Y.
Rev. Orville Reed,	Montclair, N. J.
Rev. C. S. Richardson, D. D.,	Little Falls, N. Y.
Rev. Charles T. Riggs,	Constantinople.
Rev. James Rodger,	Farmington, Minn.
Albert H. Rodgers, M. D.,	Corning, N. Y.
Rev. C. A. Savage, D. D.,	Deceased.
Rev. H. K. Sanborne,	Oakland, Cal.
Rev. Carl W. Scovel,	Newark, N. J.
Prof. Robert L. Taylor,	Hanover, N. H.
Judge C. S. Truax,	Deceased.
President E. M. Vittum, D. D.,	Fargo College, N. D.
Paul T. B. Ward,	Boston, Mass.
Ernest B. Watson,	Hanover, N. H.
Rev. Lewis B. Webber,	Brockport, N. Y.
Rev. Hezekiah Webber,	Deceased.
Prof. E. W. Wetmore,	Albany, N. Y.
Prof. S. D. Wilcox,	Deceased.
Prof. L. D. Woodbridge, M. D.,	Deceased.
George G. Wright,	Boston, Mass.
Rev. George B. Young,	Brooklyn, N. Y.

APPENDIX

F.   MR. ROBERT'S REQUIREMENTS FOR TUTORS

I

The candidate should be a man twenty-two to twenty-six years of age, of fervent, symmetrical piety, combined with a missionary spirit, a willingness to do hard work, the ability to work harmoniously with others and one who is not unyielding, stiff, or one who would be conscientiously obstinate, one who is ready to do anything which the good of the College requires, even to teaching the alphabet, though he may be versed in the most abstruse parts of the Calculus; in short a man who wants to live a Christian life and do a Christian teacher's work, desiring to do good to the souls of his pupils as well as to improve their undurstanding.

II

A good mind in a sound body, with a large share of common sense, a firm but mild temper, a warm heart readily sympathizing with those under him, keenness of perception and a cool, unbiased judgment, governing himself well and able to govern others so far as practical by love rather than force. Possessing gentlemanly habits and feelings.

III

A man of great breadth of mind, who can take broad and proper views of education, not wedded to any system, comprehending the purpose of education, knowing a great deal more than he is expected to teach.

IV

A thorough and systematic scholar, not a man who has barely "got through" college or who has been little above the average of his class, but one who has been among the very first, a real enthusiast in learning, never satisfied with present attainments but always pressing on to farther acquisitions.

APPENDIX

V

Apt to teach, with ability and tact to impart what he knows. An enthusiast in his work, determined to make better scholars than any other teacher has ever done and inspiring them with a love of learning. Not a man in feeble health who wishes to "lay off."

VI

A man who can impress himself on his pupils, who can influence them for good, whose wishes as well as his words shall be law to them, one who by his own habits of punctuality, promptness, system and neatness shall teach as well by his exemplary practice in all these respects as by precept.

VII

A mercenary person, or one who would go to make money, is not wanted.

G.   SUMMARY OF THE REPORT OF THE TREASURER OF
ROBERT COLLEGE FOR 1909

ENDOWMENT FUNDS INVESTED IN NEW YORK

General Endowment Fund $243,402.22
C. R. Robert Endowment Fund 134,080.18
Scholarship Fund 8,000.00
Lois Newton Fund 11,302.50
Museum Fund 5,997.50

$402,782.40

Real estate and other property in Constantinople 392,629.03.50

$795,411.43

The College has no indebtedness.